MARTIN O'MALLEY

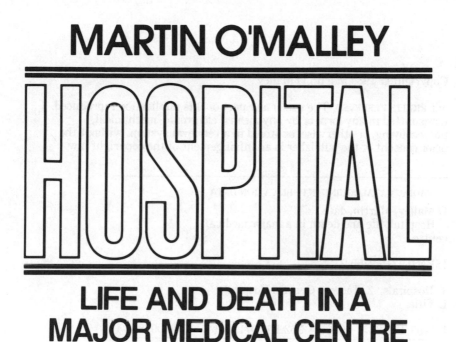

LIFE AND DEATH IN A MAJOR MEDICAL CENTRE

Macmillan of Canada
A Division of Canada Publishing Corporation
Toronto, Ontario, Canada

CANADIAN CATALOGUING IN PUBLICATION DATA

O'Malley, Martin, date.
  Hospital: life and death in a major medical centre

ISBN 0-7715-9750-9

1. Hospitals. 2. Toronto General Hospital.
I. Title.

RA983.T62T64   1986   362.1′1′09713541   C86-093865-4

DESIGN: Brant Cowie/Artplus

Macmillan of Canada
A Division of Canada Publishing Corporation

To Karen
with love and thanks

A hospital operates by the constant interplay of powerful forces pulling away at each other in different directions, each force essential for getting necessary things done, but always at odds with each other. It is an astonishment, which every patient feels from time to time, observing the affairs of a large, complex hospital from the vantage point of his bed, that the whole institution doesn't fly to pieces.

LEWIS THOMAS,
The Youngest Science

Contents

Preface

PEOPLE REMEMBER in nearly photographic detail their times in hospital, whether it was for an emergency appendectomy, a triple bypass, a birth, or vigils at the bedside of someone dying. Four times I have been a patient in a hospital, twice under the knife, and I can recall each experience as if it happened yesterday, including the tone of the receptionist in Admitting, a nurse's smile, and what I heard as I emerged from the fog of anesthesia. I have also spent hours and hours in hospitals as a worried father, worried son, worried husband, worried friend. These times are etched indelibly on my brain.

I dropped by David Allen's office at Toronto General Hospital one September afternoon in 1983. He is director of public relations at the hospital. His office is on the ground floor of the Bell Wing, which faces University Avenue. Located just south of the provincial legislative buildings, the hospital commands a splendid view of one of Toronto's most attractive boulevards, the broad and landscaped thoroughfare that leads to Queen's Park.

I am suspicious of public relations people. We need them, but we must be on our toes with them, lest they snow us with self-serving pap on behalf of their clients. Fortunately Allen is not one of these. "Sounds interesting," he remarked, as I explained what I intended to do.

My plan was to hang around the hospital for about a year, then write a book about the experience, trying to explain how a big-city hospital works. The permissions were quickly forthcoming and soon I was pretty well free to roam and watch at will. The Board of Trustees presented me with an official hospital badge that allowed me entrance to most parts of the huge institution day and night and on weekends. Allen even gave me a key to the public relations office in case I needed a place to escape to during the rigors of a twelve-hour transplant operation (which is invariably done in the midnight hours when adjacent operating rooms are available for donor and recipient). For all this co-operation I was and am grateful, and impressed, because they had no idea what I was going to write and I promised no one a veto over the manuscript. Toronto General is a big hospital in more ways than one.

When the March, 1985, deadline approached, I was nowhere near being finished. In fact, things were only starting to click into place and I was only beginning to establish rapport with enough key people to make the book work. I needed another year, and Macmillan generously agreed to delay the project.

The working title I kept in my head during the research phase was "The Hospital Assignment." "Assignment" is a familiar and honorable word among journalists, and especially newspaper reporters. We all started in a newsroom where a city editor maintained a thick and prominent "assignment book." It reminded me of the thick book priests use on the altar at mass. If you were a general assignment reporter, every morning was an adventure. Some days opposite your name you would find "obits," or "inquest," but there would be mornings when you would find "Jane Fonda," or "circus," and that day would be unlike any other. Some assignments are true adventures. Some are fun. Some are boring. Some are loathsome. One I hated as a junior reporter was visiting distraught parents and having to wheedle from them a family photograph of their child who had been killed an hour or two earlier.

I also never much liked covering politics or politicians, because I always felt as if I was fishing in a barrel. In August, 1965, when I arrived in Toronto from Winnipeg to be interviewed for a job on *The Globe and Mail*, the managing editor made a reference to Queen's Park and I asked, "What's Queen's Park?" He looked at me askance, but he had already hired me. Needless to say, I was never assigned to Queen's Park or to the Ottawa Press Gallery, or even to City Hall, which suited me fine. Fortunately, there were more than enough reporters eager to do those jobs, leaving me free to muck around with stevedores, strippers, shortstops, and surgeons.

The assignments I enjoyed most were "hanging around" assignments, which meant spending several days or weeks with a person, trying to get to know him or her, or with a place or a topic that required more than a cursory visit or a quick peek at old clippings and a telephone call.

Perhaps I am too slow, or too shy, for newspaper work, or have become so. Even now, two and a half years hardly seems time enough to scratch the surface of an assignment like this one. I could have easily, happily, hung around Toronto General for another year or two, but in the meantime there are mouths to feed and bills to pay.

Some readers will wonder why I have not mentioned this doctor, or that administrator, or this nurse, but my answer is simply that our paths never crossed. For example, Douglas Wigle is a cardiologist at Toronto General with a world reputation; but if he sat down across from me in the cafeteria I would not recognize him. Hugh Scully is one of the hospital's top heart surgeons, and also one of the young activists in the forefront of this summer's confrontation on extra billing, but he simply did not fit into the narrative I ended up using. One morning I actually stood shoulder to shoulder with Scully in an operating room and watched in admiration as he did a quadruple bypass, but this was early in the assignment and I considered it only a shakedown cruise to get used to the blood and guts of the operating room. This is an indication of just how big TGH is, and how many skilled individuals work there.

My role model for this sort of assignment is John McPhee, the marvellous researcher-writer whose prose for many years has graced the pages of *The New Yorker*. He is king of all hanging-around writers and I am an unabashed fan and disciple. As Ferris Professor of Journalism at Princeton University, McPhee for years has taught a seminar called "The Literature of Fact." I identify most with McPhee's researching methods, and especially with his interviewing technique. I had been using a similar technique for years, with considerable misgiving, thinking it was more a congenital defect than some journalistic masterstroke.

Then I read *The John McPhee Reader*, in which editor William L. Howarth explains in his introduction:

When McPhee conducts an interview he tries to be as blank as his notebook pages, totally devoid of preconceptions, equipped with only the most elementary knowledge. He has found that imagining he knows a subject is a disadvantage, for that prejudice will limit his freedom to ask, to learn, to be surprised by unfolding evidence. Since most stories are

*full of unsuspected complexity, an interviewer hardly needs
to* feign *ignorance; the stronger temptation is to bluff with
a show of knowledge or to trick the informant into providing
simple, easily digestible answers. Neither course is to
McPhee's liking; he would rather risk seeming ignorant to
get a solid, knotty answer.*

Some of the people McPhee interviewed believed he was thick-
witted because his speech slowed and his brow knitted and
often he would ask the same question again and again. And
McPhee repeated the answers, garbling them so that the
interviewed person felt compelled to provide new answers.
Reading this has convinced me that print people, book people
especially, have a decided advantage over radio and television
people, and we should luxuriate in it; we don't have to fret
about our side of the exchange. Editor Howarth goes on about
John McPhee: "Some informants find his manner relaxing,
others are exasperated; in either case, they talk more freely
and fully to him than they normally would to a reporter."
Congenital defect or masterstroke, it works for McPhee, and
it worked for me at the hospital.

Often I walked the hospital in a white coat. There was no
intention to deceive: the coat simply made it easier to get around
and avoid explanations. The white coat, I found, makes one
invisible in a hospital. It is the perfect camouflage. Without
it, I was constantly stopped, sometimes for the best of reasons,
by staff who assumed that, like almost every other visitor,
I was lost. Early one winter morning, when I was heading
to an operating room, a surly worker in one of the sub-basement
tunnels stopped me and said I was not allowed in that area.
I was in civilian clothes, so I excused myself, walked down
the hallway to the laundry room, donned a white coat, and
two minutes later walked by the same fellow. This time he
did not bat an eye. In fact he said, "Good morning."
    In nearly all my interviews with doctors, nurses, and tech-
nicians I used a small tape recorder as well as my notebook.
Medical jargon is too technical, too abstruse, and the subject
matter too important, for my slapdash stenographic skills.
Besides, most doctors are more comfortable talking to a
machine; they know they are less likely to be misquoted. A
few even taped me as I taped them, just to be sure.
    The doctors in the book are referred to by their first and
last names, and usually by only their last names in secondary
references. I did not bother labelling each one as Dr. Who or

Dr. What, because a surfeit of "Drs." tends to make the manuscript look choppy, as if bread crumbs had been spilled on it. For the patients, with one exception, I used first names only. Sometimes this was to protect their privacy, sometimes because a patient died before giving me permission to identify him or her in the book. Most of the patients would not have minded if I had used their full names, but for the sake of consistency I chose to use first names only. The sole exception is Tom Hall, the world's longest-living single-lung transplant survivor. Over the two and a half years we have become friends, and he continues to return to the hospital for various tests and checks, to make public appearances on behalf of the organ-donor program, and to advise and comfort other transplant patients. Tom Hall is a remarkable man, courageous and articulate, with a wonderful appetite for life, which is why he has done so well.

There were some harrowing and humorous moments that did not fit into any of the chapters, so I will mention them here.

Griffin Pearson, the surgeon-in-chief at Toronto General, invited me into his operating room one morning to show me how to remove a cancer from a lung. He is a natural teacher and he encouraged me now and then to step forward to peer into the chest cavity and to watch, step by step, the progress of the operation. Once I was watching from a photographer's stool, which is like one of those little step-up ladders used to reach the high shelves in a kitchen. It enabled me to watch from over Pearson's shoulders as he cut and cauterized. The stool has small wheels on the legs so it can be easily moved about, but the wheels retract when you step on it. At least they are supposed to. As I was watching, mesmerized by the surgeon's intricate work, the stool suddenly lurched backwards, probably only a centimetre, but I thought for sure I was about to collapse onto Pearson, onto the operating table, and onto the anesthetized patient. It would have been a disaster, of course, and for the rest of the morning I felt quite light-headed.

For most of 1985, I met regularly with hospital president W. Vickery Stoughton. For a long stretch we met monthly, in his office, sitting on opposite sides of his coffee table across the room from his desk. When I entered his office on Wednesday, July 17, 1985, one of the executive secretaries, wearing a long pink dress, was feeding his new baby boy, Zachary Benjamin. Stoughton waved me in and our session proceeded as usual, until the secretary caught his attention to say, ahem, little Zachary needed to be changed.

"Would you mind doing it, Maureen?" Stoughton asked.

She demurred, explaining that she hadn't changed a baby for ages.

"Well, that's okay," Stoughton said. "I wasn't the oldest of seven kids for nothing."

He walked to the couch, took Zachary from her arms, gently placed the baby on a cushion, undid the soiled diaper as he slung a fresh one over his shoulder—all the while answering my questions and responding to my observations about hospital doings. Suddenly, in mid-reply:

"Oops, piss . . ."

A stream of urine shot up in a wide arc and splattered across my left wrist and over my notebook.

"Oh. Did he get you?"

Stoughton turned crimson, then began to sputter and giggle.

"This is the bad part of it. This is the *baaad* part of it. Changing a boy . . ."

"Jeez, Vick, you ask me not to smoke, then your son pees on me."

Stoughton couldn't contain himself. He roared, teary-eyed with laughter. "I tell you," he coughed, "I'm going to be telling this story for years! Martin O'Malley's in the office and the kid pees on him!"

"So much for the press."

"I *love* it!"

Queen's Park is a restful part of Toronto. The lawns are a favorite place for downtowners to brownbag their lunches, or jog, or sit on a bench and watch the rest of the world go by. The park is surrounded by the St. George campus of the University of Toronto, and students are constantly strolling over the lawns going to and from their classes. An elderly lady regularly visits the park to feed the pigeons, and on those bright, sunny afternoons it is quite a sight to see the pigeons, perhaps a hundred of them, perched on her bench and on her shoulders and sometimes on her head.

During an eight-month spell at the University of Toronto in 1972-73, when I was on a Southam Newspaper Fellowship at Massey College, I walked through the park every day, and in good weather I used to sit on a bench and do my reading. The fellowship was unstructured, and serendipity was encouraged. It was time to indulge myself—play a lot of chess, drink a lot of port, and read and read. After slugging it out on newspapers for ten years, that is how I chose to interpret eight months away from the trenches of journalism—on full salary. Reading whatever I wanted, unfettered by any assignment, was so exhilarating that it felt vaguely sinful. As a purely personal project, I took it upon myself to read the entire works of certain authors. The one I chose first was Aldous Huxley, a favorite of Robertson Davies, then Master of Massey College. The Upper Library of the college had nearly all of Huxley's works, most of them in paperback, most of them cracked and dog-eared. There is a bench in Queen's Park I always associate with such delightful novels as *Antic Hay*, *Chrome Yellow*, *Point Counter Point*, *After Many a Summer Dies the Swan*, and, of course, *Brave New World*.

Time moves ahead.

On Monday, June 16, 1986, nearly 700 doctors, most of them in white coats, stormed Queen's Park to protest against a new law that would ban extra billing by doctors in Ontario. "Stormed" is not too strong a word. The doctors waved placards, chanted, stomped, and jeered, and a few banged wooden sticks against crowd-control barricades. The doctors became so unruly that the front doors to the legislative building had to be locked. Film of the demonstration was on all the television channels that evening and pictures were on the front pages of all three Toronto newspapers the next day.

It was the fifth day of a doctors' strike that had extended to closing even the emergency departments of some hospitals. The emergency department at Toronto General Hospital stayed open, crowded to overflowing with patients from its own broad jurisdiction as well as those who had been turned away from other hospitals in the metropolitan area. Toronto General takes pride in always keeping its emergency department open, no matter what—war, civic disaster, epidemic, plague. Even a doctors' strike.

Still, it seemed like very undoctorlike behavior, not what I had come to expect of the men and women I had encountered over the previous five years, first for the book *Doctors*, published by Macmillan in 1983, and then for this book. Over these five years I have interviewed hundreds of doctors who have allowed me into their offices, clinics, operating rooms, and homes. They are a fascinating lot, worth knowing, but in recent years they have been experiencing hellish frustrations.

For doctors, the 1970s was the decade of "doctor-bashing," when books and articles appeared tearing the hide off this hitherto widely respected, if not revered, profession. The public was encouraged to speak out against doctors, question them, criticize them, seek second and third opinions, and generally to haul them down from their lofty pedestals. The days of the dear and glorious physician are over; Ben Casey and young Dr. Kildare have made way for St. Elsewhere; the hospital itself has become the star attraction.

The faces in the demonstration at Queen's Park were those of doctors in their early thirties and middle to late forties, what a nurse in this book calls "The Big Chill Generation." They are the men and women who sacrificed a lot of money and years to study medicine only to discover that some of the rules had changed, many of the perquisites were gone, and somehow the aura of being a doctor had become a little smudged. Doctors are highly skilled, and highly paid, and they still command respect, but it no longer comes automatically. They have to prove themselves.

But the book is not about doctors, not entirely. There is much in it about doctors, of course, but there is also much about nurses, administrators, social workers, technicians, therapists, dietitians, engineers, security guards, cooks, dishwashers, chaplains, volunteers, and all who toil within this vastly popularized, frequently misunderstood, and endlessly fascinating community. More important, there is much in the book about patients, for whom hospitals were created and to whom they are supposed to be devoted.

When to stop researching and start writing? The project never ends. In Toronto General alone, a story worthy of front-page coverage happens every day. After two and a half years, there was suddenly the big news of the merger between Toronto General Hospital and Toronto Western Hospital, which I decided to include. Then the brouhaha over Bill 94, the provincial government's bill to ban extra billing, and the doctors on strike, shutting down emergency departments, threatening to shut down intensive care units. I decided not to dwell on the doctors' strike. It had a lot to do with doctors and their frustrations, but not that much to do with how a hospital functions twenty-four hours a day, seven days a week. By autumn, the smoke would have cleared, and doubtless a new controversy would be raging. Medicine and health care are a volatile field.

Early one morning last winter, well before dawn, I was with Ron Lindzon, a bright young doctor in Emergency at Toronto

General. He was sewing up a bad cut in a woman's arm and explaining the work of an emergency physician. At one point, as my little tape recorder rolled on in the pocket of my white coat, Lindzon asked me for a package of suture thread. I walked across the room, selected the proper package from the cabinet, pulled out a satchel, and cracked it open for him. When I realized what I had done, I knew it was time to start writing.

I would like to thank David Cobb, Loral Dean, and John Edward Slinger for reading the raw manuscript, for suggesting improvements, and for eliminating certain imbecilities. Also, Harley Smyth, my neurosurgeon friend, for giving it a stern, Oxonian medical read. And John Tennyson McLeod for again supplying me with a shelf of appropriate books. And Kathleen Richards of Macmillan of Canada, my editor, for her enthusiasm and "good eye." And Douglas Gibson, who encouraged me to come to Macmillan in the first place. And my children, Sean and Michelle, for putting up with an obsessed and grumpy father for the better part of three years. And the Ontario Arts Council and the Canada Council for their financial support.

I miss the place a bit these days. For a time I felt as if I had a job, a place by the water cooler. I'd go back any time, even as a patient.

MARTIN O'MALLEY
Aurora, Ontario
June 1986

CHAPTER 1

Jennifer
on Christmas
Eve

A COOL, MOIST evening and snow fell into the lights and blew across the street, melting on the windshields of the taxis parked in a row outside the hospital. The drivers sat behind their steering wheels, waiting for visiting hours to end so they could make the last run, then go home to spend Christmas Eve with their families.

From the sidewalk on Christmas Eve, the hospital looked only barely festive, like a dour and obstinate Scrooge who had condescended to wear a silly hat for the sake of the party. Colored lights strung here and there over bush-sized evergreens. Christmas cards, red poinsettias, and scratchy little potted pines on the window sills in some of the lighted rooms higher up, above the offices, labs and operating rooms, which were in darkness. On the face of the new Eaton Wing, clusters of Christmas lights looked like celestial barnacles on the prow of a ship pushing through an arctic blizzard. Two orange-and-white ambulances were parked in the curved driveway at the emergency entrance, one with the rear doors swung open.

You can tell a lot about a hospital by its emergency department, in the same way that you can tell a lot about a restaurant by its soup. Good soup can't be bluffed; neither can good emergency medicine. There is nothing subtle about a body mashed under the wheels of a subway train or a thumb sliced off by a high-speed press. There is something honest about a broken bone.

Elsewhere, in the great beyond of the hospital, things are more complex and not always what they appear. Toronto General is a teaching hospital, with some of the best equipment available in modern medicine, with some of the finest medical brains and skills on the continent; but it is intensely doctor-centred, not patient-centred. On the morning after open-heart surgery, an aching and befuddled patient must tolerate, as best he can, an entourage of solemn young doctor-trainees parading into his room behind their mentor, who conducts a Socratic dissertation on what worked and what didn't work and what might go wrong next. "And what do you see *here*, Dr. McGillicuddy?" The sicker the patient, the longer the dissertation — the worse the intrusion.

Rich and well-connected patients often are not treated as well as poor and badly connected patients. For instance, the poor alcoholic patient usually is referred to a social worker, or a psychiatrist, or the Addiction Research Foundation. The rich alcoholic patient might get a shot of brandy with his dinner every night. Hospitalized doctors and VIPs get the worst treatment of all. Nobody wants to discomfort them, or intrude too often, or ask embarrassing questions, so often they are left to languish in respectful but debilitating neglect.

People die in hospitals every day. A social worker mentions a recent study that shows that the public's perception of "natural death" is a death in a hospital, in intensive care, hooked to tubes and wires, with an oxygen mask clamped to the face and various geegaws whumping and thumping in the background. "That's considered a natural death today," he said. "Not at home, in your old bed, with someone handing you a last smoke as you listen to the Red Sox and Blue Jays in the bottom of the eighth."

And there is something more troublesome, ominous. Curious transplant surgeons sometimes wander over to the intensive care units to check on dying patients, especially the victims of accidents, homicides, and suicide attempts who have agreed to donate their organs for transplants. They ask about the patient's blood type, the medication prescribed, the dosage. The surgeons might be waiting for a kidney, or a liver, or a heart, and certain drugs administered can make a dying patient unsuitable as a donor. They have patients who are desperately in need of a kidney, or a liver, or a heart. Their transplant research has been heavily funded, and they have deadlines. They do not ever say, right out, that a certain medication be changed, or suspended — the patient might still live, after all — but their presence is disturbing and their questions bother the nurses.

Everyone is welcome in Emergency. It is open twenty-four hours a day, seven days a week, fifty-two weeks a year. It is the Department of The Lowest Common Denominator, the easiest way in. No reservations are required, no need for referrals, no need even for a family doctor. The doors, figuratively and literally, open automatically. There is a small, scuffy waiting room with coin-operated machines that dispense pop, coffee, tea, and hot chocolate. There are chairs, tables, ash trays, and magazines. Derelicts, addicts, winos, hookers, and bag ladies sometimes drop by, particularly in winter, if only to warm their toes. Some of them are known by their first names. Once a week, soon after dawn but before the cleaners start work, a young man in a three-piece suit arrives carrying a tubular gym bag. He says hello and goes about picking cigarette butts out of the ash trays. He drops them in a plastic bag, puts the plastic bag back in the gym bag, snaps it shut, says goodbye, and leaves.

A large white board faces the nursing station in Emergency that lists the evening's work in red and blue marker-pencil:

Vomiting
Vertigo, vomiting
Abd pain
MVA
GI bleed, admit
Chest prob
Assault, HI
NFW

Not too busy this Christmas Eve. In Emergency, it always is too busy or too quiet. And it can get too busy, or too quiet, in an instant. Observers, especially newspaper writers who come for color stories or television cameramen who come for stock footage, invariably are told in Emergency: "You should have been here *last* night."

Most of the ailments are obvious: abd pain — abdominal pain; assault, HI — head injury; GI bleed — gastrointestinal bleeding; MVA — motor vehicle accident; vomiting — vomiting. The ones in red are referrals, patients sent to the hospital by family doctors or transferred from other hospitals; the ones in blue are people who have walked, or crawled, in off the street, sometimes with a nosebleed, sometimes with a gunshot wound.

NFW?

"Not feeling well," Nurse Beryl Reid explained.

Nurse Beryl, in her late forties, was the night triage nurse on duty, which made her the traffic cop in Emergency, directing new arrivals to their proper rooms, scolding the obstreperous, soothing the hollerers and whimperers. Shift upon shift Nurse Beryl works up to her elbows in pain, fear, anger, blood, excrement, and meets irate spouses, worried parents, anxious lovers — all convinced *their* emergencies are life-and-death, the reason for the hospital to exist at that moment. She does it with such wonderful equanimity that visitors sometimes entertain the possibility that someone who has stopped breathing might not be in that bad shape after all.

"Look, you dumb twits!" the red-faced trucker shouted as he banged through the swinging doors to Emergency. Nurse Beryl looked over her shoulder at a colleague and rolled her eyes upward as if to say, Oh my, aren't we having a time tonight? Emergency departments could not function without smart, experienced triage nurses who can recognize real emergencies and sniff out phony ones and, when necessary, which is just about every shift, de-fuse situations that would panic air traffic controllers. It helps to have a sense of humor, a sense of irony, and a sense of the absurd, in no particular order.

Nurse Beryl is small but authoritative, and she gets along with everyone — patients, ambulance attendants, cops, orderlies, the other nurses, the doctors, even the occasional hospital administrator who comes along every now and then in a blue suit to see what a hospital is really like. Laugh lines are etched on her face like ripples in a summer pond and she has a knack of flirting without appearing suggestive. Pinned to her starched, white uniform is a jewelled timepiece, with the clockface upside down so she can check the time without having to use her hands. "In England, nurses can't wear wristwatches," she said. "Might cut or scrape the patients. Can't wear rings either, except for wedding bands."

Only weeks ago, on another night shift, a young man had walked through the doors to Emergency holding a gun to his head, threatening to blow out his brains. Nurse Beryl had walked up to him from across the room like a friendly aunt and said, "My, my, my . . ." The other nurses in Emergency still talk about it in the lunch room. The young man stared down at her, still holding the gun. "I wish you wouldn't do that," Nurse Beryl continued. "There are a lot of sick people in here and you're upsetting them." The young man looked baffled, then bemused, and Nurse Beryl took the gun away and that was that.

She arrived at the hospital in the 1960s, during the heyday of hippiedom, when Emergency regularly was crammed with youngsters in beads and headbands, some trembling with dysentery, others dreamy-eyed, some freaked out or knocked out by drugs. On some shifts the place looked like an antiseptic head shop.

"LSD was the worst of them all," she recalled. "Kids used to think they could jump off buildings and fly — and some of them did! Oh, it was riotous."

One summer afternoon a young man and a young woman were carried in, both badly strung out on LSD. They had arrived from different ends of the city and, because Emergency was crowded to overflowing, they had to be put in the same room. It is not against hospital regulations to do this, but for reasons of delicacy, males and females usually are put in separate rooms. "Right over there," Nurse Beryl said. "Room twenty-six — twenty-six A, twenty-six B. It's one room, but you can pull curtains around each bed for privacy. That's what I did, then I went off to attend to somebody else. When I came back, oh my, they were out of their beds and doing it, on the floor. *On the floor!* It was like that old movie with Clark Gable and Claudette Colbert, in the motel room, when the trumpet sounds and the bedsheet falls down — the walls of Jericho." She tilted her head and winked. "Anyway, we just closed the door. We were too busy."

Suddenly, a loud crash from one of the Emergency rooms — *kraang-awaang-awangawangawangang!* A huge pause, heads perked up in and all around the nursing station, then, as everyone recognized the noise of a metal bed pan hitting the floor, great, eye-watering howls of laughter.

Another scribble went up on the board:

Dyspnea

Dyspnea?

"Shortness of breath," said Nurse Beryl. "We used to use SOB but we had to stop doing this because too many people thought it meant 'son of a bitch' . . ." she paused, then, with exquisite timing, added, ". . . which many patients in Emergency are."

Off to the cafeteria for coffee and a sandwich, along scrubbed, tiled corridors, about as far as a city block from Emergency. Three nurses at one end of a long table were discussing

Christmas suicides. Only three so far this week. There usually are more at Christmas, as there are in spring, when people feel cheated for not feeling as hopeful as the rest of the world. "A jumper and two carbon monoxides," said a Filipino nurse who was brown-bagging it Christmas Eve. "None of them were successful." The jumper jumped off an office building and scraped his face and snapped bones in his arms and legs. Probably changed his mind after he jumped and tried to stop his fall by grabbing at the side of the building, which was made of bricks.

There was a suicide attempt last summer, another jumper who broke nearly every bone in his body and was carried in a bloody heap to Emergency. When they got the call, orderlies kept the elevator doors behind Emergency open so the man could be rushed straight to an operating room upstairs as soon as he arrived. They got enough blood and oxygen into him in time, stitched him together expertly, and after more than a week in intensive care, the jumper was recovering nicely. Everyone felt terrific about having saved a life in a most dramatic way, but the day the man was released he went directly to a subway station, dropped ninety-five cents in the slot and threw himself in front of the first train.

The carbon monoxide was a sixteen-year-old boy who had been to church with his parents, then sat down to eat lunch with them. After a time, he left the table and walked out to the garage, where his parents later found him slumped unconscious in the front seat of the car, the engine running.

"How can you be sure it's a suicide?" I asked. At sixteen years old, at that time of year I used always to grow tired of hearing Bing Crosby's "I'm Dreaming of a White Christmas" and chipmunks singing carols. Any teenager might have gone to the car and turned on the radio and, if it got too chilly, might have started the car to get some heat.

"I know what you mean," the youngest nurse says, getting up from the table to head back to her station. "I wouldn't mind some Bruce Springsteen right now."

Christmas Eve in a hospital is really no busier and no quieter than any other night of the year. Jennifer, a twenty-six-year-old telephone operator was waiting for her transplant operation in a private room on the ninth floor of the Eaton Wing. The room cost $491 a day and she had been in the hospital for nine months, waiting, while the transplant team practised on pigs and cadavers. A month ago, David Allen, director of public relations for the hospital, had dropped by her room. He had copies of press releases that the hospital wanted to issue after the operation and he wanted to explain the public relations procedure to her.

She had only recently been transferred to a private room. She had been sharing a semi-private room with a woman her own age for several months and they had become friends. The roommate had been so excited about sharing a room with someone she thought was about to become famous that she had called a friend who worked as a reporter at *The Toronto Star*. The reporter kept phoning Jennifer in her room to ask if he could talk to her and write a story about her. She wasn't interested, but the reporter kept calling, and one afternoon he called when her mother was visiting. "He seemed to be really angry at me," Jennifer said. "I had to hang up in his ear."

Jennifer's operation would be big news. It would be the first small bowel transplant anywhere in the world in fifteen years. The last one had been done in New York in 1970, and the patient lived for seventy-six days, the longest anyone has ever lived with a small bowel transplant. All small bowel transplants were stopped after that. They were considered too risky, and perhaps a luxury after it had been determined that people without natural digestive function could be kept alive indefinitely on total parenteral nutrition, TPN, which provides adequate nutrition intravenously. Jennifer had been on TPN for months. She hated it.

"Hi Jennifer."

She was drowsy, weak, and barely lifted her head from the pillow. Christmas cards hung from a string taped to the wall over the bed. There were more on shelves and on her bedside table and on the window sill. A small plastic Christmas tree, with lights and decorations, stood on another table at the foot of the bed. One of the blue lights blinked on and off.

She said she felt like having a visitor, which was a way of saying that sometimes she does *not* feel like having a visitor. Hospital visits can brighten up the day, be something to look forward to, if only as a break in the routine, but sometimes they can be bothersome and disruptive. Especially when the visits are unannounced and the visitors are shy and embarrassed. Or when the conversation is stilted and drags on repetitively, interminably. Or when the room is crammed with visitors and everyone is talking at the same time, like a mad morning at the stock exchange. Or when the patient has just awakened and feels numb and dishevelled and knows there is a bad smell in the room and it is hers.

"Any word?"

"Now it looks like it'll be after the holidays," Jennifer said. She was wearing a white cotton nightgown stitched at the bodice with tiny red and pink flowers. A delicate gold cross hung at her neck. She reached for a can of ginger ale on her bedside, poured it into a Styrofoam cup. "Oops," she said, as it fuzzed over the side. "I'm a little dopey tonight. I had to take some morphine, for the pain." Tall and slender, she was a woman who, with her hair brushed and any sort of everyday make-up, could turn heads on the street. She had been prepared for the transplant operation for months, knowing that she could be told any day or night — even Christmas Eve — that a suitable donor had been found and the operation was a go. The consent form she had signed for the operation, regarded as highly experimental, with great risks, was in the drawer of her bedside table.

"My parents were in today," she said, pulling herself upright, reaching over to the bedside table for a package of cigarettes. "They're staying at the Holiday Inn." She lighted her cigarette and exhaled a long, grey cloud of smoke that rolled into the screen of a small television set swung over the bed at her knees. "Maybe I'll be able to get out of here for a while tomorrow and see them in *their* room."

She could leave the hospital for brief periods, maybe a couple of hours. The longest she had ever stayed out, during her nine months, was twenty days. Then something went awry, the TPN tubes got blocked, and she had to be rushed back in.

Jennifer had familial polyposis, a rare and inherited disease that consists of growths of polyps, or tumors, arising from the lining of the gastrointestinal tract. The condition becomes familial polyposis when the colon, or large intestine, sprouts more than a hundred such growths, any of which could become malignant, leading to cancer of the colon or rectum.

On the bedside table was a small blue pamphlet, titled "Familial Polyposis: A Guide for Patients and Their Families." It read: "The knowledge that familial polyposis is hereditary should encourage all family members to be examined and treated at an early stage. Immediate family members at risk are the children of the patient, the patient's siblings, and the children of the patient's siblings. The earlier the condition is found, the more effective the degree of cancer prevention will be.''

As far as Jennifer knew, she was the first in her family ever to have been struck by the disease. Her father might have had it, but he died when she was very young, so she didn't know. In this condition, the polyps usually appear first in the rectum and lower part of the colon at about the age of puberty. Then there is a interval of about a decade between the appearance of the polyps and the onset of symptoms, which makes the average age of diagnosis twenty-two years. Jennifer was only fifteen, on a vacation in Europe, when she realized something was wrong in her body. When she returned, she was examined at Kingston General Hospital, but nobody there detected the problem at that early stage. The polyposis manifested itself with a vengeance years later, in her early twenties.

The first operation was to remove Jennifer's colon, part of the large bowel, in a procedure called a colectomy. The next operation was to remove the rectum, the end of the large bowel, where most of the polyps were located. The two operations had therefore removed Jennifer's entire large bowel, which meant she also required an ileostomy, a surgical opening of the small bowel onto the abdominal wall that allows body wastes to empty into a small, external bag.

Jennifer then developed episodes of small bowel obstruction, caused by adhesions, or kinks, in the small bowel. Like a garden hose which, in cold weather, can become brittle and twist in weird shapes, changes in the small bowel can block the flow of liquid through it. This is basically what happened in Jennifer, and several further operations had been required to try to straighten her small bowel.

Next she developed a large desmoid tumor, a tough, fibrous growth that infiltrated the mesentery, a suspending mantle of tissue that carries blood to the bowels. This caused more intestinal kinking. Desmoid tumors are benign, but they keep growing, slowly and steadily. They are difficult to remove, and when they are cut out, they may grow back. Jennifer's doctors decided they could not relieve the bowel obstructions without removing the tumor, but they were reluctant to do so because the tumor was too large, about the size of a large grapefruit, and diffuse. There was too great a risk of trauma and bleeding. They left it in and sewed her up.

Jennifer's doctor at Toronto General was Zane Cohen, a surgeon who had researched the procedure for a small bowel transplant for ten years. He was forty years old, a slight, quiet-spoken man who, if he weren't quite so serious, might resemble Woody Allen. His office was in the Eaton Wing, on the same floor as Jennifer's private room, down a hallway and past a bank of elevators.

Cohen also operated on Jennifer to assess the desmoid tumor, but he, too, closed her up without removing it, for the same reasons as the other doctors. The desmoid tumor simply looked too amorphous, too intransigent. She continued to exist on intravenous feeding, which she detested because of her bed-ridden dependence on the tubes through which minerals, proteins, and fat solutions trickled into her body to keep her alive. Total parenteral nutrition (TPN) is expensive, about thirty-five thousand dollars a year, and there is a constant risk of infection where the feeding tube enters the body. It also restricts a patient to a thoroughly boring, demoralizing existence, and this was especially so for an adventurous young woman.

Jennifer kept asking Cohen if he could try again to remove the desmoid tumor. He finally agreed, and although this time he managed to remove it, the operation also involved the removal of her entire small intestine: this meant she would be dependent on intravenous feeding tubes for the rest of her life. Cohen called it a major operation. "It wasn't that difficult to do, but it was an extremely unusual procedure, and it left her with no small bowel, no large bowel, no rectum. She has 'nothing' in there."

The next step, which Jennifer was eager to take, was a small bowel transplant. Cohen and his team of transplant surgeons had been practising the procedure for months, first on labor-atory animals, mainly pigs and dogs, then on newly dead human cadavers. Teaching-hospital cadavers kept in cold storage are useless for transplant research. Even dead bodies that have been around for a day or two are no good because small bowel cells die off too soon and the bowel quickly turns gangrenous. For the purposes of transplant research, the best corpses are brain-dead and tissue-alive. These can be the victims of car accidents, suicides, murders, and other assorted mayhem without which transplants would be impossible. During the "practice runs," when the surgeons removed a small bowel and then put it back in again, blood was kept pumping through the corpse. It is a gruesome, eerie procedure.

For Cohen, the small bowel transplant presented two addi-tional problems. It had never been done successfully before.

Nor was it an emergency operation, like a kidney transplant, or a heart or lung transplant. A person can live indefinitely without intestines on intravenous feeding, which made this operation a ticklish affair for the hospital's ethics committee, which must approve all surgical research. When Cohen appeared before the committee, he explained how cyclosporin, the new immunosuppressive wonder drug, would be used.

Cyclosporin appears to have facilitated a new era of transplant surgery, enabling surgeons around the world to transplant kidneys, hearts, lungs, livers, and other vital organs with remarkable early success. More than a year ago, Tom Hall, a fifty-eight-year-old Toronto businessman, had had a single-lung transplant at Toronto General. Today he is the world's longest-surviving single-lung transplant patient, and every day he stays alive, Toronto General makes medical history.

Cohen told the ethics committee that a small bowel transplant would be easier than most other transplants because rejection of the new organ could be detected more quickly. This was because part of the new bowel would be exposed, brought outside the abdominal wall in an ileostomy. This would enable daily biopsies of the new organ to determine if rejection was taking place. Cohen told the committee that if he detected signs of rejection, he would be able to re-operate to remove the new bowel.

Still, he worried. If something went wrong, if Jennifer died — he had explained the risks and she had accepted them — Cohen could be criticized on ethical grounds for going ahead with an operation that amounted to a form of human experimentation. Every night, as he fell asleep, Cohen ran through the operation in his head.

Jennifer reached for another cigarette, as the blue light on the little tree at the end of her bed blinked on and off. "I'm quitting next year, when I'm out of here."

"Anything you'd like me to bring next time?"

"Maybe a 7-Up."

"It's okay to drink pop?"

"Yeah. Liquids are okay. What I'd really like is a Big Mac — a hot, juicy Big Mac."

Because she had virtually no digestive system, she couldn't eat anything: she had developed a keen sense of food. She often thought not only of how food tastes, but of how it looks and smells, how artfully it can be arranged on a plate, how vegetables can be soft or crunchy, how sauces can be tart or sweet, how biting into a fresh stick of celery squirts a cool spray of mist at the roof of the mouth. Food, like music — like cigarettes, for that matter — evoked a nostalgia for other times and places. Sometimes Jennifer ordered a meal just for the satisfaction of waiting for it, then chewing it, tasting it, even if she had to spit out every mouthful. "I still do it with an orange once in a while." The last food she remembered actually swallowing was a piece of dry toast, about a year ago. From a radio at the nursing station down the hall came Liona Boyd playing Bach's "Sheep May Safely Graze." "Another thing I really want is to go swimming, somewhere where it's warm and breezy."

"You used to be a big swimmer?"

"No, I hardly ever went swimming. Funny."

It was time to go. A clumsy attempt to kiss her on the cheek but the bed and the paraphernalia of the TPN were in the way so I squeezed her big toe through the blanket. She smiled.

"Merry Christmas, Jennifer."

"Yeah. You too."

CHAPTER 2

Maybe I Couldn't Run a Thousand-Bed Hospital

HOSPITALS NEVER look inviting. Welcome, perhaps, when you need one, or when someone close to you needs one, but never inviting. They always feel cold, as if someone had left a door open. They always make you feel exposed, as if you had awakened in a train station in your pajamas. Too many memories of waiting, worry, fear, the anticipation of fear, or worse. ("Your tests are back, and I'm sorry to have to tell you . . .") The bigger the hospital is, the less inviting, the more likely to conjure the thought: *Something could go terribly wrong in here.*

This one, Toronto General Hospital, sprawls over a large downtown block, the different wings in different shades of brown brick, each evoking a different era. It is one of the oldest hospitals in North America. It began as a military hospital in 1812, the creation of a citizens' group known as "The Loyal and Patriotic Society," but the following year, invading United States troops captured what was then the Town of York, took the supplies and equipment from the hospital, and burned it to the ground. It went up again, in another neighborhood, then another, until it finally moved, like an upwardly mobile family, to its current address (across from what are now the treed and verdant lawns of Queen's Park, the provincial Parliament building).

This is TGH. It is "The Big House." It is "The Flagship Hospital," one of the largest hospitals in North America. It is a massive and bewildering complex, truly a town within a city: 1,000 beds, 4,000 employees, its own police force, its own purified air, its own germs (more lethal than germs outside).

For the year in question, the annual budget was $169 million, which would rise by $8 million the next year, and certainly by another $10 million the year after that. There was a merger in the works with Toronto Western Hospital, a mile or so to the west, which would make all the figures bigger still.

On every shift, someone in one of the rooms confronts one life crisis or another: cancer, a new baby, open-heart surgery, a new kidney, a new lung, loneliness, sorrow, fear, pain, death. There are needles and knives, vile-tasting medications, soothing analgesics — morphine, cocaine, heroin — and tools that look like they belong in an auto-body shop. There are tubes people want to push up your nose, down your throat, in your ears, up your ass, until you do not think more is possible. People remember for the rest of their lives, in eidetic detail, the times they had to *go to the hospital*.

Some arrive feeling like characters in a Russian novel, or a soap opera. They were somebody worthy of attention, and now it mattered not if they were relegated to a bed in a corridor for five hours while orderlies walked by discussing baseball's infield fly rule. Something serious happened and they were not in control of their own lives, so off they went to the hospital in a trail of woe and worry. Nothing is quite as self-absorbing as hearing the wail of the siren from inside an ambulance.

People who have worked at Toronto General for a decade still manage occasionally to get lost in the maddening labyrinth of corridors, tunnels, wings, operating rooms, intensive care units, nursing stations, offices, boardrooms, laboratories, lecture theatres, cafeterias, freezers, and storage rooms.

Patients sometimes get lost here, too. Usually they are found quickly, in an hour or two, probably watching television on the wrong floor, but sometimes it takes longer.

On March 24, 1981, patient Howard Grossman, who had undergone brain surgery, was reported missing. The hospital's public relations office issued a press release that began: "A thirty-year-old male patient is missing from Toronto General Hospital. While the patient is not considered to be dangerous, it is imperative for medical reasons that he be found and returned to the hospital." Then a massive search began, a search that involved every available person in the hospital, as well as police and police dogs; that extended to the dark, wet tunnels that lead under the streets to the Hospital for Sick Children and Mount Sinai Hospital; and that was accompanied by an increasingly hysterical news coverage.

Grossman's brother, Allan, took part in the search with a security guard, who had been hired only two months earlier. They started in the basements, then explored some of the hospital's abandoned wings. Allan Grossman came upon a tunnel that looked as if it had not been used for years. He asked the guard where it went. The guard had no idea. They followed it until they had walked entirely under College Street to the Banting Institute, the famous research centre that gave insulin to the world.

Allan and the guard entered an abandoned lecture hall, then a dissecting room, then a huge, walk-in freezer filled with jars of specimens. There was blood on the floor. They backed out and found themselves in a boiler room, then a room with cages of rats and mice. They could hear dogs barking, thrashing against cages, and somewhere in the dark Allan heard a cow mooing. Frightened, the two men ran out, only to find a series of open doors all marked RADIOACTIVE MATERIAL — DANGER.

In one of the sub-basements, they encountered a mechanic who told them he had seen a patient wandering around in a backless hospital gown two hours earlier. Allan questioned the mechanic thoroughly until he was convinced that the man the guard had seen was not his brother. It was *another* patient.

It was a public relations nightmare at the time, of course, but years later nearly everyone at the hospital can recount a favorite story of the big search. One night a policeman and his dog, a German shepherd named Bronc, prowled a basement corridor and, as they passed what looked like an ordinary closet, the dog suddenly stopped and sniffed loudly and began to growl. The policeman told a security guard to open the door, but the guard assured the policeman that the door already had been checked, more than once. Bronc kept sniffing and growling.

"I want that door opened — *now!*" the policeman demanded.

The guard reluctantly opened the door and behind it they found another guard, sound asleep.

Twelve days later, the searchers found Howard Grossman in a small mechanical room on the fourth floor of the new Eaton Wing, naked and dehydrated, lying on a grating with his head resting on a pillow made from his rolled-up, blue-and-white pajamas. He was dead.

For such a hulk of a place, Toronto General is remarkably efficient and creative, with a legacy of stunning medical breakthroughs, any single one of which could have made it famous. In 1906, it was the first general hospital in Canada to open a psychiatric unit. The first diabetic patient in the world to be treated with insulin was treated here in 1922. The blood thinner heparin, developed in the labs at Toronto General, was used here in 1935 — another world first. Also, North America's first artificial kidney was created here. Researchers at Toronto General perfected the therapeutic use of hypothermia, which lowers the body temperature and reduces the patient's need for oxygen, making open-heart surgery possible. The first human heart valve transplantation was done here. The world's first coronary intensive care unit opened here.

The hospital is part of a huge downtown medical complex in Toronto, known unofficially as Bedpan Alley, that includes Toronto General, the Hospital for Sick Children immediately to the south, Mount Sinai Hospital across University Avenue to the west, and Women's College Hospital to the north. Every hospital has its own constituency, the community to which it is accountable, and which in turn contributes money and volunteers.

The Hospital for Sick Children, whose research labs gave the world the gummy nutrition of Pablum, is accountable to both younger patients and the families of the children. It is one of the finest pediatric hospitals in the world, though its reputation was besmirched by a horrible and tragic series of still-unexplained baby deaths — murders, some are convinced — in the early 1980s. Mount Sinai's constituency is Toronto's Jewish community, and, as the fabric and texture of the neighborhood changes, Toronto's Chinese community. Further to the east, in the downtown core, is St. Michael's Hospital, serving primarily the Roman Catholic community. Toronto General's constituency? "Queen's Park," replied a senior hospital executive, referring to the provincial Parliament building just north of the hospital, but also, obliquely, to Toronto's powerful White Anglo-Saxon Protestant community. "If a cabinet minister's lover gets pregnant, she comes here for the abortion."

W. Vickery Stoughton is president of Toronto General Hospital.

His office is on the ground floor of the Bell Wing, down an august corridor lined with heavily framed portraits of his illustrious predecessors, most of them full-bearded, with solemn, Smith Brothers faces that befit the great healers and captains of industry who have guided the destiny of the old and honorable institution. The reception area of W. Vickery Stoughton's office is tiny, with four oxblood-leather chairs squeezed in front of a partition — behind which is the skittering sound of someone typing on a word processor — and a small table with newspapers still cold from the winter outside.

Waiting, one expected a hospital president named W. Vickery Stoughton to be as imposing and solemn-looking as the faces in the corridor outside, and then a young fellow with good teeth and a shock of brown hair stepped around the partition, extended a hand in greeting, and said, "Hi, I'm Vick Stoughton." It was a surprise, for W. Vickery Stoughton vaguely resembled the childhood comic book character Superboy.

Stoughton's office is not grandiose, hardly even presidential. It is large enough, but it is rather plain, functional: venetian blinds; a leafy green plant in a large pot by the window in a corner; a sofa and coffee table against the wall opposite his desk, which is clear and tidy. He sat across the coffee table from his guest and crossed his legs. It was four o'clock on a cold December afternoon, still three hours to go in the president's twelve-hour day. He wore a brown three-piece suit, pin-striped and well-pressed, with a light-blue shirt. His gaze was direct, with bushy eyebrows over deep brown, smoky eyes that seemed never to blink. "I'm coffee'd out," he said, as he poured water from a silver-plated pitcher into two small crystal glasses on the coffee table.

Before any questions were asked, Stoughton moved from his chair to the sofa, as if to make his guest feel there were no barriers between them. Inevitably one remembered comments made in the public relations office earlier: "Stoughton is the new-breed administrator," said David Allen, public relations director for the hospital. "If you want to know him, read *In Search of Excellence*, the book on how America's best-run companies are managed. Stoughton could have written it." It was what a director of public relations would be expected to say, but for Stoughton it was not an exaggeration.

To begin, Stoughton hunched forward and shuffled some papers on the coffee table. They were sheets of statistics, part of the hospital's latest financial report that lists the number of admissions, patient-days, average occupancy, and dozens of other statistical references. The figures showed that the average length of stay at Toronto General for the year just ended had been 9.7 days, with an average occupancy rate of 86.42 per cent. Stoughton studied the statistics like a baseball fan poring over the Saturday morning batting averages. Then he got right down to business.

"If the average occupancy reaches 93 or 95 per cent, problems start," he said. "We need those extra, vacant beds for flexibility, for emergencies. Occupancy is highest in the middle of the week, lowest on weekends. Saturday is the big discharge day, Sunday the big admission day. When the average occupancy slips over 90 per cent, we start postponing elective surgery, things like gallbladders, cysts, hemorrhoids, and simple hernias. If the average occupancy is 90 per cent every day, we have problems getting patients in and out, which results in beds having to be set up in corridors and spare rooms and broom closets.

"The optimum average occupancy rate is 85 per cent. We don't like to postpone elective surgery because it's hard on people who have taken time off from work because they've been told they would have an operation on a given date, but we've got to have the flexibility for emergencies. We don't close Emergency under *any* circumstances."

More statistics: Every day, 87 patients are admitted, 108 walk or are carried into Emergency, 100 surgical operations are performed, 420 X-rays are taken, 4,282 meals are served, 14,576 pounds of laundry are washed, 3 patients die, 9 babies are born, 10 are aborted. Yearly operating expenses for the year Stoughton was studying amounted to $169,306,180: salaries and wages, medical and surgical supplies, gases, drugs, dietary provisions, housekeeping supplies, plant operation, security, employee benefits, telephone, stationery, depreciation, bad debts — nearly half a million dollars a day.

Anyone who runs a hospital has to be able to look at big dollar-signs without twitching. Requests keep coming in from the various departments for new machines, because a sprocket has worn out, or because there is a newer, better machine to do the same job. One of the more expensive items may be a CT (computerized tomographic) scanner, a machine that X-rays the entire body — up, down, sideways — and for nearly a decade has been *the* prestige item at any hospital worth its salt. The CT-scanner is to the hospital what the stereo video recorder is to the mid-town reno. A good CT-scanner will run about $900,000, tops, and cost about $500,000 a year to operate.

The priorities at the moment were not overly daunting. Nursing needed two phototherapy lamps, at $1,750 apiece. Clinical Biochemistry wanted a blood glucose analyser, $6,672. Also an automatic urinalysis dipstick reader, $7,640 — a number-one priority. Microbiology requested a letter-quality printer, $3,488 — given a number-three priority. The Blood Transfusion

Lab needed a $10,200 countertop freezer. Cardiology wanted a 16-channel arrhythmia monitor which cost $75,435 — another number-one priority. Stoughton scanned them as he would weather reports from across the country.

The benefit rates for various medical procedures are constantly changing, but they are all set down in page after page of a booklet published by the Ontario Hospital Insurance Plan. To have an arm amputated costs $219.40 (same for a leg). An appendectomy is $180; a cornea transplant $417.50; a simple mastectomy costs $200.85, and a radical mastectomy, $370.80. A caesarian section costs $204.70 (with a hysterectomy, $502.10). A coronary bypass costs $648.75, a double bypass $881.25 (each additional bypass, $138.75). A hemorrhoidectomy with the dreaded sigmoidoscope costs $169.95. To circumcise a male infant costs $26.30, an adult male $67.20.

It is easier to be a big hospital than a little hospital when it comes to bottom lines, or financial survival, or "zero-based budgeting," as hospital administrators prefer. Savings tend to be "redirected," which is another way of saying to the outside snoops to whom you may be accountable — try-to-find-it-if-you-can. Put simply, big hospitals have more money to throw around, to hold back, to tuck away, to invest, to roll over. A good hospital accountant can make more money from money in a day than a top neurosurgeon could earn in a year.

Every month, the board of trustees meets in the boardroom down the hall from Stoughton's office. One of the regular items of business comes under the heading *Security Transactions*, which represent financial wizardry of the highest order.

Three items from one meeting listed under the subheading *Sundry Trust*:

3 OCTOBER, 1985: *Purchased $700,000 discounted Canada Treasury Bills for 169 days to mature 21st March, 1986, to yield 9.10%. Discounted at $671,699. Purchased from proceeds of Bank of Montreal $700,000 discounted Banker's Acceptance at 8.99% matured same day.*

10 OCTOBER, 1985: *Purchased $900,000 discounted Government of Canada Treasury Bills for 176 days to mature 4th April, 1986, to yield 9.02%. Discounted at $862,488. Purchased from proceeds of Montreal Trust $891,000 Guaranteed Investment Certificate at 9.25% matured same day.*

29 OCTOBER, 1985: *Purchased $800,000 discounted Toronto Dominion Banker's Acceptance for 177 days to mature 24th April, 1986, to yield 8.82%. Discounted at $767,184. Purchased*

*from proceeds of Toronto Dominion $1,200,000 Term Deposit
at 9.45% matured same day. Balance of funds credited to
account to cover operating expenses.*

The three transactions produced $98,629 from interest alone,
merely by spinning dollars. And they were only three of ten
such transactions reported at the board meeting that month.
The ten transactions reported at the October meeting generated
a total of $268,551 — money from money. It is all possible because
of the large amounts involved, and because of Toronto General's
unofficial policy of delaying payment of bills for sixty days,
which frees up a lot of dollars. Also, the hospital, modern as
it is, has been reluctant to switch to a system that would
automatically deposit cheques in employees' bank accounts.
This is because it has been estimated that most employees,
if paid on a Thursday, do not cash their cheques until the
following Monday, which allows the hospital three more days
to work with it.

The administrator responsible for the magic is William
Louth, the hospital's genial if parsimonious executive vice-
president. At some hospital social functions, often held at
Toronto's finest hostelries, most staffers drive their cars to
the front door and use the valet service, but Louth is regularly
seen walking briskly along the sidewalk to the party because
he managed to find a flat-rate parking lot several blocks away.

The modern teaching hospital is the most complex organization
in society. It is a business, a corporation, a hotel, a school,
a restaurant, a charity, a supermarket of balms and medications, a self-contained community that functions seven days
a week, twenty-four hours a day. It is new, as these things
go, a phenomenon of the twentieth century, really only of the
past fifty or sixty years, when, as Yale University's pioneering
neurosurgeon Harvey Cushing once said, medical and biological
discoveries were bursting like "popcorn in the pan."

The hospital's three-fold duties are to cure, to teach, and
to do research. Daily, nightly, within its walls, there are birth
and death, joy and sadness, fear and pain. There are doctors
and nurses roaming the corridors whom patients regard as
candidates for beatification, and others they see as misan-
thropes who might want to remove their gallbladders just for
the heck of it.

The hospital must meet and maintain standards of excellence
despite the budget limitations and restraints imposed within
a highly regulated health profession, despite public scrutiny,

criticism, and the everyday crises of life and death. There are power plays involving all levels of government, labor unions, and physicians and surgeons, some of whom have barn-door-sized egos and wince every year when they discover they are not on the short list for the Nobel Prize. Most of the doctors are not even hospital employees, but highly paid, powerful entrepreneurs provided with inexpensive office space, with nurses and interns and technicians and orderlies as support staff, with discounted meals, free work clothes, billions of dollars' worth of equipment with which to tinker, and nearly unlimited freedom to order drugs and medicine, all paid for by the hospital. Hospital doctors do not have to go out in the cold to drum up business. They are provided with an inexhaustible supply of clients, most of whom are ready to agree with anything the doctors say and submit to anything the doctors wish to do, even if it kills them.

It wasn't always so. Hospitals used to be regarded as anything but the respectable institutions they are today, the miracle palaces depicted in books, movies, and television. They were pesthouses, poorhouses, refuges for the homeless, the feeble, the insane, and the dying poor. There were no Ben Caseys or Dr. Kildares. By the late nineteenth century, with the advent of asepsis — the use of sterilized instruments — hospitals began to be constructed with operating suites for surgery. At the beginning of the twentieth century, the hospital as we know it emerged, with the doctors afforded the greatest status and prestige. They were plainly in charge. They dominated the institutions because of their superior education and because the early hospital administrators came from less prestigious fields and could easily be dominated. Nurses were expected to serve breakfasts in the doctors' lounges and to rise whenever a doctor approached a nursing station. Still, most people, certainly the influential and well-to-do, preferred to be treated at home by their own doctors and nurses.

By the 1920s the upper crust of society began to recognize the advantages of hospital treatment, with the new gizmos and geegaws invented to detect and treat what used to be regarded as cursed ailments best left to prayer, or, for the less spiritual, leeches. Medicine always has been as much art as science. Wilhelm Konrad Roentgen, the German physicist who discovered that electromagnetic radiations could penetrate solids and thus serve as a useful diagnostic tool, did not know what they were or how they worked, so he called them X-rays.

Hospitals grew, more inventions were invented, wonder drugs were discovered, aggressive and bloody treatment procedures became commonplace, and hospital budgets moved toward the stars. This could change, of course, and the rich and influential may head home again, even for their dying days.

There is a discernible trend in the United States away from hospitalization, a trend documented by Alvin Toffler, author of futuristic tomes such as *Future Shock* and *The Third Wave*, and co-founder of a U.S.-based organization called The Institute for Alternative Futures. Heart patients will likely be treated more with drugs and less with operating-room legerdemain such as the coronary bypass, which is becoming yesterday's medical hemline. Cancer patients who receive intravenous drugs in hospital may also be sent home, because of new technologies such as implantable pumps that will deliver the requisite anti-cancer medication at the touch of a button. The burgeoning hospice movement has already resulted in thousands more dying patients being transferred to restful, caring, non-hospital environments where they can prepare to leave the world while enjoying bridge or euchre — even sex — fending off their pain with adequate doses of morphine or heroin or marijuana or whatever new analgesic sacrament becomes available.

On the other hand, hospitals could become bigger and more bewildering than ever because of the latest medical fashion: organ transplants. Eyes, kidneys, bones, bowels, hearts, lungs, livers, pancreases — you name it — are much in demand and the hospitals of tomorrow could become therapeutic supermarkets. The dangers of abuse are obvious and everywhere. What are the guidelines? Where are the safeguards? How to enforce them? What is to stop the rich and powerful from indulging in all manner of persuasion, manipulation, and corruption in order to buy life?

Kidney transplants, the longest-established organ transplant procedure and the one with the highest success rate, have already made the world black market. Documented cases include a thirty-two-year-old man who was flown from the slums of New Delhi to England where he had a kidney removed and implanted in the wife of his employer. The man explained that he had no choice if he wanted to keep his job, which paid him a dollar a day. A West German industrialist, a former medical doctor, offered to buy kidneys from Third World donors for thirty thousand dollars apiece. The stakes are often too rich for a hospital ethics committee, or a hospital board of trustees composed of the rich and powerful, to resist.

By the 1980s, the hospital itself had become a personified institution, full of intrigue and glamor, and it began to over-shadow the role of individual physicians and surgeons, usually to their chagrin. The Ben Caseys and Dr. Kildares had exited with the spear carriers and Paddy Chayefsky's *The Hospital* and television's "St. Elsewhere" took centre stage.

When you are running a hospital, as W. Vickery Stoughton does, no two days are the same. There was the young woman, a psychiatric patient, who climbed out on a ledge at the top of the Bell Wing — twice on the same day. The second time, Stoughton arrived, told everyone to back off and more or less took charge of the rescue himself.

Another day, a woman patient in a room in the Eaton Wing was found cut from throat to stomach, in what was first considered an attempted suicide, until one of the nurses reported that earlier she had seen a "shadowy figure" hurrying down the hall. Police were called, the woman recovered, no charges were ever laid, and no newspaper story was ever written about it. Another front-page story that never made the front pages.

Then, early on an April Saturday morning in 1985, at Toronto's Queen Elizabeth Hospital, a young woman visited another woman who had been in a coma for six years. Two nurses watched as the visitor swiftly pulled a knife from her sleeve and plunged it into the patient's throat and stomach. The nurses held the attacker until security arrived, then the stabbed patient was rushed to Emergency at Toronto General. A general surgeon and someone from administration who happened to be on call debated whether or not to operate. They called the patient's husband to get his consent and he said don't bother, let her go in peace. The woman had been a vegetable for six years. They decided not to operate, but, against all the odds, the woman clung to life.

Now what? If she dies, a murder charge can be laid. Or can it? What if she dies because the hospital decides not to operate? Is the hospital to blame? Is the husband to blame?

"It was a messy one," said Stoughton, who thinks the stabbing may have been prompted by a full-page feature story that Saturday in *The Toronto Star*, a retrospective account of Karen Ann Quinlan, the woman in Morris Plains, New Jersey, who had been in a coma for ten years. "That often triggers something like this."

There was the sparkling June morning when Stoughton arrived at his office in good spirits, fresh from his morning tennis, to be told: "We have a case of Legionnaires' Disease." The call was from Virology. The patient, an elderly woman with leukemia, had been transferred to Toronto General from Etobicoke General in the west end of the city. "Just our luck," Stoughton remarked. "We might have to shut down the place." The disease first made headlines at the fifty-eighth annual convention of the American Legion at the Bellevue-Stratford Hotel in Philadelphia in June 1976. A week later, Virology and Microbiology reported that the causative agent was a gram-negative bacillus called *Legionella pneumophila*, and that it had probably come from the hospital's water supply, specifically from stagnant water in the shower heads.

The woman survived, the hospital never found a sample of the *Legionella pneumophila* that had infected her, and the hospital didn't shut down. Workmen scrambled around the hospital, thumping on pipes, draining faucets, checking water temperatures, occasionally replacing pieces of derelict tubing. Microbiologists examined the shower stalls and latrines.

Six months later, a team of surgeons at Toronto General performed the hospital's first liver transplant. It seemed a great success, at first; then, weeks later while the patient was recovering nicely, he contracted Legionnaires' Disease, probably from stagnant water in the shower heads, and died.

Stoughton tries to keep in touch with all departments. He wanders the hallways, drops by Emergency, visits Public Relations. Every Friday, shortly after dawn, he goes on a walking tour with the nurses to inspect the front lines. Sometimes he stops by Infectious Diseases for a chat with Jay Keystone, the doctor-researcher in Tropical Medicine who has a current case load of sixty-three lepers. In Cardiology today, Stoughton is told that $600,000 is needed for a new piece of equipment for Digital Subtraction Angiography. Gastroenterology tells him it does not have nearly enough consulting and examining rooms to handle the three hundred and thirty in-patients and out-patients who tromp through every month, resulting in a waiting list two and a half months long.

Neurology says in a report to Stoughton: "The ethical and legal aspects of care of patients dying with incurable neurologic disease is an increasing problem for the service." Specifically, Neurology's complaint is the high rate of turnover of young, inexperienced nurses who are physically and emotionally drained and suffering from what the vocational therapists call "burnout."

On to Orthopedics, where John Kostuik, an orthopedic surgeon with a world reputation — he has worked on skier Steve Podborski, cyclist Jocelyn Lovell, and former hockey star Bobby Orr — has good news. Kostuik is making progress in developing an artificial disc, which would be a world breakthrough in orthopedic medicine, offering relief to the 70 per cent of humanity who suffer low back pain. It is exciting work, but he is not anxious for the news to get out. Neither is Stoughton.

There is terrific competition in the world of industrial medicine and Kostuik does not want anyone to jump the gun. A patent on an artificial disc could be a huge money-maker for Toronto General. Kostuik actually has solved the problem on paper. What remains is only a matter of testing, which might require another four or five years.

W. Vickery Stoughton exudes unquenchable enthusiasm. He enjoys the company of doctors, and the doctors respect him, though he knows working with doctors can be tricky, even perilous. He is the chief executive officer, and he can be tough, but his authority over the doctors is limited.

"The politics are such that the only way I could fire a doctor is if he's medically incompetent. If he creates a disaster because he can't get along with anybody — because he's the biggest jerk in the world — I can put a real squeeze on him, but I'd have a tough time firing him. I've had some shouting matches, sure, but I keep them private, unless I'm attacked personally.

"What's nice about them is they are a group of people of above-average intelligence. They like good information, and usually they will sit down and listen. But the politics can be *horrendous*. You don't get into ego battles with them, because you'll lose. You've got to *tease* them. Watch me in a situation. It's instinctive."

When Stoughton agrees with you, he will blurt, "You got it!" When something pleases him, or excites him, he will say, "Unbelievable!" He calls himself "people-smart," which he says can't be taught in any business-administration course. He is a delegater and a decentralizer. Over the years, Toronto General has tended to alternate between chief executive officers who are builders and those who are consolidators. Stoughton is a builder. He likes to get things moving, get things done, likes to see holes in the ground and cranes hoisting steel and ribbon-cutting ceremonies. He likes to win, though he tries not to be seen hogging the limelight.

"You never want to be perceived as making all the decisions," he said. "You never want to be too powerful in an organization like this. You find people who can pull things off. They're the ones you bet on. It's like a manufacturer betting on a new product. There are a lot of talkers, but few doers and achievers."

When Stoughton took on the job of president of Toronto General, in January 1981, he was only thirty-five years old, an exceptionally young age for the chief executive officer of a $169-million operation. He was confident and eager for the challenge, though some regarded him as a bit too brash.

Three mornings a week he plays tennis with the mayor. He threw his personal support behind one of the contenders for the leadership of the Ontario Progressive Conservative Party (when the Tories were in power).

Once he let it be known that he would welcome an invitation to join Toronto's York Club, a prestigious, old-boy watering hole for the community's upper crust. He managed to find someone willing to sponsor him, but, to his surprise and chagrin, he was rejected. He had most of the requisite credentials, of course, but word got out he was a bit of an upstart, a little too "new." Never one to quit, Stoughton kept trying and eventually made it to the York Club, this time sponsored by a long-time member who happened to be one of the hospital's veteran urologists.

When it came time to include a new Stoughton in the family, W. Vickery cut through all the red tape, made the necessary arrangements with Obstetrics upstairs, and soon he was the proud father of an adopted baby boy — Zachary Benjamin. Stoughton sometimes keeps Zachary in his office, wrestling with diapers and bottles. "He's a healthy little guy," he said. "I'm told the father was over six feet."

Even on the playing field, on occasions when he pulls on a T-shirt and goofs around with the hospital softball team, he is forever driven to take command. An easy grounder bounces to the shortstop, the shortstop boots it, and Stoughton walks across the diamond from first and says, hey, maybe I'll play shortstop for a while. He rarely waits to be asked. He is a doer, or, as he prefers to say, a "pro-active" person, as distinct from "reactive," which he regards as a distressingly Canadian personality trait.

Stoughton is an American. At St. Louis University in Missouri, he majored in chemistry, and for a time considered studying to be a doctor, but his father convinced him to try the business side of medicine. At the University of Chicago, he studied hospital administration and industrial relations, then went to the Massachusetts Institute of Technology for a post-graduate course in health administration. Three months later, he was drafted. He spent three years in the army, during which time he worked in various military hospitals, and in 1971, at the age of twenty-five, he was discharged with the rank of captain. He returned to graduate school, finished his post-graduate studies, and started work in 1973 as assistant administrator of the Boston Hospital for Women. In 1975, still in his twenties, he moved over to the Peter Bent Brigham Hospital in Boston, where he was appointed assistant administrator.

The director of Peter Bent Brigham, a man Stoughton liked and respected, moved up to become the chief executive officer of a corporation established to oversee a merger that was in the works involving Brigham and two other smaller Harvard University teaching hospitals. Under normal circumstances, an international search would have been launched to find a new director of Peter Bent Brigham, but because of the proposed merger, the position of director would end when the merger was completed. Brigham required only an interim director, but Stoughton saw it as the opportunity of a lifetime. He put his name in for the job.

"People kind of blinked," he said. "Like, who are you kidding?"

It was a risk, applying for a dead-end job, but for Stoughton, it was a chance to show what he could do. Besides, he had worked closely with the hospital director on many of the early details of the merger. As Stoughton explained, "I was the person who went around and got all the department heads from each of the three hospitals and hammered out the space and physical requirements for the new facility. We got into all the issues of how to run the place, all the controversial and emotional issues that a merger involves."

Stoughton approached his former boss, who was then arranging the merger, and said he wanted to be considered a candidate for the job the man had vacated at Brigham. "He was one of the ones who blinked," Stoughton said. "I told him that if I couldn't get the support of the medical staff, I wouldn't even submit my name." He got the job and in 1978, on his thirty-second birthday, he became director of the hospital.

It soon became apparent that Stoughton's former boss was not up to the job of handling the complex merger. "In many ways he was like a Winston Churchill character," Stoughton said. "He was the right man at the right time, but the time had changed. He hadn't lost his enthusiasm, he'd lost his legs. And he couldn't delegate. So they brought in a *physician*-administrator, which probably was a face-saving move, but he turned out to be a very good administrator. It became increasingly awkward when I heard he was going to ask me to be the new chief executive officer of the merged hospital. It was a position that logically should have gone to my former boss, whom I felt a strong loyalty to.

"I was in a bind, so I started looking around and I was offered the job of chief executive officer of a teaching hospital in Chicago. When word of the offer got around, they asked what it would take to keep me in Boston. I said I'd like to make peace with the man I used to work for, with the same responsibility that the Chicago hospital offered me. We sat down and worked it out, the three of us, but when the merger was completed I ended up second in command, responsible for operations. I wasn't *totally* in charge."

Stoughton had strong, definite ideas on how a hospital should be run, but he had to be the man in charge, "the focal point of the institution." One morning in August 1980, when he was at his desk at the newly merged hospital, he got a call from Thomas Bell, who was chairman of Toronto General Hospital's board of trustees. Bell explained that Toronto General's president, James McNab, was leaving and had designated his own replacement. The replacement had been acceptable to the board, but the hospital's medical staff had objected vehemently, so the trustees had backed off and agreed to a search for a new president.

"Would you like to come up to Toronto and talk?" Bell asked Stoughton.

"I'm not really looking for a job," Stoughton replied, "but why don't you tell me something about your hospital?"

Bell told him as much as he could over the telephone, and Stoughton was impressed.

"I had a lot of contacts across the country, people I respect in academics and medicine, and I checked out Toronto General with them, trying to determine if it fit into the academic mainstream of medicine. Consistently, the answers were, yes, it did. On any medical map of North America, I was told, Toronto General would be up in the top five — with Stanford, Duke,

Johns Hopkins, and Massachusetts General. Essentially, what Tom Bell was telling me was that Toronto General was the Massachusetts General of Canada."

Joel Cooper, one of the star surgeons at Toronto General — he has a world-class reputation for lung and lung-heart transplants — encouraged Stoughton to take the Toronto job. Cooper is an American, too, a graduate of Harvard, and he knew what reservations Stoughton might have. He knew Stoughton was ambitious, and that he really wanted to be chief executive officer of a place like Massachusetts General Hospital, a huge medical emporium that doctors and hospital administrators regard as the Yankee Stadium of hospitals.

Stoughton remarked, "If the Toronto General was in the United States, my salary would easily be more than $200,000 U.S. That's what the guy who runs Massachusetts General makes — actually about $250,000. I'm a long way away from $200,000."

"It's actually not much bigger than Toronto General, but it's number one in the world," Cooper said. "Those who know simply call it *The General*. What we spend on research, they spend on toilet paper. Anyway, when I talked to Vic before he came here, I told him, 'You may not have heard of TGH, but it *is* a world-class hospital. You go a hundred miles outside of Toronto and no one's ever heard of Toronto Western or Wellesley Hospital, but go ten thousand miles away and everyone's heard of Toronto General. It's all here for the asking, all the resources on a platter. They just don't know how to put it together in Canada.' I told him, 'With your background, if you come up here and work in a government-run health care system, who could touch you in ten years? No one in North America.'"

As Stoughton remembered, "I was overwhelmed. Here was a challenge to come to a new organization, a huge place, and see if I really had it." It was the risk that appealed to him most of all. W. Vickery Stoughton looked down at the tips of his steepled fingers, and said, "Oh yeah, the risk. You have to keep testing yourself. That's what makes administration interesting. Maybe I'd find I couldn't run a thousand-bed hospital."

CHAPTER 3

The Pathology Show

TUESDAY MORNING, nine o'clock, and the whitecoats were assembling in a classroom on the fourth floor of the Eaton Wing for the weekly pathology show. Before crowding into the classroom, some slipped into an adjacent staff lounge for quick, almost furtive, coffees in Styrofoam cups.

The whitecoats came in both sexes and all ages, doctors who have been practising for decades, gruff with experience, and nervous young residents anxious to display their learning and perhaps also their brilliance.

It is worth noting that at Toronto General, Pathology is on the fourth floor, that in the corridor outside the classroom sunlight actually washes in from the east-facing windows. This is a progressive move. It is an archaic and unfortunate tradition in most hospitals that Pathology is regarded as somehow shameful and is therefore tucked away in some Stygian corner, usually in a basement where one expects to dodge stalagmitical columns and hear droplets ploink into fetid pools. This is because Pathology is where the dirty deeds are done; it is the medical discipline whose raw material is death; the one in which the first cut lays open the cold, undraped body from neck to pubis.

Every Tuesday morning, for an hour, one or two cases are reviewed. Each case is that of someone who died within the past week because of an ailment that was intrinsically fascinating, or because of a procedure that was either experimental or routine enough to be a textbook example, or under circumstances shrouded in mystery. This is a teaching hospital, and death always has much to teach.

That morning, the day after the worst blizzard of the winter, we examined the death of a sixty-seven-year-old man who died in Toronto General on January 6, 1985. A male resident stood at the front of the room holding a pointer. He cleared his throat and asked that the lights be turned off.

The first slide listed the basics: age, height, weight, disease, date of admission, dates of significant operations, date of death. The opening credits. Personal habits were listed — whether he drank too much, whether he did drugs, whether he smoked. This man was a smoker. He had been admitted first to a suburban hospital on November 22, 1984. He was transferred to Toronto General on December 18, 1984, because Toronto General has better monitoring equipment. He looked "well" when he arrived at Toronto General. The resident had an irritating habit of standing so that his body blocked most of the screen for anyone watching from the right side of the room.

He described the drugs administered — digoxin, lidocaine, mexiletine, dopamine. The drugs got progressively more potent and adventuresome as the man's condition deteriorated and towards the end his condition was getting desperate. One of the last drugs administered, the resident suggested, tentatively, glancing warily at the line of senior doctors seated along the south wall to his left, might have caused a heart attack. Altogether, the man had eight heart attacks, represented by eight small red dots in a row at the bottom of one of the slides, like grade school rewards for penmanship. One of the procedures tried was a triple bypass, which included a heart valve replacement. The man survived the operation, which lasted six hours, but then his kidneys began to fail. He was connected to a pacemaker to increase his heart rate. When that didn't work his chest was reopened for another procedure, one considered highly experimental.

The man had severe coronary artery disease, atherosclerosis, and the series of heart attacks had destroyed parts of the heart muscle. Because the arteries were plugged, he was not getting enough oxygen to the heart muscles, which were contracting in a wild, irregular manner. The heart is a muscle, to be sure, but it is also a complex electrical system, what a senior pathologist describes as "a big bag of wires that intermix within the muscle and carry impulses that make the heart contract in a nice, regular manner — the body's own pacemaker." Because the heart's electrical system in this case was not getting enough oxygen, it fired off commands at random, crazily, like a drunk plunking on a piano. The experimental procedure was an attempt to freeze the microscopic areas of the heart triggering the erratic impulses. It failed. The man survived the operation, barely, and died forty-two hours later. "He had just about everything done to him you could have done," the resident said, and then the lights in the classroom flicked on again.

Another resident walked to the front of the room and the lights flicked off again. The show went on, this time with slides showing the heart photographed from various angles against a royal blue background, but the terminology was bewildering — "recurrent ventricular tachycardia" — and more and more the heart began to look like a salmon steak. As the layman's mind drifted — "pulmonary edema" . . . "myocardial infarct" . . . "arrhythmia" — other organs set against the deep blue began to look like a stale roast, a grey pork chop, coiled knockwurst in a meat shop window. Soon we were watching slides of cells.

Cells! What a marvel it would have been a hundred years ago, fifty years ago, to sit in a classroom and see clearly and in color what was considered infinitesimal, body innards only to be guessed at. Some of the slides were beautiful, swirling, impressionistic paintings, but there were no "oohs" and "aahs" from the audience. Click, next slide. No toothy graduation portraits. Nothing to show ol' Henry as he used to be, standing by the boathouse with his arm around his wife. Hans Selye, the great Canadian authority on stress, made the seminal observation while still in medical school that sickness has its own general symptoms — that one simply *looks* sick — which can be recognized even across the breakfast table: pallor, listlessness, vacant eyes. Nobody here much cares if poor dead Henry liked Beethoven or trout fishing or if he wore his baseball cap backwards, but ears perked up if he smoked a pack a day or if whisky turned his liver into hockey pucks. At least he was interesting enough for the pathology show. This part over here looked "pretty good," the resident said, tapping his pointer at a section of lung not far from the necrosis which did the killing. Click, next slide. How astonishing it would have been to an eighteenth-century anatomist to see the minutest beginnings of these lethal irregularities, the tiny, inchoate cancers that might as easily be beaver dams in a wilderness from thirty thousand feet. What would Galileo make of it? Click, next slide.

The show ended, the whitecoats hurried out of the classroom in a flutter, like laundry flapping on a clothesline. Jim Cullen, the senior pathologist in charge of autopsies, wandered out and headed to his office down the hallway. He was in his early forties, a slender, bearded man with inquisitive blue eyes. He wore desert boots and on most days he cycled to work on a one-speed bicycle. He had been at Toronto General for fifteen years and was well liked and respected at the hospital. He took the chair at his desk, swivelled it around, and sat down with his back to the open door.

"Yes, it's a nervous-making situation in there," he said, propping up his chin on the tips of his fingers as he talked. "They're residents in training, from medicine and pathology, and they have to get up in front of their bosses and think on their feet. They can be made to look very bad. It's a pressure situation. The chief of medicine is there. I'm there. Some of them handle it extremely well, others not so well. The ones this morning handled themselves okay."

But, isn't pathology a discipline that attracts scientist-doctors, loners who don't wish to mingle much in the medical market place? Why the showbiz? Why should a pathologist be expected to perform?

"Yeah, there's a little showbiz, but really it's trial by fire. They have to learn how to think on their feet. If they can't get up there and explain their results, then they shouldn't be in pathology. They won't be able to function, not even in the small hospitals. They're going to have to do medico-legal autopsies, attend at coroners' inquests, explain their results to a lay public, to a legal public."

Some four hundred autopsies a year are done at Toronto General, more than one a day, or between thirty and forty per cent of all patients who die at the hospital. Cullen would like to have autopsies done on every patient who dies in hospital, which is the practice in some large European teaching hospitals. Here the hospital needs consent for an autopsy from the patient's next-of-kin. There are exceptions, of course, such as when someone dies in hospital after having been shot or strangled or bludgeoned, in which case the coroner can override the next-of-kin. Coroners' autopsies are not actually done at Toronto General, but at the Forensic Sciences Building several blocks away.

"Theoretically it's possible for a doctor to botch something up and never have an autopsy done, but I doubt there's much of that," Cullen continued. "Thoracic surgeons get autopsies on most of their cases. They review their cases with us and discuss what went wrong and they can be very critical of themselves. If a patient dies on the operating room table, it's almost always considered an unnatural death, and the coroner would be called. It's up to the coroner to order an autopsy. Surgeons who do the most intensive types of therapy have high autopsy rates. Patients who sort of die quietly, who've been in hospital three, four, five weeks and for some reason the doctors decided to cease being aggressive in treatment, those are the ones we don't get so often. Next-of-kin can always insist on an autopsy. If they're contemplating legal action, I let the coroner know about it. Politically, it's usually better to have an autopsy like this done outside the hospital."

Autopsies are not pretty to watch, and the popular stereotype — street-hardened cop keels over in dead faint at first incision — is not that fanciful. There is also the smell, especially the smell of a "dirty" autopsy, where there is much dead bowel and infection in the peritoneal cavity of the abdomen. It is far more noisome than anything encountered in an operating room. And when the hospital airflow system breaks down, as it had done that morning, before the pathology show, the smell wafts from the autopsy rooms and drifts into the offices along the fourth floor, reminding secretaries and receptionists that they are not working in a bakery.

"The cutting can be a bit of a shock for some people, too, probably more so than in an operation. It's because we're not dealing with a contained, compact, operating zone. We have the entire body lying there, undraped. You get used to it, though, especially when you stop thinking of the sights and smells and think of an autopsy as a problem-solving exercise."

The attraction?

Cullen laughed. "It's not the smell," he said. "Pathology attracts people who want more of the science of medicine, who don't want the hassles that go with patients and patients' relatives. It's a way to avoid the emotional and social aspects of disease. We don't get the immediate gratification and feedback from patients and relatives, like the surgeon who finishes the operation and calls the wife or husband and everybody thanks him and says, 'What a great job you did!' I'm sure that's a big part of why people want to do clinical medicine. We don't get that. If you need that you probably shouldn't go into pathology. We don't cure anybody, but we also don't lose anybody."

Cullen led the way to one of the autopsy rooms, down the hallway and around a corner. It was not busy that morning, only a woman sitting on a tall stool, wearing a lab coat and a surgical mask. She was examining a dead heart, probing it, turning it over and upside down, making notes. The heart had been cut in half and looked the same color and texture as a giant mushroom. She was wearing the mask, she said, because she is allergic to the formaldehyde used to preserve organs.

"It's the same formaldehyde used in that insulation that's been banned," Cullen said. "That smell can get very strong and it can be a hazard. We get concentrations of it much stronger than in any house." He mentioned a radiology resident who spent three months in pathology and reacted so violently to the formaldehyde that he had to be admitted three times to hospital.

Across the room, which had been scrubbed to gleaming, water from a tap splashed over two brains in a sink. "We're running water over them to flush out the formaldehyde," Cullen explained. The brains were a dull, pale grey and looked soft and crumbly. "They look fairly recent. Probably taken out about two weeks ago. Brains are soft when they're taken out. You can't cut them when they're too fresh." He sniffed at the sink. "No smell. They're probably just about ready." The brains would be washed overnight and would be ready for cutting the next day.

We sat at one end of the autopsy room and Cullen talked at length about his specialty.

"We can be much more invasive here because we don't have to worry about things like blood loss. We see something every day that's different from what we've ever seen before — a new kind of tumor, or a new distribution of tumor. A lot of our work is in cancer and you'd think after fifteen years it would start to become simple, but it isn't. There's always some new wrinkle. Thirty or forty years ago, we only saw the end of it, when the patient was ready to die and tumor was all over the place. It's easy to tell what's going on when the patient is nearly dead. That used to be the criterion — you'd find nothing or you'd find a lot of tumor. Now we see it much earlier, and we're not always sure it's cancer. The electron microscopes we've been using for the past fifteen years are giving all sorts of information on what's going on in the cells, but sometimes it creates problems because we don't always know what to do with the information.

"I think pathologists, because they see so many cancers, could be on the leading edge of a discovery — a cure. Unfortunately, too much of our day-to-day work bogs us down. We should really be given more time and facilities to be able to sit down and examine, oh, the last five thousand lung cancers we've had. Put them in a computer. Try to determine what's common about all the lung cancers that survived.

"There was a big study in Boston a few years ago when coffee was suspected of causing cancer of the pancreas. The study asked people with pancreatic cancer what coffee they drank, how much, whether it was instant or real or decaffeinated. And did they add milk, sugar, or cream? And did they smoke as well? They had to do it retrospectively, but people really aren't good at remembering this information. It would be better to do it prospectively, having people filling out sheets every week.

"Cancer has become one of the obsessions of pathology, because we see so much of it. It's here, it exists, and I know it's not something only other people get, but I'm less frightened of it than I was fifteen years ago. I think it can be beaten. It will probably be a slow solution, but my gut feeling is that we'd know a lot more about cancer if a good epidemiology was done. With stomach cancer, we don't have that much of it, but people in Japan and China have lots of it. With cancer of the colon, it's the reverse. It's almost epidemic here, and there they hardly see it. It has to be related to diet.

"There's no question smoking is a factor in lung cancer, but the public doesn't want to hear about it. We never see ordinary lung cancers in a non-smoker, and these common-variety lung cancers probably are the most virulent. And I keep seeing physicians, even chest surgeons, who are chain-smokers! There are always some people who will get away with it, same with drinking and liver disease, but it's as if you got up every Sunday morning and drove the wrong way up the Don Valley Parkway. You'd get away with it quite a few times, one or two might make it, but most people won't."

The woman on the stool, a pathology resident, was still examining the heart at the counter across the room. It came from a thirty-year-old woman who had died a week ago. She had had open-heart surgery and a bovine heart valve, a cow's heart valve, had been implanted, which probably was a mistake, for the woman had been known to take drugs intravenously. The resident showed the artificial valve, which was badly rotted and looked deader than the rest of the dead heart.

"Anything artificial like that gets infected easily," Cullen said, examining the woman's heart up close. "Once you start shoving all kinds of bacteria through, which happens with intravenous drugs, it compounds the problem. Things start to grow on the valve and it falls apart. The valves are one-way valves, but when they rot and start leaking the flow goes the wrong way and she'd start to go into heart failure." It raised the serious question of whether the woman should have been given the artificial heart valve, knowing her background. It would be a good question for the pathology show the following Tuesday.

Cullen stared down at the grey, lifeless heart on the counter, and then he said, "She was here last October. She was a prostitute. Her name was Nicole."

CHAPTER 4

14,000 Doors, 500 Hamsters, 218,000 Pounds of Bananas

THERE ARE 14,000 doors in Toronto General Hospital. These are not little doors on medicine cabinets, or doors to the liquor cabinets in the executive offices, or doors to the laundry and garbage chutes. They are not even those flimsy doors to the closets in patients' rooms. These are doors big enough for a grown man to walk through.

The man who knows everything about doors at the hospital is Phil Garment, manager of Plant Engineering and Plant Maintenance. He knows all there is to know about doors because he has seen and walked through all of them. Garment has nearly a hundred people working for him at the hospital and two of them are men who work full-time on the doors. That's all they do, maintain the doors.

"The reason I know there are 14,000 doors is because I was asked for that information at the inquest that was held over the fellow who got lost and died in the shaft." He was referring to the great search at the hospital for Howard Grossman, the neurosurgical patient who wandered from his room in 1981 and was found twelve days later, dead, in a duct shaft off a mechanical room on the fourth floor of the Eaton Wing.

Garment played a key role in the great search because he knew the place better than anybody. At one time or another he had walked or climbed or crawled through pretty well every square inch of the hospital, from the tunnels to the roof-tops. But the matter of the door to No. 1 Duct Shaft, South Mechanical Room, fourth floor, Eaton Wing, continued to irritate him years after the search. It was a matter of pride. It irritated him because he knew the place like the back of his hand, and because that particular duct shaft was his responsibility, and because he knew he had checked that door during the search — more than once.

"Would you like to see the shaft?" Garment asked, his big engineer's hands planted on the desk in his office in the squat, two-storey maintenance building just outside the hospital's front entrance. The walls of his office were painted an industrial cream color, the floor covered with thin, grey, wall-to-wall carpeting. He wore a brown tweed jacket with leather patches at the elbows. He is a transplanted Englishman in his mid-forties, with the hearty demeanor of a rugger player. "Tell you what then," he said. "We'll work our way over there, and I'll show you."

He led the way from his office, along a corridor, then down a series of stairs to a basement, then another basement. He walked briskly, carrying a large, jangling ring of keys. Keys to the doors. First he headed to the hospital's steam-generating plant, of which he seemed inordinately proud, probably because it is inordinately important for the manager of Plant Engineering and Plant Maintenance. The steam-heating system heats not only Toronto General, but the Hospital for Sick Children, Mount Sinai Hospital, and Women's College Hospital.

"It's a total underground distribution system," he said, pointing to various pipes and ducts that carry heat through a network of tunnels, many of them under the city streets and boulevards. The plant generates 500,000 pounds of steam an hour, which Garment said is a "tremendous" amount of steam. The steam causes more corrosion problems than hot-water heating and rigorous checks and controls are necessary to make sure the pipes are holding and bringing warmth to the cafeterias and patient-rooms and operating rooms.

Garment is always relating his job to the people "upstairs," the doctors and nurses and patients. He takes a fatherly concern for their comfort and wellbeing, in the same way that a man comes down in his housecoat late at night to tinker with the family furnace while outside a winter storm howls.

One of his concerns on this morning late in March was static electricity, which he tries to keep to a minimum by raising the humidity level. It is a problem in winter because the air is drier. "It's also important that the operating rooms be as close to a perfect environment as possible," he said. "The ORs must be kept cooler than other places because the lights and equipment in them can raise the temperature. The air in the ORs is exchanged nearly 100 per cent. It's flushed out, expelled, not merely recirculated. We change the air about fifteen times an hour in the ORs. All the air comes from outside, but it's filtered to remove as much dust as possible, then it's humidified and heated. We can't do much about the smell. Charcoal filters could remove the odors, but it would require too much pressure to push the air through the filters."

There is a central system that supplies "medical gases" to the hospital, another of the responsibilities of the manager of Plant Engineering and Plant Maintenance. The Toronto General plant supplies three types of these gases — oxygen, nitrous oxide, and "medical air" — and "vacuum." The oxygen and nitrous oxide, an anesthetic gas, also go to the Hospital for Sick Children across the street to the south and Mount Sinai across the street to the west. The medical air (outside air that has been cleaned and compressed) and the vacuum function (used to suck up blood and other fluids and bits of human tissue) go only to rooms in Toronto General, a vital service. In a year at the hospital, patients unable to breathe on their own spend nearly 200,000 hours on ventilation.

Garment checked equipment in each room he entered and as he walked along the corridors, his nose in a large hospital floor plan, the ring of keys jangling from his belt. He paid special attention to the fire alarms and the fire-fighting equipment.

The biggest worry in a hospital, day and night, is fire. Fire in a hospital is the worst calamity imaginable, worse even than fire on a ship at sea. Garment has three men whose only job is to patrol the hospital to inspect fire alarms. There are fire zones throughout the hospital, with special fireproof doors that automatically close to seal off areas, pockets, which are designed to contain any fire for at least an hour.

About twice a week a fire alarm goes off somewhere in one of the wings in one of the buildings. Heat detectors throughout the hospital are sensitive to any extremes in temperature, hot or cold. An open window in a patient-room in winter can sometimes set off an alarm. At the other extreme, an alarm automatically sounds in any area when the temperature rises above 57 degrees Celsius.

In the case of a fire on the thirteenth floor of the Eaton Wing, for example, the code announced over the hospital's intercom system would be: *Dr. Red, Dr. Red, Thirteen Eaton Wing.* . . . "Most of them are real fires," Garment said. "Cigarette fires, trash-can fires, lights falling on beds, fan belts burning out. It's a constant source of danger. Once there was a pyromaniac on staff who went around setting random fires, including one that nearly destroyed a cardiovascular unit. He was caught and arrested, but it didn't get any publicity. Not long ago we had an elderly woman patient, desperately lonely, who discovered that she could get attention by setting off fire alarms. About 15 per cent of all the calls we get are for fires.

"Cigarettes are the prime cause of fires, but I'm not convinced that banning smoking in the hospital would help matters. It could be more dangerous because it could force more people to smoke where they shouldn't."

Garment pushed opened a heavy metal door to another room where the hospital's power supply is located. There are two power supplies, one hydro-electric, the other two back-up diesel generators. "Altogether," Garment said, "they provide enough power for a town the size of Cobourg, Ontario, which has a population of about 12,000." He looked over the equipment with respect, with a certain awe, as if he had rolled open a garage door and found two Ferraris parked side by side. Thick, insulated wires and pipes, all different colors, wind around the walls of the vault-like room. The high-voltage wires are yellow, the lower-voltage wires blue. "Anything that's yellow is dangerous," Garment explained. "The big yellow pipes are for steam. Anything that's green is okay. If it breaks, it won't hurt you."

In some of the tunnels, Garment had to walk on his heels to avoid soaking his shoes in the puddles. "It's a lost cause trying to keep this place clean," he said. As he walked by a chute in one of the basements, an avalanche of garbage rumbled overhead and crashed into a bin beside him. "There are set times for dirty linen and set times for garbage, but sometimes the two clash and you get total chaos. I've never seen any bodies come down the chute, but sometimes you'll see a rat or a mouse."

Through another door, we came upon a 3,000-gallon tank that occupied nearly the entire space, as if someone were building a submarine in the oversized laundry room. This was the standby diesel tank, with enough fuel to run the hospital for a week. "The diesel generators are always on standby and click on automatically when there is a power interruption of five seconds. If we've got a total power failure, both diesels come on. If half the system goes down, only one diesel kicks on. Twelve seconds after they kick on, full power's restored to the hospital. They come roaring on at first, then there's an automatic phase control. We have a three-phase system and if you're not in complete balance with the phase, you'll blow the system apart."

Twelve seconds without power is all the hospital can tolerate. It is merely a matter of life and death. In the operating rooms upstairs, during open-heart surgery, or a transplant operation, a sustained power failure would be disastrous. The rooms would go black. Surgeons hovering over a half-resected lung would not be able to see what they were doing. Anesthetic equipment would shut down, patients on the tables would stop breathing. "We had a couple of brownouts last summer," Garment said. "In the ORs, they were hollering, 'What the hell! That was a *minute*!' We said, uh-uh — twelve seconds. We timed it. We use stopwatches. But when you go black in OR, it seems like half an hour."

Up an elevator in the Eaton Wing until the elevator went no higher, then Garment trudged up a flight of stairs to the roof, muttering imprecations at the architects who designed the building. "It's one of the frustrations between engineers and architects," he complained, puffing as he reached the top of the stairs and opened the door to the roof. "Architects don't like the esthetics of a bulky elevator shaft on top of their new buildings, so you always have to walk up that last flight of stairs. Isn't that ridiculous? In a hospital! And it's always the engineers and maintenance men, people carrying tools and equipment, who have to do the climbing."

Outside, on the roof, a stiff, wet wind whipped over the gravel as Garment tried to explain the vents where outside air is sucked in to be filtered and cleaned and turned into medical air. "AFTER IT'S GONE THROUGH THE FILTERS," Garment shouted into the wind, "IT'S 85 PER CENT PURE." He walked to the edge of the roof to the south, holding on to the protective railings, and pointed to the helicopter landing pad emblazoned on the roof of the Hospital for Sick Children across the street, where emergency patients for all the neighborhood hospitals arrive, often from thousands of miles away. That day it was too windy, we were too high up, so Garment decided to head back inside. He shouted, "LET'S GO DOWN TO THE FOURTH FLOOR. I WANT TO SHOW YOU THAT DUCT SHAFT."

He tromped down the stairs to the elevator, down in the elevator to the fourth floor of the Eaton Wing, then along a series of corridors until he came to a door on which a sign said: "Authorized Personnel Only, Door Must Be Locked At All Times." Garment used one of his keys. At the inquest into the death of Howard Grossman four years earlier, it was determined that the door had not been locked when the patient, dazed and disoriented from his neurosurgery, had wandered along the same corridor.

Garment opened the door and walked into the two-storey mechanical room, which was bright and noisy and crowded with ventilation equipment and air ducts. Retracing Grossman's route, he turned to the left, walked up to one of four concrete-block structures in the room and opened a small, unlocked door. He had to step over a metal vent about a foot high just inside the door, then he was inside the room, which was fifteen feet long and eleven feet wide. He stood on the grate floor as warm air rushed upwards, riffling the cuffs of his trousers.

There were two large, floor-to-ceiling circular ducts, each about five feet in diameter. They looked like oversized hot-water tanks. Garment edged over to one of the ducts and squeezed himself between it and a wall, as, he guessed, Grossman had done when any of the searchers came along and opened the door to the room. The room was harshly illuminated by a bare light bulb. In order to simulate what it had been like when Grossman had entered the room — the inquest had determined that the light bulb was burnt out at the time — Garment switched off the light, pitching the room into darkness. Witnesses at the inquest said when Grossman entered the room the heavy door would have swung shut behind him, leaving him in the blackness, unable to find the door to get out. But, it is a movie-theatre darkness. The eyes soon become accustomed to it and begin to see things.

"Just wait here and you'll see what I mean," Garment said. "A hell of a lot of light comes in through the cracks. In twenty minutes it'll be like daylight in here."

Sure enough, in a few minutes, the pipes, the air ducts, the ventilation equipment and Garment all became visible.

"I think he was hiding from us. We checked this room four times. I think he squeezed behind one of these tanks when he heard us coming. The door wasn't locked. He could have walked out any time."

Garment flicked on the light, opened the door and stepped out of No. 1 Duct Shaft, South Mechanical Room. "The odd thing," he said as he walked along the corridors back to his office, "is that Grossman's room was only three floors up, directly over the duct shaft."

Helen Hood, manager of Nutrition Services, stood in the main kitchen, in the basement of the Bell Wing, beside a line of shiny soup cauldrons big as kettle drums, one of them bubbling with a fresh batch of mulligatawny. "Our biggest concern is food poisoning," she said. "More and more food coming in is contaminated, especially the chickens." If fire is the biggest calamity in a hospital, food poisoning is a not-distant second.

"Cleanliness is paramount here," Hood emphasized. Spread out in the noisy, cavernous kitchen — it is about half the size of a football field — workers went about their steamy duties wearing sterilized smocks, hair nets, and disposable gloves. Signs on walls and pillars reminded workers to keep clean. There were hand-washing basins, with soap and towels, in nearly every corner.

Cleanliness *is* paramount. It was proven long ago, back in the mid-1800s when Ignaz Semmelweis, a Hungarian physician, first recognized that unsanitary conditions in hospitals were killing people. His suspicions were aroused by the large number of women who died of puerperal fever giving birth in hospitals. Many of them had been infected by doctors who had come to them directly from autopsies without washing their hands. Semmelweis eventually was proved right, and his nostrums on cleanliness became standard medical practice, but only years after he had died frustrated and heartsick in a mental asylum.

Hospital-acquired infections (called nosocomial infections) can come from anywhere — sneezing, coughing, an inadequately scrubbed surgeon's hand, dirty instruments, dirty linen. Bacteria, viruses, and organisms crawl the floors and walls and fly in the air, attacking people already severely weakened and susceptible to invasion. Hospital germs are more virulent and are everywhere, but they are impressively under control at TGH. There are regular inspections, announced and unannounced, and Toronto General has one of the best records in the country — Ottawa Civic Hospital and Vancouver General are also very good — but inevitably, once or twice a year, some sneaky staphylococcus creeps in and there is an outbreak of vomiting and diarrhea on one of the floors upstairs. When that happens, all fingers point to the kitchen.

"The trouble with chickens is that they're filled with salmonella when they come in," Hood said. "It applies to any kitchen, not just hospital kitchens. We have to make sure chickens are stored properly, and we cook them very, very well. Gravy can be a problem, too. If we don't keep it at the right temperature, something's bound to start growing in it.

Gravy goes bad very quickly. We're careful with eggs, too. We don't use raw eggs in anything. You'll never see eggnog here, not even at Christmas. And we never use frozen eggs or cracked eggs — only top-grade fresh eggs."

The term "hospital food" has come to be a pejorative, but Toronto General, big as it is, has an enviable reputation for preparing food that is nourishing and palatable. Every so often a restaurant critic from one of the newspapers visits the cafeteria (or shows up as a patient) and reviews the food. Most of the reviews have been favorable, with the food served to patients rated slightly higher than the food served in the cafeterias. "Cheesecake is our most popular dessert, and it's all made from scratch," Hood said. "We buy a lot of our desserts now because we don't have as many bakers as we used to have. We used to bake everything — breads, rolls, cakes. We still make most of our entrées and all our salads and sandwiches. We always try to have fresh fruit available. And we make vegetarian meals. We prepare more of our own food than most other hospitals."

Occasionally a bedridden patient will throw a tray of tepid victuals against a wall, but usually it is more a protest against the institutionalized service than a thumbs-down on the crispness of the carrots. Most of the ingredients are fresh, and the meals are prepared with care, despite the large volume.

Chef Szabolcs Mendel came to Canada from Hungary in 1957 and has been working at Toronto General for twenty-five years, fourteen of them as chef. Before that, he worked as a chef on Canadian Pacific Railway's transcontinental passenger trains.

"When I started at the hospital, we prepared *everything*," he said, sitting at a table in the rear of the large cafeteria, smoking a cigarette after the lunch hour. "The spinach was washed and cooked fresh. Same with the potatoes and carrots and turnips. We used to make our own mayonnaise and sausages, but the emphasis today is on safety and foods like mayonnaise and fresh eggs and homemade sausages tend to encourage salmonella. The kitchen is a lot more sanitary than even five years ago, but you'll occasionally get complaints. We'll serve 900 shepherd's pies for lunch and maybe two patients will come down with diarrhea and say it was because of the food. When that happens, I always ask what happened to the other 898?"

Nothing annoys Mendel more than waste. It is because of growing up in wartime, in a Communist country, he said. "I remember saying to myself as a boy that if I could ever eat well, boy, that would be real riches. These things stay with you. Food is a precious commodity and people here don't realize this because it's plentiful and cheap." The day before, the menu called for 850 suppers, with two choices: macaroni and cheese, or roast beef and vegetables. The hospital always provides one "soft" meal that is easy to chew, in this case macaroni and cheese. Mendel had estimated that 40 per cent of the patients would choose the macaroni and 60 per cent would choose the roast beef, "We only had seven meals left over yesterday," he said proudly.

In a year, the hospital serves 1,563,000 meals, about 4,262 a day. Up go the color-coded plastic trays on rumbling conveyor belts, onto large, multi-shelved trolleys that are trundled to all the floors in all the wings. An hour or so later, back they come, empty and encrusted, heading to the automatic washing chambers.

The kitchen functions seven days a week, from seven o'clock in the morning to ten o'clock at night. Five times a week a truck arrives with a cargo of milk. Three times a week other trucks deliver ice cream, fresh meat, fruit, and mixed vegetables. Once a week a truck arrives with frozen food.

In a year, the kitchen orders:

Meat	*285,000 pounds*
Fish	*210,000 pounds*
Poultry	*252,000 pounds*
Carrots	*62,000 pounds*
Beans, frozen	*46,000 pounds*
Celery	*18,720 heads*
Lettuce	*2,030 cases*
Potatoes	*158,000 pounds*
Bananas	*218,000 pounds*
Apples	*31,200*
Oranges	*68,640*
Orange juice	*65,000 litres*
Apple juice	*66,000 litres*
Milk	*200,000 litres*
Eggs	*53,000 dozen*
Bread	*20,500 loaves*
Cheese	*15,675 pounds*
Ginger ale	*7,000 cases*

Helen Hood is one of the hospital's longest-serving employees. She joined the hospital in 1948, after graduating from McGill

University in Montreal with a Bachelor of Science degree in home economics. She never wanted to be anything but a hospital dietitian. Her mother was a dietitian. Her office is in the basement of the Bell Wing, next to the hair-dressing salon, across the corridor from the main kitchen. She has blonde hair, blue eyes, wears glasses and dresses primly, usually in a jacket and straight skirt. When she joined the staff at Toronto General, she had to spend a year interning in the kitchen, working with the pots, pans, and dishes, preparing food, loading the conveyors.

"It was entirely different back then," she said. "We had public wards in the College Wing — large, forty-bed wards, male and female wards. There were three kitchens then, one for the public wards, another for private patients, another for diabetic patients. There were separate dining rooms for doctors, nurses, and student nurses. The Bell Wing used to be the Private Patients' Pavilion and patients there had their own fancy menus. For breakfast, they could choose from two or three fruit juices to go with individually cooked bacon and eggs. At dinner, there was always a choice of two or three entrées. They could order steak, oysters on the half shell, brochettes of beef, duck à l'orange. Lobster wasn't listed on the menu, but if someone in the Private Patients' Pavilion wanted lobster we would get one and cook it — steamed, broiled, boiled. Doctors often prescribed wine and brandy for the private patients, who often brought their own nurses with them. The private-duty nurses carried the trays to the rooms and served them their meals. That was long ago, before medicare."

Hood worked her way up, slowly. Soon after her internship, she was put in charge of the diabetic kitchen, then moved to the main kitchen, then became assistant director. She became manager of Nutrition Services in 1968. Much of her job now involves overseeing the departmental budget, which runs to nearly $8 million a year, and includes salaries for the two hundred full-time and thirty part-time kitchen workers. She has twelve full-time therapeutic dietitians on her staff. Then there are the chefs, cooks, porters, and dish washers. The kitchen prepares food for employees, patients, and visitors — $2.5 million worth, of which about $1.5 million is for patients' food.

In a small room off the kitchen, a butcher carved healthy slabs of ten-ounce steaks for a dinner that evening in the small Private Dining Room off the main kitchen, one of two eateries at the hospital with a liquor licence (the other is the Graduate

Students' Lounge, a popular hangout for young doctors, nurses, and middle managers who crowd the place to overflowing for the weekly Thank-Goodness-It's-Friday gathering).

"New York cuts today?" Hood asked. "Must be Dr. Langer."

"No, it's for Orthopedics," the butcher said.

On a counter near the sink there was a pile of fish thawing — sole. "We get 500 pounds of fish a week," Hood said. "We don't get fresh fish any more. It all comes frozen. We used to buy meat carcasses, too, but now we get small cuts, and we cut off what we need from that."

Across the kitchen in another room a woman named Gladys was weighing the ingredients for a batch of seventy dozen bran muffins. Gladys is not fussy about the Toronto General's vaunted cheesecake. "Too heavy for me," she said. "Butterscotch rolls are my favorite. Chocolate cake used to be my favorite, but we don't make it any more." Gladys started in the kitchen twenty years ago. She also likes the carrot cake.

Hood is especially meticulous about the trays sent to the new Eating Disorders Centre in the College Wing, where anorexic patients attend a day clinic. "If you make the slightest mistake with these trays, they won't eat their lunch," Hood said, standing by a conveyor watching gowned workers prepare trays for the day's lunch. The choices included French-Canadian pea soup, tomato juice, grilled cheese sandwich, salad, cheesecake, an orange, and ice cream. The demands of the 1980s probably are more onerous than any of the demands from the influential sick who inhabited the well-appointed rooms of the Private Patients' Pavilion in the 1930s. These days, Hood said, there are special high-fibre diets, vegetarian diets, restricted-fat diets, low-calorie meals, kosher TV dinners, and requests for Oriental and Polynesian food. Every day the kitchen gets thirty-five to forty requests for special meals — Chinese food, sole, filet mignon, shrimp — and if the ingredients are available, the meals are prepared in a special corner of the kitchen. Only a few patients know the service exists. There is even a new fast-food pizza outlet in the basement of the Bell Wing called (after an in-house naming contest) *The Grand Rounds*.

Szabolcs Mendel recalled a patient from northern Ontario who asked if he could have a raw fish for dinner. "We found a white fish and served it up for him, raw," he said. "No problem."

The walk from the hospital across University Avenue to the Medical Sciences Building on the campus of the University of Toronto is an especially long one in pouring rain. The university building is where the future doctors are taught, where they first cut into a cold cadaver, and where the research animals are kept. All sorts of animals: mice, rats, hamsters, dogs, cats, pigs, monkeys, sheep, frogs.

It was the day of the big "Open House and Media Tour" of the animal facilities, the university's bold move designed to counteract recent public relations gains by animal rights activists in the community. Newspaper reporters, photographers, radio and television reporters and cameramen assembled in a room as Peter McCann, a veterinarian, explained how the tour would work. McCann chatted comfortably with the newsmen, displaying none of the nervous mannerisms of other workers in the office who were convinced that once again they would be depicted as heinous butchers of all that is soft and cuddly on the planet. He puffed on a pipe as he talked. On a wall behind him was an impressionistic painting of a cat.

"It's raining cats and dogs outside," one of the reporters joked.

McCann smiled, then turned and rolled his eyes to the ceiling.

More newsmen arrived than were expected, so they were divided into two groups, which set off ten minutes apart. Jack Almeida, co-ordinator of laboratory animals, headed one of the groups. He is a short, bald man with a moustache, and wore a shirt and tie under his white lab coat. He is an amiable man, but he appeared more nervous and fidgety than his colleague about being the centre of attention. He explained that there would be a live operation on a pig. "Anyone who wants to watch it will have to be scrubbed and gowned," he said.

"What's the operation for?" a reporter asked.

"It involves removing a liver from a pig, which will be transplanted to another pig later in the day."

"Can we photograph it?"

"No, I'm afraid it's harmful to the animals to be filmed. The bright lights and the flashes bother them. The lights disturb their breathing cycles."

A television cameraman explained that his camera is quiet and requires very low lighting. "I can probably get by with available light in the operating room," he told Almeida, who pulled at the lapels of his lab coat and said perhaps then it would be all right. Co-operation was the order of the day.

Strolling along the first corridor, Almeida explained that the cages are made of stainless steel because they are easier to sanitize than galvanized metal. And there are sixteen to eighteen air changes an hour in most of the rooms. "Normal air-conditioning is five, six air changes an hour, but that's because it's designed for humans. With animals, you need more — because of the odors." A photographer pushed his shoulder into one of the doors, opening it a crack, then grimaced and stepped back. "Hoo, boy!" he muttered. Almeida continued, "Most visitors can only take the odors for about half an hour." A few chuckles from the inquisitive horde. Almeida was loosening up.

Next room, rabbits. Almeida lifted one from a cage by the scruff of its neck and held it against his chest. "This is the proper way to hold a rabbit, so it won't struggle unduly," he said. The rabbit, struggling unduly, wriggled down to his feet and nearly escaped out the door. Almeida recovered it and hustled it back into the cage.

Next room, mice. It was one of the rooms the reporters were not allowed in because, as Almeida explained, the mice were "nude" — shaved for various surgical experiments. "You'd have to be scrubbed and gowned to go in," Almeida continued, adding that most of the workers routinely knock on the doors to the rooms before entering. "It disturbs the animals if you just barge in. It helps if you talk to them, too."

Next room, more mice, these ones not nude. "Some of these mice don't exist anywhere else," Almeida said. "They are specially bred for cancer research. They're all from Rochester." A minor scrum developed as photographers and television cameramen jostled for vantage points. A television soundman held a microphone to one of the cages, hoping for — what? An interview? "I just want to get some chirps for my report," he explained.

Next room, rats. Big, white rats called Wistar rats. Almeida picked one up by the tail and a reporter asked if that was the correct way to pick up a rat. "This is the best way," Almeida replied.

"Will it bite?" the reporter persisted.

"No."

Almeida picked up another rat by the tail, this one a big, black rat called a Black Hooded Long Evans rat. It pooped on the floor, just missing Almeida's right shoe.

There is some sort of test going on in the next room to determine the effects of alcohol on a species of rat called C-57 rats. The room is in darkness. Almeida explained that the lights in the room are controlled by a clock, so that they go on and off automatically. A photographer, trying to be funny, said, "So we're looking at a bunch of drunken rats." Nobody laughed.

Next room, hamsters. They looked weak, lethargic. "They look sickly," a reporter observed. One of the workers in the room with the hamsters replied, "That's because they *are* sickly." The hamsters all had white spots on their tongues — calcium deposits. They were all born with heart disease. "They are difficult to breed, but we have five hundred of these hamsters," Almeida said. "They are very gentle and easy to work with."

Next room, food. Shelf upon shelf of food. Bags and bins and boxes of food. There seemed to be enough food to feed all the animals for a semester, but Almeida said all of it would be gone in four days, eaten up by the dogs and cats and monkeys and pigs and sheep and hamsters. He said the monkeys need more vitamin C than the other animals and so every day they get apples, a banana, or an orange. On a blackboard, someone had scrawled special instructions for Dr. Julien's monkeys. "No. 244 and No. 243 get pills in apple juice. No. 163 gets pill in banana." Special "rat chow" is regularly served to all rodents because they like food they can crunch.

Next room, sheep. About a dozen of them stood in their tall, wire-mesh cages, making terrific pictures. Despite the crash and clatter and flashes, the sheep stared placidly at the visitors. One walked out of the cage and roamed about the room. Almeida gently ushered it back to the cage, talking to it all the time, saying, "There, there." The animal replied, *Baaa-a-a-a*.

Next room, monkeys. They hunkered at the far end of the room, staring at the humans studying them through the small window in the door. The monkeys looked startled, as if they had been enjoying a wild party that had just been busted by narcs. One of them stood up, hung by an arm, and made a rude gesture toward the window. The rest chattered and scrunched their snouts and bared their teeth. They had wonderful teeth, all of them. The monkeys were part of a dental experiment to determine the long-term effects of brushing and flossing after eating.

"Hi George! How are you?" Almeida asked the monkey hanging by one arm.

"Do they all have names?" a reporter asked.

"No, they all have *numbers*," Almeida replied. "But that one is George."

In the next room, a German shepherd dog was lying on its side on an operating table, anesthetized. A gowned worker shaved the dog's neck, behind its ear, in preparation for an operation to implant a new type of heart pacemaker that morning.

Down the corridor, four gowned and gloved surgeons were preparing to operate on the pig. One of the surgeons was Len Makowka, an up-and-coming star at Toronto General who was preparing to leave that summer to go to Pittsburgh to join Thomas E. Starzl's liver transplant team. Starzl is acknowledged to be the world leader in liver transplants, having done the first one ever back in March 1963, when he was at the University of Colorado. Starzl's success rate had reached 75 per cent, and liver transplants in Pittsburgh were no longer considered experimental, but an effective therapy for various types of end-stage liver disease, including primary biliary cirrhosis, biliary atresia, sclerosing cholangitis, inborn errors of metabolism, and certain primary malignancies.

The liver is the largest organ in the body and a liver transplant is a complex, arduous procedure, usually requiring more than twelve straight hours in the operating room. Many things can go wrong. One of Starzl's first liver transplants failed because the donor-liver was too large and Starzl could not close the abdomen at the end of the operation. The new liver was functioning splendidly, but the patient died because he couldn't breathe.

Toronto General had been researching liver transplants for fifteen years and was preparing for its first liver transplant. Makowka and the other surgeons in the corridor were going to practise on the pig to refine the technique. As an anesthetist in the operating room put the pig to sleep, Makowka, a big man, leaned against a wall in the corridor and talked about cyclosporin, the new immunosuppressive drug that was making all these transplants possible. He worried about some of its side effects.

"The major concern is the kidney damage it causes," he said. "There's also some liver toxicity attributable to it. The problem with cyclosporin is over-immunosuppression, which is the same with any immunosuppressive agent. There have been some funny viral diseases, infections. . . ." His voice trailed off as he shook his head, watching the juggernaut of notepads, cameras, and tape recorders roll on to the next room down the corridor. "You know," he remarked, "it's going to take some of these animals weeks to recover from this thing."

Makowka and others were also concerned about the long-term effects of cyclosporin, which all the latest transplant patients were expected to take indefinitely. "With research like this," Makowka said, pointing his thumb back at the pig on the table in the operating room, "we can experiment with lower doses, or stop the cyclosporin altogether and see what happens. Cyclosporins are a family of compounds. There are other immunosuppressive agents. They're working on one that they hope has less toxicity. One day we'd like to be able to take transplant patients off immunosuppression. Right now, you can't do that with humans. No one in the world has been on cyclosporin longer than five years. Tom Hall's only been on it for a year and a half, and we're not going to take him off cyclosporin just to see if he'll reject his new lung. It's one of those questions that will have to be worked out in animal research." No one yet knows what the long-term effects of cyclosporin are.

When the tour ended, everyone assembled around a long, polished table in a conference room where coffee and cookies were served. Harvey Anderson, the medical faculty's associate dean of research, explained that most of the animals used in medical research are rats and mice, as if an anthropomorphic hierarchy existed in the animal kingdom, with rodents at the bottom. "We hardly use cats and dogs at all," he said. Brochures were distributed, one of which listed the various animals and how they were used in medical research at the University of Toronto in one year:

Rodents   *92%*
Rabbits, sheep, pigs   *3.5%*
Frogs   *1.4%*
Cats and dogs   *1.3%*
Primates   *0.03%*
Fish and birds   *1.75%*

The brochure also listed "a few of the recent advances made possible by experiments on animals that have allowed millions of people to live longer, healthier lives." The list included:

Vaccines against polio, diphtheria, smallpox, rubella, measles
   and mumps.
Blood transfusions.
Antibiotics.
Anesthetics and pain-killers.
Radiation and chemotherapy for cancer.
Insulin.

Heart pacemaker.
Medications for high blood pressure.
Medications for epileptic seizures.
Artificial joints.
Microsurgical techniques.
Cataract removal and artificial lens implants.
Surgery for atherosclerosis.

In addition to medical breakthroughs for humans, Anderson explained, much of the animal research has resulted in breakthroughs that have advanced veterinary medicine. Cats and dogs live longer, too. He referred to the Judeo-Christian heritage that places a premium on human life. Down the table, Tom Harpur, a former Anglican priest who writes a column on ethics and morals for *The Toronto Star*, nodded sagely. (And gratefully, because Anderson's offhanded remark had provided him with a full-blown column. "I must say," Harpur wrote the following Saturday, "I was somewhat surprised . . . to hear an eminent surgeon justifying the use of animals in experimentation by citing the Judeo-Christian tradition. Since he is a practising Christian, his appeal to religion made sense for him. But to put this kind of faith forward as a defence of the scientific community's animal research seemed far-fetched.")

Anderson continued, "We have not been delinquent in abusing animals, but we *have* been delinquent in communicating our work. One of the problems is that scientists tend to be bright, practical, and humane, but a little shy and reticent." As pencils scribbled and tape recorders rolled and cameras whirred, Anderson announced his personal office number and said, "If you want to know anything, call me any time."

When Anderson finished, a film on animal research was shown. It began with George Connell, the president of the university, sitting in his living room, stroking his two Welsh terriers under the ears. There was also a segment that showed a rabbit in a sling, then moved in to a close-up of the rabbit's nose. "Notice that the rabbit's nose is wiggling," the narrator said. "That is what rabbits do when they eat well and drink well and sleep normally. That is what we call happiness, in a rabbit."

Off in the distance: *Baaa-a-a-a. . .*

CHAPTER 5

We Have
a Lung

As HOSPITALS GREW and became ever more complex and complicated, someone had to explain all this new-fangledness to the outside world, which was expected to pay for it. At Toronto General, public relations is the domain of David Allen.

The hospital's Public Relations office is on the ground floor of the Bell Wing, immediately inside the front entrance, to the left. It does not look like the place where a Public Relations office should be, more instead like where you might expect to find a government appointments secretary, probably a snooty one at that. The foyer is elegant, dimly lighted, mostly in dark wood and marble — floor, pillars, walls — and a high ceiling makes the most tentative footsteps echo, as if you had entered a museum.

Unlike many public relations people, Allen never worked for a newspaper or trade magazine or concerned himself very much with advertising or any of the other related activities. He used to be a forester. Whenever he can, winter, spring, summer, and fall, he heads northwest of the Muskokas to a small island in Georgian Bay and a cottage he built himself, piece by piece, painstakingly ferrying the wood and stone and glass and furniture over miles of open water. He is short and square, nearly bald, and one of those fellows with a warm smile and a bright, take-charge confidence. He likes to drink dark rum and Coca-Cola, then dig into a hot roast beef sandwich slathered with gravy, French fries and green peas on the side — bus depot food.

Allen's public relations technique is to co-operate with reporters, not bar the door, which serves only to arouse suspicion and often results in carping, negative stories. Allen's is more an American than a Canadian public relations technique but not so American as to co-operate to a fault. He does not load down the reporter with so much information — pamphlets, speeches, mimeographed biographies, magazine excerpts, books — that the reporter staggers under the weight of it, feeling enormously grateful but so awash in facts that he forgets why he came in the first place. Until it is proved otherwise, Allen assumes that a reporter is honest, curious, and intelligent. He does not always volunteer information readily, but he makes it a point to answer each question succinctly and openly, even if sometimes it puts the hospital in a bad light. The good reporters know this, and respect him for it.

Allen's job is to make the hospital look good, but he knows he can't be a pimp for the institution and the people in it. As often as he must educate the media about the hospital, or at least steer experienced medical reporters to the right people, he must also explain the sometimes esoteric processes of media to medical professionals who feel mostly disdain for the wretches.

He works in a no-man's-land, always in the crossfire, and sometimes he gets burned, as he was a week ago when a local television station called to ask if a crew might drop by Emergency to take some stock footage. This means shooting some standard medical videotape — doctors, nurses, ambulances, scalpels, sutures, intravenous lines, oxygen masks — that can be used as the pictures for an upcoming medical program, perhaps one that hasn't yet been scripted. Allen said sure; the crew arrived that evening, spent several cumbersome hours in Emergency, and the footage later was used to illustrate a news report on medical malpractice. It was an unconscionable breach of ethics, for the story had nothing to do with Toronto General, and Allen felt betrayed. It will be a long, long time before that television station gets access to the hospital again.

On Allen's desk that day was a "patient consent form," one of those missives routinely sent along to public relations, this time from general surgery, for Allen's perusal. It was titled, "Consent Form for Percutaneous Gastrostomy Placement of Gastric Balloon for Morbid Obesity." It is one of those forms that may befuddle a patient who must sign it to give the surgeons the go-ahead on an experimental procedure — this *is* a teaching institution — which protects the hospital if anything should go wrong.

The text read:

I understand that my weight is so great that it is a serious threat to my health and that dieting alone has failed to control my weight. There are a number of potential approaches to this problem including Stomach Stapling surgery but the long term results of this are as yet unknown. I understand that an alternative approach to my problem is to place a balloon into my stomach for an indefinite period of time. This balloon is pulled into the stomach from mouth by means of a catheter and/or guide wire placed in the stomach from the skin by a technique called percutaneous gastrostomy. The balloon will limit the amount of food which I can eat at one time. The procedure will be performed under local anaesthetic + sedation. There will be a minor degree of discomfort when it is done and probably for a few days afterwards. I understand there is a small risk of bleeding or of leakage from the stomach related to the gastrostomy and that these might require an emergency operation to correct. I also understand that there is a small risk of the tube dislodging and producing an intestinal obstruction which would also require emergency surgery. The likelihood of any of these complications occurring is probably small, but is actually unknown. . . .

Scrawled across the top of the form, in Allen's neat handwriting, was the clearly rhetorical question: "Would *you* sign this?"

Another of Allen's duties is to help arrange "think-ins" for hospital staff, retreats where they can ponder their errors and attitudes and perhaps return to work properly chastened and renewed, the milk of human kindness coursing again in their veins, white and pure as their freshly laundered lab coats. Fortunately, Allen has access to a mother lode of material for the staff to think about. Letters from disgruntled and outraged patients and their families and friends regularly are forwarded to Public Relations from lower and upper echelons of the hospital, sometimes for a felicitous reply, sometimes to avoid a lawsuit big as the Ritz.

For instance, the seventy-two-year-old woman who went downtown on a brisk, wintry morning to do some shopping, fainted in a department store, and was taken to the hospital where, following a Kafka-esque series of blunders, she died. Three months later, the woman's daughter was as puzzled as ever. "No one seems to know anything," she said in a letter to David Allen. "I am not interested in starting a lawsuit against the hospital to gain some satisfaction and peace of mind. All I want to do is to speak with those responsible for my mother's care. Is there any one individual who can help me? Are you that person?"

Here is what happened.

Someone at the hospital had called the daughter to tell her of her mother's accident when her mother was brought into Emergency. When the daughter arrived at the hospital, a doctor told her that her mother had only bruised her forehead when she fell but she should stay in hospital for a few days. The daughter agreed and tried to calm her mother, who wanted desperately to go home. Four days later, the daughter arrived to visit her mother and heard that she had been transferred to Orthopedics. She asked a nurse what this was all about and the nurse said she wasn't sure but thought it had "something to do with a broken hip." Apparently her mother had gone for a walk and slipped on some loose tiles left in a corridor by maintenance workers. The daughter asked to see a doctor — she wanted to know if the broken hip required surgery — but a nurse said that all the doctors were in the operating room. That night, after dinner, a nurse called to say her mother had suffered a heart attack and was in Intensive Care.

"Oh my God!" the daughter gasped. "When did it happen?"

The nurse said it had happened about noon.

The daughter rushed to the hospital and found her mother in Intensive Care, conscious but terrified of all the machinery around her. A few days later, the mother was transferred from Intensive Care to Urology, not because she had any urological problems but because there were no other beds available. The daughter arrived the next morning, this time to find her mother unconscious. She called for help and a nurse arrived, then a doctor. They pushed the daughter out of the room and told her to wait outside in the corridor while they examined her mother. Minutes later, the nurse and the doctor came out and said her mother had probably suffered a stroke and that a specialist would have to be called and, no, she couldn't go into the room. The specialist arrived an hour later, went in the room, stayed about two minutes, then started yelling at the nurse. "Why did you call me to look at a dead patient? This better not happen again!" he shouted, then walked away stiffly down the corridor.

"In my shock and grief, I neglected to ask some important questions," the daughter said in her letter to Public Relations. "I simply assumed that she had had another heart attack as well as a stroke. No one offered a different explanation. Now I'm no longer certain of anything."

The letter prompted an official inquiry, which determined that: a CT-scan had not been performed when the patient arrived because of repairs being done to the scanner; the patient had not been examined by an attending physician during her entire stay; an autopsy report, completed three weeks after the autopsy, indicated the patient died of heart failure following a stroke; X-rays of the broken hip indicated that surgery should have been scheduled promptly; the patient's lab tests were never located; maintenance crews repairing floors had been reprimanded on two previous occasions for not removing materials after their work; the identity of the specialist could not be determined because the nurse who attended at the woman's death had only been working at the hospital for a week and had not completed her notes; when the patient kept asking to go home, a resident prescribed a sedative, which was administered an hour before she fell and broke her hip.

It all contributed to a troubling but useful think-in.

Allen's domain is vast, but his public relations department is tiny and chugs along with a staff of three, including himself. His assistants are Jane MacGillivray, a registered nurse with a degree in journalism, and Carol Saunders, who writes press releases, fetches coffee, and directs traffic, ushering neurosurgeons, nurses, graphic artists, maintenance men, hospital administrators, security guards, and the odd crazy in and out of the busy PR office.

Other departments struggle to meet budgets by cutting expenses, by circling their wagons, but Allen realized long ago that his small department does not have much room to manoeuvre. When in doubt, his strategy is to take the offensive, like Rommel grinding over the sands to Tobruk with the rasping command, *Angreifen!* — Attack!

When he needed word processors to replace outdated typewriters and found there was not enough in the kitty, Allen launched his own fund-raising campaign. He sent personally addressed letters to some thirty thousand patients who had been discharged during the previous year. It was a remarkable success, with a 5 per cent response rate and an average donation of seventy dollars, which raised twelve thousand dollars, more than enough to equip public relations with handsome new Apple word processors and printers. A senior surgeon, hearing of this, stormed into Public Relations to complain vociferously of begging letters being sent to his patients. Allen reacted with equanimity, for he knew that the surgeon himself had used the same technique to solicit donations for a pet research project. When he reminded him of this, the storm quickly subsided.

Allen unleashed a more elaborate offensive in the spring of 1985, when the hospital administration ordered an arbitrary, across-the-board budget cut of 2 per cent. He knew he didn't have the flexibility to cut his own budget by 2 per cent, so he decided instead to raise money, which he did by allowing hospital property to be used for the television mini-series *Kane and Abel*. He often gets requests from television and movie producers to use the hospital for shoots. In his office, among other memorabilia, is a photograph of Hollywood star Jack Lemmon with his arms draped over the shoulders of two Toronto General nurses. The photograph was taken during the filming of *Tribute*, one of many movies filmed at the hospital.

The property the *Kane and Abel* people wanted to use was across the road to the east, on College Street, a building which once had housed the Hospital for Sick Children, but which for years now had stood empty and decrepit. It is a magnificent old red-brick building. Allen had once thought great things could be done with it, but eventually he realized that it would be an inordinately expensive reclamation project. To install a mandatory sprinkler system alone would have cost $2 million. Worse, the city had declared it to be a historic property, which meant it could not be razed and would remain a useless, hulking monument occupying some extremely valuable downtown property.

Allen grew to loathe the building. He charged the television company $10,000 to use it for a scene involving a fire at a turn-of-the-century Chicago hotel. With any luck, Allen thought, the fire might get out of control and burn the old dinosaur to the ground.

On the night of the filming, crowds lined the street to watch the action. The old building had been given a superficial facelift, with new awnings and some adroit sandblasting. Old-time fire trucks and firemen and old-time newspaper photographers with box cameras clustered about the front entrance, which was strewn with hoses. Propane jets sent real flames shooting out the windows and portable smoke machines filled the night with clouds of soot as actors and extras rushed out of the hotel in their housecoats and pyjamas.

Many startled passers-by were convinced they had come upon a major disaster. Some of the spectators were medical staff who had lingered at the hospital to attend a party celebrating the hospital's thousandth open-heart operation. In order to prevent any panic, Allen's office notified patients in rooms overlooking the scene about the movie beforehand and some of them watched the extravaganza from their windows. Allen himself got caught up in the excitement and watched from a director's ladder across the street. From time to time he climbed down and strode brusquely through police lines to enter the apparently burning building to see how the effects were done.

At one point in the filming, pieces of paper fluttered down to the street from an upstairs window. One of the extras, dressed as an old-fashioned newspaper reporter with a press card stuck in his fedora, picked up one of the papers and noticed something written on it. He began to laugh uproariously and passed the paper to one of his colleagues, who passed it to another, until the laughter spread like a grass fire among the crowd in the street.

The papers were old hospital index cards that had evidently escaped the shredding machine. The one that caused the commotion recorded information about a nurse who had been hired by the hospital in 1955, and who had resigned a year later. The card listed most of the pertinent details of her education and training and concluded that she "is not endowed with a brilliant mind but she has other qualities which overcome this fault. . . ." Mercifully flames had eaten away the rest of the note.

Alas for Allen, the building survived the fire scene.

The latest thorny problem for Allen and his staff involved missing narcotics. Someone had been stealing the drugs from a cabinet near one of the floor nursing stations and replacing them with other prescribed drugs — antibiotics and anti-arrhythmic drugs like digoxin, the drug that had caused the spate of baby deaths across the street at the Hospital for Sick Children. The discovery of the thefts could not have happened at a worse time: the press was ravenous for more news of heinous hospital wrongdoings.

"The press has wind of it," Allen said, looking down at a yellow scrap of paper on his desk as if it might jump up and bite him. On it was the name of a television reporter from the Canadian Broadcasting Corporation. "She called me and asked about the narcotics, and she's got it pretty well down." He muttered a small blasphemy. "Really, I'm *dumbfounded*! She must have got to some pretty key people. All I could do was answer her questions and try to correct some of the information. I told her that these things happen, that steps are being taken to bring the situation under control. I also told her she should be careful because if it's aired, if the shit hits the fan, well, it might harm our internal investigation."

That was on a Friday. At home that night — at the time, Allen was living across the street in a suite at the nurses' residence — he watched the news on television, preparing for the worst, but the missing-narcotics story didn't run. He watched again Saturday and Sunday, but there wasn't a word.

The CBC reporter later said she thought it was because it was too much a Toronto story. Besides, there was no indication anyone had mistakenly taken the wrong drugs. Perhaps the story was too much a "word" story and not a "picture" story — news with pictures rates higher in television than news without pictures — but it was more likely another instance of the press censoring itself.

Sometimes the press can be responsible to a fault. Perhaps if the missing-narcotics story had run, the CBC could have alerted the public to a grave situation, one that might have involved life and death.

Allen stepped briskly into his office Monday morning, all smiles.

"Win some, lose some," he said.

Allen was on a roll, and he knew it. If there are times in public relations when things just won't go right, when every silver lining has a cloud, there are times when things just won't go wrong, and the autumn of 1983 was one of those times.

It was all because of a suburban Toronto salesman, a victim of pulmonary fibrosis. Tom Hall is an irrepressible man, a salesman's salesman, and he was about to become Toronto General's most famous patient, a world-class medical superstar. At first glance Hall looks rather ordinary: short, thin to the point of being scrawny, with silver hair and dark, bushy eyebrows. He is quiet and well-mannered, all of which serves to disguise the personality of a Patton. His eyes are luminous blue lasers that look as if they could penetrate bricks.

In January 1983, doctors gave Tom Hall eight months to live. Even to survive that long, he had to be hooked to an oxygen tank twenty-four hours a day. He could switch off the oxygen for brief periods, such as when he washed his hair, but it always made him gasp and his lips started to turn blue. The tubes to the oxygen tanks were cumbersome and often he inadvertently stepped on them, cutting off his supply, or tripped on them, risking broken bones as well as suffocation. He kept an oxygen tank at home, switched to a portable tank in his car on his way to work, and switched again to a third tank when he got to his desk at the office. The oxygen alone cost $1,200 a month, most of which was covered by insurance, but Tom didn't realize that there was a limit — $8,000 over three years — and he exceeded the limit by $3,000. The insurance did not cover the tanks, which cost $75 for a large size, $50 for a medium, and $25 for a small. "I mean, how the hell do they expect the gas to get here?" he blurted one day, exasperated. "In green garbage bags?"

Pulmonary fibrosis is a disease of the lungs that causes scarring and hardening of the lung tissue. Normally the lung is soft and spongy, but with pulmonary fibrosis it becomes fibrous and rigid, leather-like, and the lungs can't do the job of transferring oxygen and carbon dioxide across the membranes. The result is that not enough oxygen reaches the bloodstream and the victim gradually suffocates.

Tom had first noticed shortness of breath five years earlier, when he was recovering from an operation for a hiatus hernia. It was his first time in a hospital for anything serious. He had always been in excellent health. As a boy, growing up in Toronto's Parkdale district, he had enjoyed track-and-field sports, especially pole-vaulting and running hurdles.

"I really didn't know what a hiatus hernia was, but I'd eat something for lunch and somehow it always seemed to get stuck deep down in my throat, in my gullet, and I couldn't dislodge it. Then it'd go away and I'd feel fine. Once I was at a hockey game at Maple Leaf Gardens and something I ate before the game stuck in my throat, worse than ever. I kept getting up and running to the washroom, trying to cough it up, throw it up, but it wouldn't budge, so I decided to stand at the railing and watch the game from there. I remember thinking I wanted someone to give me a good whack on the back, so as to jar whatever it was loose.

"Later, I went to my doc to find out what was bothering me. He took some pictures and the way he explained it he said it was like a blow-out on an inner tube, one of those soft spots . . ." (Here Tom blurted out the proper medical term

— *diverticulum* — which he often does, even in the midst of a rambling, homespun narrative.) ". . . a soft spot that catches the food, keeps it stuck down in the esophagus. The food only regurgitates to about here" — he pointed to a spot just below his sternum — "and these gastric juices give you this terrific heartburn. It's like there's a drawstring on your esophagus and it keeps the stomach fluids in, but as you get older this drawstring starts to relax and doesn't hold the stomach juices in.

"Anyway, they decided to go in and repair it. It's the same as a lung operation. They take the back right out of you. They just cut down on the shoulder blade — lift it right out. They don't do it unless you're in pretty bad shape. The operation left a numbness in my chest and instead of getting better, it got worse. The thought's always lingered that that's where I got this thing in the lung — pulmonary fibrosis. But they said no. The theory with the medical people is that it might have been something common like the flu that went through the population and everybody was able to shake it off but somehow I couldn't."

Tom blamed his shortness of breath on age and overweight, maybe booze and cigarettes too. He used to smoke a small package of cigarettes a day, but he had quit twelve years earlier, when he noticed his youngest daughter, Carolyn, smoking. "There I was lecturing her on the terrible things about smoking and I was smoking all the while I was doing it," he said. "I realized how stupid it must have looked, so I made a pact with her. I told her, 'If you quit, I'll quit.' It was very lucky for me, or I'd be dead by now for sure."

However, his breathing got worse, and by 1981 he could barely climb three steps without having to stop and cling to the banisters. His family doctor referred him to a chest specialist, who diagnosed his condition as asthma and prescribed various medications, all of which made Tom so sick that he ended up in hospital, where he discovered he had pulmonary fibrosis. "They let me listen to my lungs," he said, "and they sounded like cellophane rattling." The diagnosis was a death sentence, but Tom persisted, going about his life and work tethered to an oxygen tank, which he often used to say made him feel "like an animal." With the portable tanks, he and his wife, Barbara, even went on vacations and in March 1982, they drove down to Florida. The weather there was exceptionally hot and humid that spring, which made Tom's breathing worse than ever.

When they returned, his doctor asked him how he had fared on his vacation and Tom replied, "Terrible," adding, "I just can't cope with that moist night air."

Barbara was with him in the doctor's office and, during a pause in the conversation, she casually mentioned that what Tom needed were new lungs. "It's too bad they don't do lung transplants," she mused aloud.

"Oh, but they do," the doctor said. "They've already done a couple here."

That was all Tom needed to know. He pestered the doctor for more details, but the doctor fended him off, saying the age limit for lung transplants had been set at fifty and Tom — who was fifty-seven years old at the time — was too old.

"Why should that matter?" Tom asked. "What the hell difference does it make? Who says chronological age is the only measure of a man? I've got a lot to live for. I've got four kids. I really *want* to live. I'd probably make a better candidate than some single guy living alone in a room."

The age limit for lung transplant candidates remained at fifty, but Tom finally persuaded his doctor to arrange an appointment with the "big-cheese thoracic surgeon" at Toronto General who was doing the transplants.

Joel David Cooper was the surgeon Tom Hall wanted to see. He is a brilliant, assertive doctor, forty-six years old, but in the twenty years since he graduated from Harvard Medical School, *cum laude*, he has accomplished more than some entire thoracic departments. His *curriculum vitae* was nine pages long and in one ten-year span he had produced more than seventy articles for various medical publications covering a range of surgical techniques and studies of the chest.

His specialty-within-a-specialty is lung transplantation. In recent years, transplant surgeons around the world have progressed to "heart-lung transplants," replacing the entire unit of heart and lungs rather than the heart or lung individually. The heart-lung transplant was pioneered at the Stanford Medical Center in California. Just as it is simpler, and usually more effective, to drop an entire automobile engine into a car than to tinker with the individual pistons of the old engine, so the heart-lung transplant is a simpler operative procedure than the replacement of either part separately. An apparent resultant absurdity is that a heart-lung transplant for a patient who requires only a new lung means discarding a perfectly good heart for a transplanted heart. Cooper prefers the single-lung transplant for patients with lung disease because the operation avoids the added rejection problems of a new heart. In this situation, the patient keeps the other lung, which may keep him alive if the transplanted lung fails. In years to come medical historians doubtless will look back on this period favorably, if not fondly, as a time of great break-throughs, but also as a time confounded by inevitable gaucher-ies.

Cooper does heart-lung as well as single-lung transplants, but because he is a thoracic, or chest, surgeon, and because of his spectacular results, some now call the procedure a lung-heart transplant. It is a little joke of his. One of Cooper's planned projects is a double-lung transplant, which could be a lifesaver for victims of emphysema, largely a smokers' disease that kills millions of people every year, and is said to cost some $10 billion annually in medical care and loss of productivity in North America alone. A single-lung transplant for emphysema would be useless because the new lung and the old lung can't work together. Too much inhaled air flows to the emphysematous lung, causing the new lung to collapse, while blood flows only to the new lung, starving the old lung. The result is a fatal mismatch. Cooper's experimental work with lung transplants could also lead to its application in the care of cystic fibrosis, which causes many of its victims to die slow, relentless deaths by their mid-twenties. While cystic fibrosis might also attack the new lungs, the invasion would be slow, taking possibly fifteen or twenty years, which could buy enough time for a cystic fibrosis cure to be found.

It is a measure of the esteem in which Cooper is held at Toronto General that the entire eleventh floor of the Norman Urquhart Wing, where thoracic patients are kept, is known as "Joel Cooper's floor." He prefers to do his work away from the heat of publicity. It is not that he is overly modest — far from it; he regards himself as the greatest thoracic surgeon in the world, and he may well be. Allen of Public Relations admires Cooper, and works well with him, but it took some time before Allen knew what keys to play. "I have found the best technique with these huge egos is to walk up and say, 'I am the world's greatest expert on public relations.' That's what I did with Cooper. Now we get along fine."

Cooper actually enjoys publicity, but not at the beginning of a case, not during the time of the operation when the pressure is most intense and when things can go badly wrong, quickly. Cooper regards the operation itself as only part of a process, and not necessarily the most important part. Today's transplant operation is not the glamorous operating-room *tour de force* portrayed in movies and books, with the heroic surgeon single-handedly pushing back another frontier of medicine as an adoring nurse wipes his brow.

Neurosurgery presents more intricate technical challenges than transplant surgery. Heart bypasses, plastic surgery, and certain orthopedic procedures may demand more virtuosity. But greater teamwork and logistics are involved in transplantation medicine, teamwork that involves not only surgeons and nurses and anesthetists in the operating room, but immunologists, respiratory technologists, perfusionists, lab technicians, and negotiators. These latter are the people who must somehow be able to persuade a grieving mother in Montreal that her thirteen-year-old son's lungs may keep a fifty-seven-year-old salesman in Toronto alive, if she'll allow the arrangements to be made. There are also pilots who will fly off on a moment's notice, usually in the middle of the night, to pick up and transport a donor-corpse from somewhere often thousands of miles away.

Cooper hates watching transplant surgeons staging press conferences hours after the operation, when it is far too early to know if it is successful or not. He calls it the "Christiaan Barnard syndrome," after the flamboyant South African surgeon who performed the world's first heart transplant in the 1960s, and then embarked on a tour of press conferences and public-speaking engagements.

"It diminishes your reputation with your colleagues," he says. He prefers to wait at least a year before pronouncing on the success or failure of any of his procedures.

There is drama in transplant surgery — the most experienced surgeon still feels a *frisson* when a newly transplanted organ flushes from lifeless grey-blue to pink with the patient's own blood — but basically all it is is taking an organ out of one body and replanting it in another. It involves life and death, to be sure, but there is a certain paint-by-numbers element to it.

"He chased after me, which tells you something of the sort of man he is," Cooper said, recalling the day he met Tom Hall in February 1983. "Patients come in two categories. There are those whose doctors thought that maybe they should talk to us, but who really are suspicious, reluctant. We don't try to convince them they should have a transplant operation. Quite the contrary, they've got to bang on the door. They've got to really want it *bad*. Like Tom Hall. They seek us out, sometimes despite their own doctor's opinion. They're insistent and persistent — tenacious. They *demand* to see us. I like that, because it means they'll have a better chance for survival before, during, and after the operation."

Cooper waited six months before he met with Hall again. "His situation was that much worse, but he was persistent as ever. He knew he wasn't going to die in a week. He probably could have gone on for another year, but he didn't like *the way* he was living. That's a good sign for a prospective patient. It's not enough just to come to me on someone else's suggestion. You've got to have a real *desire* for life."

Tom checked into the hospital in the summer of 1983 for a series of tests and interviews, which included sessions with each of the twenty members of Cooper's transplant team. He also met with the hospital ethics committee, whose function is that of a secular devil's advocate. Its role is to raise every conceivable objection to the procedure, to make certain the patient knows of all the dangers, and to protect the patient and the hospital from an overzealous transplant team. When he appeared before the committee, Tom was told, again, that lung transplants, which began in the early 1960s, had a remarkable record of failure. The numbers of such transplants peaked world-wide in the late 1960s, then there was a moratorium on them. Cooper performed one in 1978, went back to the drawing board, and tried again in the summer of 1982, but in each case the patient died.

Tom was unperturbed by reports of such early disasters. In September 1983, he heard he had passed the tests and was the next candidate for a lung transplant. He was issued a Bellboy paging device, which he was to carry with him at all times, and told never to leave town for more than two hours. Cooper's transplant team put the hospital's Multiple Organ Retrieval and Exchange office — it uses the acronym MORE — on alert for an available lung. All Tom had to do was wait. There were some false alarms, when Tom's Bellboy sometimes erupted while he was on his way to work or late at night when he was asleep. "It was an odd sensation," Tom said. "Part of my mind would say, 'Hey, great! The waiting's over . . .' And then the other part would cut in and say, 'What's the rush, Tom? Like, tomorrow morning you could be *gone*.'"

When the time finally came, Cooper called Tom at his home, deciding that for such an historic occasion, a telephone would be better than the cold, impersonal beeper. Cooper's own Bellboy had sounded earlier, when he was at a neighborhood rink watching his children at their skating lessons. There was a call from MORE to say that a thirteen-year-old boy and his father had been killed in an automobile accident in Montreal and should the boy's mother be asked if she would donate his lungs? Cooper checked a card he carried with him to see if Tom's measurements and blood type matched. They did.

"It was Sunday afternoon and Barbara had a roast in the oven," Tom recalled. "I was chopping apples to make an apple pie. Dr. Cooper phoned and asked, 'What are you having for dinner?' Roast beef and apple pie, I told him, and then he said, 'No you're not. We have a lung. I think we're on for tonight.'"

CHAPTER 6

Jennifer
on Easter
Saturday

DOWNTOWN was respectfully quiet and nearly deserted except for some taxis and the occasional streetcar that rattled by, its tocking racket conspicuous in the silence. The afternoon was dark, spitting rain. A raw wind pushed through the old, begrimed buildings of the hospital and rippled puddles on the asphalted mezzanine roof outside the windows of the operating room.

Windows. There weren't supposed to be windows. Richard Selzer, the surgeon who writes so eloquently of these matters, begins his book *Confessions of a Knife* with a chapter titled "An Absence of Windows." He laments the bricked-up windows of the modern, hermetically sealed operating room and reminisces about the time when it was common for a doctor to look up during surgery and see the moon and stars, even lightning, all of which provided celestial pomp to match even a surgeon's self-esteem. "It did no patient a disservice to have Heaven looking over his doctor's shoulder," writes Selzer.

Pigeons roosted on the brick balconies of the Norman Urquhart Wing some two hundred feet across the way. If they had been interested, they could have looked in through the windows and watched the goings-on in Operating Room 220. On that grey Easter Saturday, at ten minutes to three, Jennifer was lying on her back on a thick patch of sheepskin in that OR, staring up at two large blue discs that washed her in a bright, bluish light. She was awake. She blinked.

She looked sideways towards the glassed-in scrub room, where Mark Bernstein, gloved and masked and clothed in green, operating-room linens, had escaped to blow his nose. He had a cold. Tears ran from his eyes into his surgical mask. Bernstein is young, in his early thirties, and on that afternoon he was part of Zane Cohen's transplant team. Cohen was about to attempt only the eighth small bowel transplant in the world, and the first since 1970, when a patient in New York City had received part of a small bowel from a living, related donor and had survived for seventy-six days, the longest anyone has ever lived with someone else's small bowel. Small bowel transplants were stopped after that because they were considered too risky, even a luxury. People without natural digestive function could be kept alive indefinitely with "total parenteral nutrition," which makes the operation ethically delicate. It is a matter of quality of life, not life or death.

At two minutes to three, the anesthetist, standing by his cockpit of controls behind Jennifer's head, reached forward to hold a black latex mask over her nose and mouth. Her eyes had been taped shut, because in the deep sleep of anesthesia the eyes do not close and any impurities in the operating-room air would fall into them. A thick tube protruded from her mouth. Sensors the size of quarters rested at strategic points on her rib cage for the cardiac monitor to record her heart beats, which appeared on a television screen as spikes darting up at intervals from a luminous green baseline, the audible signal of which filled the room with a shrill continuous *eeep* . . . *eeep* . . . *eeep*. Other tubes were inserted into her torso. A thick yellow tube in the left side of her abdomen was the ileostomy that drained the body wastes. Her right arm was extended, palm up, on a leaf that jutted from the table. Her fingernails were long and well kept, doubtless because she had had so much time to do them during the numbing hours on TPN.

One of the doctors inserted another tube in her right wrist and blood squirted from the incision, forming a bright red rivulet that trickled into her cupped hand. A few drops splashed on the floor of white-flecked black tile. From a speaker in the ceiling, an FM station emitted a faint: *Some day soon, going with him, some day soon* . . .

Jennifer's skin was a ghostly white, and from across the room she looked like a figure made of fine-grained alabaster. Lying prone on the table, she looked taller than she was, with small breasts and good long legs. But her hip bones protruded like tent posts on each side of her stomach because she was nearly hollow inside. (During the operation, a doctor gaped in surprise at the size of the cavity and quipped, "Jeez, you could park a car in there!") On the operating table, naked under a small pile of sterile linen resting on her stomach, she looked girlishly innocent and vulnerable. It seemed an intrusion to be watching, having come to know her a little, but it was not embarrassing. What came to mind was Jennifer in a bathing suit, wet and glistening and turning brown on a tropical beach, freed at last from the dreaded tubes. On a counter by the window ledge, an official green sheet stated, "Small bowel transplantation, Miss Jennifer. . . ." Nothing to indicate anything unusual. The doctors brushed an iodine solution over her body where they would be working, staining the white skin with a garish yellow-red from below her breasts to her knees.

"What's the original disease?" one of the anesthetists asked Bernstein.

"Gardner's Disease," he replied.

A nurse, trying to be light, asked, "What's that? Garbage disease?"

Bernstein did not smile. "She presented with polyposis," he said to the anesthetist.

While doctors and nurses arranged the coverings on the table under Jennifer, an orderly stood at the foot of the table, lifted her legs straight up over his head, then perfunctorily rested them on his shoulders as a nurse pulled a plastic bag over each foot. A thin plastic film was stretched across her midsection, over the surgical zone, where it adhered and pulled the skin taut. Over the intercom came a message from Cohen, who was across the street at the Hospital for Sick Children. He and another medical team were removing the small bowel from the corpse of a ten-year-old boy killed the day before, on Good Friday, in an automobile accident in Mattawa, Ontario. At twenty-six minutes after three o'clock, Bernstein and Wayne Johnston, the tall, lanky vascular surgeon, stood on each side of the sleeping Jennifer. Both were in high spirits, ready to start.

Bernstein turned to John Brebner, the senior anesthetist, and asked:

"Okay to cut?"

"Yeah," Brebner replied.

The scalpel, held between the tips of thumb and forefinger (as one holds the bow of a cello, Selzer says), was aimed first at the middle of the belly, and with no effort and in hardly any time a thin red line ran downward to the pubis, opening her. The cavity was eventually widened and a circular metal device about the size of a steering wheel was installed over the opening where it was used to hold retractors and other surgical utensils.

Soon the clinking, clanking sounds of surgery began, then tiny snaps as wisps of smoke curled up from the exposed innards as the electro-cauterizing scalpel cut and sealed off blood vessels. "A little buzz, please," Bernstein said to the scrub nurse, who was wearing a floral surgical cap and stood near two pedals, one labelled "CUT," the other "COAG." Each surgeon has his own mannerisms, his own way of giving instructions, and cauterizing often is requested by the instruction "Burn ... burn ... burn. ..."

At this point, the operation was all business, but not something to make even a layman queasy or uncomfortable. The operating zone was clearly marked, obvious, like a roped-off work area. Everything else was covered in green, which means sterile. Jennifer's face was hidden behind a tent-like drape, by the anesthetist's arsenal of equipment. Under all the sterile covering, her short dark hair fell down from her head toward the floor. Sometimes, after an hour or two of surgery, it is a surprise to catch sight of the patient's face down there — a person, after all. The same operation conveyed with the intensity of television is much more difficult to watch. In a McLuhanesque way, television seems to magnify and intensify the experience. The burden is too much for the eyes alone to bear. In the operating room, everything is in context: sights, sounds, smells. It is a room that permits no gratuitous interruptions. There is a peculiar, relaxing peace.

At fifteen minutes after four o'clock, the intercom crackled. Cohen wanted to know how far they were into it in OR-220. Johnston told one of the nurses to say they were waiting, then, *sotto voce*, he muttered: "What the hell do they think we've been doing?"

Another message. The bowel would arrive in OR-220 at five o'clock.

"That's Cohen time."

"Better send in a deck of cards."

Mohan Kulkarni, a fourth-year medical student, was in the operating room as an observer. He asked if he might scrub up so he could get closer. "I want to feel part of the energy," he explained.

At four forty-five, the small bowel still had not arrived and some of the medicos wandered off for a break. A sheet of green sterile linen covered the opening in Jennifer's belly during the wait. There is a coffee machine in the Anesthetists' Lounge down the corridor.

In the kitchen of the lounge, tacked to a bulletin board, hung a newspaper story with the headline: "Mom-to-be Paralyzed After Injection Error." It told of a pregnant woman in Albany, New York, who was irreversibly paralyzed from her neck down when a doctor misread the label on a syringe and injected Vincristine, a cancer drug, into her spinal column. A similar error had happened four days earlier, in Miami, when a man being operated on for facial cancer had died from an injection of chemical preservative. The anesthetist's lot is not a happy one. "Too much responsibility, not enough respect," is how one has described the job.

5:50 — Still waiting. Eating doughnuts and sipping cans of Coca-Cola in the Anesthetists' Lounge, discussing Registered Retirement Saving Funds with a junior anesthetist and a nurse.

6:20 — A telephone call to the lounge for Johnston, who has just made a pot of coffee thick enough to stand a spoon in. The call is from Bernard Langer, one of the surgical superstars at Toronto General, who is in the operating room and wants to show Johnston a piece of tissue.

Langer is a distinguished-looking surgeon — tall, balding, hawk-nosed — and Kulkarni, the medical student, brims with unabashed admiration for the man. "He's the best in his field in North America," he says. "He knows the belly like the back of his hand." Johnston hurries to the operating room and asks for his loupes, eyeglasses with a customized magnifying lens that he keeps in a wooden box on which is stencilled: Dr. K. Wayne Johnston.

6:36 — Cohen still has not arrived. Johnston says he expects no problems with the anesthesia, or from anesthesia build-up in the operating room. In some hospitals where the ventilation is not good, an accumulation of the gases can cause headaches and drowsiness in the operating-room staff.

During a "practice run" the day before, when surgeons removed a small bowel from a brain-dead, body-alive corpse and re-implanted it in a cadaver, they found that the donor bowel was too large. It was probably good that the donor was a ten-year-old boy, Langer said.

6:56 — Rob Smith of the hospital's Multiple Organ Retrieval and Exchange program arrives carrying a red-and-white picnic cooler containing the small bowel. "Lunch has arrived," someone shouts. Smith had not bothered to use the tunnel that connects the Hospital for Sick Children to Toronto General.

He had simply walked across Gerrard Street, carrying the cooler by the handle. He places it on the floor, in front of the scrub room, and Langer sits by it and whistles, drumbeating a rhythm on his thighs with his hands. Meanwhile, Cohen and two other surgeons scrub up in the sinks on the other side of the window.

"How does it look in here?" Cohen asks, striding into the room.

"Fine," Johnston answers.

"Wayne!" Cohen is pleased to see such an array of talent in one room. "Heeey! Great!"

The cooler is opened and he lifts the doubled bags out of the cooler. Using scissors to snip through the plastic, he allows the six metres of small bowel to slither into his gloved hands like a pile of wet, raw sausages. He places the organ into a stainless-steel basin containing a cooling solution and the nine doctors and nurses gather around to stare at it. One of the doctors drops to his knees to photograph it through the legs of the huddled group.

"Oy Vay!" Cohen shouts. "I love it! I love it!"

The condition of the bowel seems ideal. The vessels and nerve-endings are large and long, which will make the organ easier to sew into the body. Cohen lifts it out of the basin and carries it in both hands, writhing, jiggling, to the table where he places it on Jennifer's midsection. He studies the juxtaposition for a few moments, then carries the bowel back to the basin, which he places into another basin containing a frozen slush. He covers it with sterile green linen. If warmed to room temperature, the bowel cells, lacking nutrition, will begin to die. The surgery must also be quick, because only when the bowel is safely connected inside the body can the patient's blood nourish it. At a critical point of the operation, as Langer manipulates the bowel into position so he can stitch an artery into place, he is delighted to find it a perfect fit, as if the final piece of a jigsaw puzzle has suddenly clicked into place. With his hands deep inside the body, he talks to the new bowel as if it can hear him. He says, "Come, little mama! Oh, you little cutey!"

8:10 — The bowel has been hooked up, connected to Jennifer, but it remains clearly visible lying on top of her opened belly. Slowly, as her blood begins to flow through it, the bowel turns from a drab grey to a light shade of pink, then darker pink. "Ha! I don't believe it!" Cohen says, laughing with joy.

8:27 — Langer is concerned that parts of the bowel are not as pink as others, that perhaps the blood is not reaching all parts of it. Using a Doppler ultrasound tool about the size of a thick pencil, he tests the blood flow, passing over different parts of the long, circuitous organ, most of it still in a wet heap outside Jennifer's body. A scratchy, static noise, like a faraway station on shortwave radio, fills the room like music as the Doppler ultrasound detects blood flowing through various sections of the bowel. It confirms a complete and adequate blood flow to all parts of the bowel.

8:48 — A slit is cut on one side of Jennifer's abdomen where part of the new bowel will protrude, so that it can be biopsied regularly to check for rejection. The bowel now is part of Jennifer, receiving her blood, but not yet connected to her stomach and thus not functioning as a bowel. That will be done in another operation in two or three months, when doctors are satisfied that her body is not rejecting the new organ. For now the bowel is stuffed inside the body, gently, but the procedure looks casual and almost clumsy. Piece by piece, the swabs and instruments and equipment are removed and the routine sewing-up begins.

At five minutes after nine o'clock, Cohen reaches over Jennifer's body to shake hands with Langer. He doesn't say a word, but he brings his other hand over and pats the top of Langer's hand, still gloved and smeared with blood.

Later, he walked from the operating room to the elevators, which deposited him on the second floor of the Eaton Wing, where Jennifer's parents were waiting. It is one of the surgeon's great satisfactions to be able to encounter the loved ones and say, "It went very smoothly. She's doing well." Their relief was palpable, their eyes filled with tears. Jennifer's mother looked as if she had seen a vision. She stepped forward and clumsily embraced Cohen in her motherly arms.

The story of the transplant appeared on the front page of *The Globe and Mail* on Monday morning ("Rare, risky transplant attempted in Toronto") and all day it had been on radio and television. Cohen enjoyed the attention, even the interview with the tall woman reporter from CBC-TV who asked him to stand on a stool while she questioned him.

Later, thinking he might do some good, he called the reporter to say that she might like to know she got part of the story exactly backwards when she said that future small bowel transplants probably will involve only child recipients. He told her she should have said child *donors*, because it is important that the organ be able to fit comfortably into the recipient's body. "That's not what my notes say," the reporter snapped at Cohen, then hung up in his ear. Cohen stared into his telephone, mystified as ever by the strange workings of the media.

Late Tuesday afternoon, three days later. Cohen, Bernstein, two residents and Philip Halloran, an immunologist from Mount Sinai Hospital across the street, were in Jennifer's room on the ninth floor of the Eaton Wing. All the doctors except Halloran wore white lab coats. Halloran wore a business suit. They discussed the levels of cyclosporin, the anti-rejection drug that was enabling Jennifer's body to accept the new organ. Prescribing the proper amount is an imprecise art; sometimes the doctors have to watch how the body reacts, then add or subtract from the dosage.

Jennifer lay under the covers, restless, trying to sleep. A white towel had been draped across her forehead. Her face was badly swollen, puffy, as were her wrists and forearms. She wriggled under the sheets, rolled over to lie on her right side as the doctors conferred in low voices at the foot of the bed, in a corner of the darkened room.

She had gained twenty-five pounds since the operation, most of it in retained fluids, though the new small bowel alone weighed five pounds. The doctors were trying to get her to lose the liquid weight by flushing her system, "irrigating" it they called it. Two stuffed toy dogs sat on the shelf over her bed.

Late Wednesday afternoon, the same doctors convened again in Jennifer's room. This time the door was closed. When they emerged, Cohen said Jennifer was doing fine and had lost eight pounds in twenty-four hours.

On Thursday, Cohen reported that Jennifer was doing "extremely well . . . perfect as can be." Biopsies of the transplanted organ were being done every day and so far there were no indications of rejection. She had lost more weight. She was walking around.

On Friday, there were reports that Jennifer's white blood cell count had risen substantially, indicating she was fighting off some sort of infection, but the daily biopsy showed the bowel was not being rejected.

David Allen, director of public relations, said the hospital wanted to do something special for Jennifer because her birthday would be on Wednesday the next week. Someone suggested baking a birthday cake in the kitchen and having a small party in her room, but this was rejected because her new bowel was not connected to her stomach and she still couldn't eat.

On Tuesday, ten days after the operation, Jennifer suddenly took a turn for the worse. Something in her system was destroying her red blood cells. Cohen brought her to the operating room again and removed the small bowel, then examined it closely. It appeared to be normal. There was nothing to indicate that the body was rejecting it. He thought the problem might be a peculiar reaction to the cyclosporin, or something foreign in the boy's small bowel that Jennifer couldn't handle, something that might have been "liberated" from the bowel. A virus? Maybe. It might have been something that spread to the brain. There are always strange and potent viruses in a hospital, stranger and more potent than the viruses outside. The lack of answers distressed Cohen. "If there's a substance circulating in the blood that affects the brain," he said, "we'll never find out why."

On Wednesday, at ten o'clock on the morning of her twenty-seventh birthday, Jennifer died.

In the spring issue of *Monitor*, a handsome quarterly published by the hospital, there was a letter from Jennifer's parents, who live in Orillia, a small town where Stephen Leacock once lived, which Jennifer used to describe as surrounded by beautiful lakes and rocky shores. The letter thanked the doctors and nurses, even the public relations people, who had arranged for them to stay in a room at the nurses' residence during the operation. "Through Jennifer's courageous will to live," the letter continued, "we hope that this operation some day will be a success and give hope to many people. We will continue to pray for this work. We miss Jennifer and so many who loved her will also."

No one has yet found out why she died.

CHAPTER 7

Emergency!

HARRY LEVINTER and Bill Fulop, the paramedics, had just brought in Gilbert, a young man, twenty-eight years old, severely emaciated, curled up on the stretcher under a pile of blankets, knees nearly to his chin. Levinter and Fulop had picked him up at his apartment near Avenue Road and Dupont Street. On instructions from the radio room in Emergency, they had given Gilbert an injection of Narcan, an anti-narcotic.

They wheeled him by the nursing station, by the big board, across to Room 522, the three-bed room. Gilbert was nearly comatose, moaning softly. He wore only blue socks and the bottoms of cream-colored pajamas. He had a digital watch on his left wrist.

Everyone in Emergency knew Gilbert. They called him by his first name, usually in stentorian tones, which is how medical people talk to nearly unconscious people. They said, "HELLO, GILBERT." And, "WHERE ARE YOU, GILBERT?" And, "WHAT DID YOU TAKE, GILBERT?" He had been in two days earlier, on the weekend — another overdose. Before that, he had been a patient in Toronto General for more than a year, much of it in intensive care. He had tried to kill himself by swallowing acid. It had torn through his throat like lava, and he had required major surgery to reconstruct his esophagus — thick, wine-colored scars showed just beside his collarbone. Within days of being released after his long stay, they wheeled him back in, this time with a Tylenol overdose.

Charles Ramesar, the doctor in charge on the evening shift, said Gilbert should be watched carefully. "He can be hostile,"

Ramesar said. Gilbert was a loner and a loser, but he liked it at the hospital. It was home.

At four o'clock on a Tuesday afternoon, the big board in Emergency read:

Foot prob
Back pain
Vomiting
Dyspnea
Rectal bleed
Abd pain
Epileptic
Back inj
Dizzy and R eye prob

Busy, but nothing too serious.

Cathy Ryan, an emergency room nurse in a bright pink pantsuit, attached an intravenous tube to Gilbert's right arm to start flushing his system with a saline solution. Linda Braceland, another nurse, took a sample of blood and sent it to the lab to see what Gilbert had OD'd on this time. He had mumbled something about Seconal. A glob of grey-yellow sputum trickled from a corner of his mouth. "ARE YOU GOING TO BE SICK, GILBERT?" Ryan asked, cheerfully but loudly. Braceland placed a kidney basin by Gilbert's pillow, then walked out of the room to the big board, picked up a blue marker-pencil and added to the list:

Hepatic coma, O/D

Bruce Rowat, director of emergency services at Toronto General, explained, "We impose on everybody. For an emergency department to function effectively, you need a strong group of emergency physicians who can transmit the emergency imperative to all other services in the hospital. Nobody likes being interrupted. When you're upstairs assisting in an operating room and you get a call from Emergency, you know what it's like — 'Oops, Emergency. Here comes trouble!' You have to have people in Emergency who are insistent and persistent. They've got to be patient advocates."

The doctors on duty in Emergency at Toronto General are all full-time emergency specialists. They work set hours. One of the advantages of this is that they know that when their shift ends they can go home to their families. They encounter a rich variety of medical problems, on a moment's notice, and they have to think quickly and act quickly. One of the disadvantages is that emergency physicians never get to enjoy an enduring doctor-patient relationship. In the patients come, total strangers, and out they go. The greatest variety of medical problems are referred on to the neurosurgeons, cardiologists, gastroenterologists, psychiatrists, and other specialists upstairs.

"Hospital emergency departments were neglected for many, many years," Rowat said. "They were staffed by the most junior of the house staff, interns right out of medical school. You're on duty, you're it. It's not much of a problem when someone comes in to Emergency with a Zulu spear sticking out of his back. It's the subtle stuff that requires judgement, professional experience — real savvy. You've got to be careful not to send home an indigestion that might be a coronary. And even with the Zulu spear, you've got to know about resuscitation, infection control, and you've got to be able to manage those first few minutes."

Rowat is a small, personable man in his early forties. He calls himself "an evangelist for emergency medicine." It is a tradition at Toronto General never to turn anyone away from Emergency and Rowat does everything he can to maintain the tradition. Some other hospitals, when busy and heavily booked with elective surgery, will send word down to Emergency not to take in any more patients until the backlog is cleared. The same hospitals often redirect patients to Toronto General, knowing that the patients will not be turned away. For the same reason, hospitals in the Ontario countryside far from downtown Toronto sometimes arrange for patients to be flown by helicopter to Toronto General. The helicopters land on the roof of the Hospital for Sick Children across the street, then are taken down an elevator and through a basement tunnel to Toronto General. Some of the hospitals do this regularly, usually on Fridays, most often before a summer long weekend. It frees the local medical staff for less onerous diversions.

Rowat was born in upstate New York, in a small town named Malone, south of the border from Montreal. His father was a Presbyterian minister and Rowat remembers the day when he was very young, toddling after his father on a visit to Malone's volunteer fire department. "I remember how impressed my father was by the fact that one of the local doctors donated his time to train the volunteer firemen in the rudiments of paramedical work. I think that's when I became an evangelist in this. Even now, there's nothing I enjoy more than spending an evening with ambulance workers we're training to be paramedics. I'll go out on my own expense, as long as they've got popcorn for me."

The Rowat family moved to Quebec when Bruce was ten years old. At university he studied geology, working summers as an amateur paleontologist; then he decided on medicine and enrolled at McGill University's School of Medicine, eventually specializing in internal medicine. But it was the emergency department that captured his enthusiasm. "I found medical school really dull," he said. "You were always presented with patients who had been seen by a million other doctors. It wasn't much of a challenge. If they were on the hematology ward, you knew it was a hematology problem. If it was on the cardiology ward, you knew it was a cardiology problem. And the patients were tired of having to repeat their stories. When they did, they had the stories so refined that you didn't have to ask any questions. In Emergency, it was a challenge. When someone came into Emergency with a problem, it was up to me to put it all together."

The ambulances arrive at Emergency by a covered, curved driveway at the south end of the complex. The hospital doors open automatically for the stretchers. The attendants push the stretcher into the lobby, then make a sharp right through two swinging doors that lead directly into Emergency. The nursing station is in the centre of the room, with rooms all around. On each side of the big board are rooms with two beds, around which curtains can be drawn for privacy. At the east end of the room is the large, three-bed room. Behind the station are three single-bed rooms, each with windows and venetian blinds. They are reserved for serious cases, patients who need to be watched more closely than the others. Behind the private rooms are the resuscitation rooms, the suture room, the radiology room, and the emergency operating rooms. The further north a patient goes in Emergency, the worse his condition.

There is continuous motion in the department, always a low babble and a clamor, even on quiet days. In many ways, the pace in Emergency resembles the pace of a baseball game, long periods of lolling about, punctuated by feverish activity. Monitoring devices emit piercing tone signals. Ambulance attendants and policemen chat up the nurses. Doctors hunch over charts at the far end of the nursing station. Distraught spouses, children, mothers and fathers wander and wait, clutching handkerchiefs, smoking cigarettes in the lobby outside by the coin-operated vending machines. Orderlies in white uniforms with red stripes down the legs wheel beds in and out of the rooms, usually bearing patients stunned by the sudden upheaval in their lives and the assault upon their dignity and privacy.

An hour earlier they were at home reading, watching television, then pain or nausea or dizziness or tightness in the chest overwhelmed them and someone said, "You're going to the hospital!" By car, by taxi, by ambulance, carrying small bags of essentials, they sped through the city streets to the hospital, to Emergency. When they arrive they are told by the receptionist to sit in a chair, even when the lump on their forehead is the size of a walnut and blood drips on the floor.

"Name?"

"I want to see a doctor *now*."

"Do you have your OHIP card?"

Type, type, type.

"I'm bleeding!"

"Have you been here before?"

"Look, blood!"

Type, type, type.

If the problem looks serious, they may be stripped, issued backless gowns, wheeled about like groceries in a supermarket, gawked at by complete strangers, examined by doctors and nurses to whom they may never be properly introduced. If Emergency is crowded, if their ailments do not rate a high priority, they may be left for an hour or two or three on stretchers pushed against a wall by the nursing station, like exhibits. In moments of distress body functions are not always easily controlled and sometimes an arc of urine rises from the bed and splatters into the face of a nurse who did not get a catheter in quickly enough. *"Damn! Pissed on me! God Damn!"* The pace can be frenetic. Diseases like hepatitis-B can kill in forty-eight hours. And there is AIDS. It is a worry.

Linda Braceland remembers the shift she worked when two ladies in their late sixties sat waiting in the lobby of Emergency. It was about eleven in the morning. The ladies had arrived separately, for minor problems, and at first they were frightened and confused by all the commotion. After an hour in the lobby, however, they became chummy and soon were discussing aches and pains and grandchildren. As they chatted, a tall young man walked in through the automatic doors and headed directly to the bathroom, just inside the lobby. There he removed his clothes, then walked out to the lobby and sat on a chair across from the ladies. They kept chatting. The scene all seemed so normal that Braceland actually walked through the lobby without noticing, then did a doubletake. She briskly ushered the naked man out of the room, got him dressed and escorted out of the hospital, then approached the ladies and asked why they did not report him. The two ladies looked at her quizzically, not sure what to say. "They hadn't been here before," Braceland said. "They thought that's how things are in Emergency."

Nurses in Emergency wear nametags that display only their first names. They are Cathy, Linda, Christine, Debbie — and that's it. It is a safety precaution. Emergency nurses often deal with rough, sometimes seedy, clientele, and they all do shift work, which means going home late at night, alone. Cathy Ryan said, "I've had more than one patient who waited outside after being discharged and then followed me home."

A manual for emergency room workers starts by listing five reasons why anyone comes to Emergency:

1. *For expert medical care for acute life-threatening illness.*
2. *For convenience.*
3. *For lack of a personal physician.*
4. *For a second medical opinion.*
5. *For reassurance in a comprehensive institutional setting.*

"In approaching the patient," the manual continues, "it is useful to think in terms of serious, life-threatening illnesses that require prompt diagnosis and treatment." The manual urges workers to think of the *Horrendo Principle*. For example:

In assessing the older male with acute abdominal pain, it would be important not to miss a leaking abdominal aneurysm. For the patient with indigestion . . . the diagnosis of acute myocardial infarction or dissecting thoracic aneurysm should be entertained. . . . The well-looking infarct or impending abdominal aneurysm are not infrequent. Beware! Look for pathology. Assume the worst.

The manual warns of a common error in Emergency, which s to delay decision-making while waiting for laboratory data.

Laboratory data are no substitute for clear thinking. You are encouraged to question what you are told and to develop a healthy skepticism in all things medical. . . . Neglect these principles and the final equation may be a brilliant diagnosis with a dead patient. . . . Your patient may be less concerned with what they have than your opinion as to what they don't have. . . . Beware of the bizarre, derelict, psychotic, abusive, alcoholic patient. They may have significant underlying organic disease (hypoglycemia, subdural hematoma, drug ingestion). Do not let your gut reaction interfere with your professional assessment. . . . In times of tragedy, you may learn that you must stop being a doctor and start being a person. . . .

In a year, some forty thousand patients enter Emergency, about 110 a day. The days and weeks have rhythms. There is the pre-dawn quiet when there is time to sip a coffee and fill out reports. There is the little peak during morning rush hour when people wake up feeling worse than when they went to bed, and there are the commuting accidents. Then the slow, steady arrivals during the business day, the referrals from family doctors. The next peak comes before the supper hour, when doctors' offices have closed and the pain, nausea, dizziness, or tightness in the chest suddenly are magnified and feel vaguely fatal — and there are the commuting accidents. The next peak comes between the late news and midnight, when it is time to go to bed, when the distractions of daytime have receded and one can meditate more thoroughly on the pain, nausea, dizziness, or tightness in the chest.

There is also the burst of activity when the bars close, especially on Fridays and Saturdays. The drunks stumble in — cuts, bruises, gunshot wounds, broken noses, automobile accidents, falling down, overdoses, commuting accidents. They arrive whimpering, cursing, singing, apologizing, bragging, confessing, roaring, flailing. Some are familiar customers. "BEEN A NAUGHTY BOY TONIGHT, HAROLD?" For the drunks, Emergency is the whore with the heart of gold. Some of them can take fifteen stitches without an anesthetic.

And then, at various times, there are the expectant moms.

David Williams was the emergency resident on duty Tuesday. He is a big man with a moustache, thirty-two years old. He wears Nike running shoes on duty. In Emergency at Toronto General, there are three residents, doctors who have finished medical school and a year as an intern but who still have to log an arduous apprenticeship before they are regarded as fully qualified doctors.

It is not easy to become a resident at Toronto General. First, there is the competition to get into medical school. Williams studied medicine at McGill, where every year between eighteen hundred and twenty-five hundred students apply for 160 positions. "A lot of people feel once they've made it through that rigorous selection process they've got it made, but it's not true at all," Williams said. "With government cutbacks and reduced hospital funding, there are fewer postgraduate positions available, fewer internships and residencies, which means an ever-expanding pool of applicants for an ever-shrinking number of positions."

What this means is that it is possible — rare, but possible — for a person to be accepted as a medical student, complete four years of medical school, then find there are no suitable internships available. This, Williams said, is the horror called "not matching." He explained, "In fourth-year medical school you fill out applications and send your *curriculum vitae* to the hospitals where you want to work, then you make the rounds for the interviews. The hospitals rank-order you, and you rank-order the hospitals. If you're an extremely good medical student, in the top 5 per cent in your class, you might rank-order a list of four or five hospitals, and you'll probably get your first or second choices. If you're an average medical student, you rank-order ten to fifteen hospitals and hope to get one of your top five choices. If you were at the bottom of the class, it would be prudent to rank-order at least twenty hospitals. I've heard of some students who rank-ordered thirty hospitals."

Williams finished in the top 5 per cent of his class at McGill. He did an internship in family practice at Ottawa Civic Hospital, where he worked 100 to 110 hours a week. He was one of a hundred applicants who applied for three positions open for an emergency resident at Toronto General. His residency had begun the previous July, nine months earlier. It was for a three-year period, renewable each year. The hours were better, only fifty hours a week, at a salary of $26,000 a year.

That Tuesday in Emergency, Williams had come upon an interesting case, a woman in her early twenties who had clusters of deep red rash on her arms and legs. She had been to Emergency the Sunday before with diarrhea and a fever of 103 degrees. She had spent three weeks in Jamaica on vacation and, ten days after she had returned to Canada, she developed diarrhea, which lasted three days. The diarrhea stopped, she felt better, but in a few days she developed a high fever. Her family doctor didn't know what was wrong, although, because of her stomach pains and diarrhea, he suspected a severe gastroenteritis, which usually subsides in a day or two. He told her to go home and rest. If it had been constipation instead of diarrhea, then he would have suspected appendicitis, and she would have been admitted to hospital.

"When I saw her on Sunday, I thought she had some form of travellers' diarrhea," Williams said. "It's spread by bacteria, which invades through the wall of the gut. We did the appropriate blood work and stool cultures, then sent her home. She called earlier today and said she had these red rashes on her stomach and arms and legs, so I told her to come in again. I just finished examining her, and I think she has typhoid fever. I'm almost sure of it."

In the Doctors' Lounge in Emergency, where Williams had been studying, a thick book titled *Cecil Textbook of Medicine* was cracked open at page 1,589, at the section on typhoid fever. The article, written by someone called Sherwood L. Gorbach, begins: "Typhoid (cloudy) fever is a febrile illness of prolonged duration marked by hectic fever, delirium, enlargement of the spleen, abdominal pain and a variety of systemic manifestations . . . caused by *Salmonella typhi* . . . 500 cases annually in the United States. . . ."

The textbook goes on to describe other illnesses: botulism, plague, tularemia, anthrax, cat scratch disease, rat bite fever, Rocky Mountain spotted fever, malaria, Lassa fever, and — most dreaded of all — Marburg-Ebola disease. With "sophisticated medical management," the mortality rate for Marburg-Ebola disease is between 25 and 30 per cent, but in parts of rural Africa the mortality rate ranges between 50 and 90 per cent.

Jay Keystone, the doctor who runs the Tropical Diseases Unit at Toronto General, and who is a world authority on leprosy, said what would really make the alarm bells ring would be someone who arrived in Toronto diagnosed as having something like Lassa fever or Marburg-Ebola. "Back in 1976, a lady at Etobicoke General Hospital in west-end Toronto was tentatively diagnosed as having Lassa fever and the hospital had to be closed down." The procedure for such a patient is to call the armed forces, order a transport plane, and fly the patient to Ottawa, where there is an isolation tent available for anyone with such a dangerous infectious disease.

For more than two years, Toronto General has had a world-class, state-of-the-art isolation unit on the eleventh floor of the Norman Urquhart Wing. The unit is sealed off from the rest of the hospital, with its own air supply, its own electrical system, its own high-efficiency, particulate filtering system designed to remove 99.9 per cent of any impurities in air discharged from the unit into the environment. An élite hospital team has been trained to work in the unit, which was built to handle the most lethal infectious diseases known to man, including Lassa fever and Marburg-Ebola disease. The special isolation suits for the team look like space suits. Planning for the unit began in 1978, and construction finally was completed early in 1984. The hospital spent nearly $2 million on it. According to Keystone, who has travelled the world studying tropical diseases, it is as safe an isolation unit as he has seen anywhere.

But it has never been opened.

Why? There are many reasons. Vickery Stoughton, the president, said it is because of an irritating number of bureaucratic regulations. Government inspectors come along to check it out, knowing that what they are checking out is a unit for handling the most dangerous diseases in the world, so no one wants to be the one to say it is safe. Instead, they recommend that another $100,000 or $200,000 be spent to make absolutely sure. "It's a matter of back-up systems on back-up systems on back-up systems," Stoughton said. In government inspection circles, this is called "covering your ass."

Probably the only way the unit will ever be opened, according to David Allen of Public Relations, is for someone from Africa to step off a plane in Toronto with a burning fever, be rushed to Emergency at Toronto General, diagnosed as having Lassa fever or Marburg-Ebola disease, and assigned immediately to the isolation unit. It would be a case of "we're here because we're here."

For Stoughton, it remained an annoying problem. At a time of cost-cutting and government cutbacks in public health, it is difficult to justify having spent $2 million on an isolation unit that stands empty and idle. "Sooner or later," Stoughton said, looking down at his telephone as if it would start ringing as he spoke, "someone's going to ask, why'd you spend all that money and just let it sit there? I mean, *The Toronto Sun* would have a field day."

It was almost a relief to confront typhoid fever, which, next to the killers in the *Cecil Textbook of Medicine*, seemed almost innocuous. Typhoid is not the scourge it once was, though serious complications can result, with mortality rates of up to 15 per cent in untreated patients. Since the introduction of the drug chloramphenicol, the mortality rate has fallen to about 1 per cent, and most of the fatally ill succumb to intestinal perforations and hemorrhaging. Good primary medical care is crucial, and the patient must be properly nourished so that the diarrhea does not waste the body.

David Williams suspected the young woman had probably contracted the fever from the water in Jamaica. "She stayed in one of the big tourist hotels, but she spent a lot of time eating and drinking with Jamaicans. She should be able to stay at home, but she'll have to be isolated and wash her hands after bowel movements and before eating. If the diarrhea persists, or if she can't keep solids and liquids down, we'll have to admit her to hospital and isolate her here."

"*Arrrrgh!*" Two young policemen wrestled a rough young man into Emergency. He wore jeans and a T-shirt and a headband. He was handcuffed. He was screaming, roaring, as if in terrible pain. Beryl Reid, the evening triage nurse, having determined that the young man's name was Al, said to him in a calm voice, "Al, we've got to put you up on a stretcher." Al balked, then swore. "*Please*, Al," Reid scolded him sharply. "Don't scream like that. There are a lot of sick people here." Al looked up at her, startled, then meekly climbed aboard the stretcher and Elderfield Carr, a tall black orderly, wheeled him off to a room at the back. The policemen walked on either side of the stretcher, their nightsticks clinking against the metal struts.

Charles Ramesar, the tall, laconic doctor in charge of the evening shift, sat at the table in the Doctors' Lounge poring over reports. The paper work added another hour to his working day, but it had to be done. In the suture room down the hall, a doctor struggled with a recalcitrant patient who had been conked on the head in a bar earlier in the evening. "PLEASE SETTLE DOWN RICHARD SO I CAN SEW YOU UP." It was shortly before midnight.

Ramesar's paper work consisted of entering in a register the names and ailments of all the patients who had arrived at Emergency during his shift. The hospital was negotiating a new per-patient fee with the provincial government, which now gave the hospital a yearly lump sum of $23 for every patient treated in Emergency. With forty thousand patients, that amounts to $920,000. The hospital prefers to do this instead of billing the province's public health insurance plan for each emergency patient, which would require more office staff. Besides, the "catch-rate" would not be 100 per cent, as it is with the yearly-lump-sum method.

As he tallied the names and numbers, Ramesar, who is from Trinidad, mused aloud. "We don't realize how spoiled we are in this country. People don't appreciate the standard of care they're getting. In Third World countries people look at medical care differently. When you go to a hospital in Ethiopia and wait eight hours and can't find a bed, you go home to die. Here, it's not okay to get old and sick and die. Foreign students who come here are always struck by this. It leaps out at them."

Ramesar studied medicine at Queen's University and started at Toronto General in September 1977. On working in Emergency, he said, "At first it's a blur, like driving a car at 150 miles an hour. You're concentrating so hard you can't see things like trees or people by the side of the road. Then you get used to it, and you begin to notice shapes and patterns, and then you begin to see things you couldn't see before. It's a matter of getting used to the pace. . . ."

From the suture room: "YOU CAN GO NOW RICHARD. YOU'RE CURED."

Ramesar continued, "You won't see many emergency doctors who are smug or arrogant. We tend to be a humble lot. We depend on the nurses because they keep us out of trouble. The nurses in Emergency are a special breed — very experienced, bright, aggressive. We need them. We can do something great one day and botch it up terribly the next." Ramesar planned to work three more months at Toronto General, then try something else, perhaps psychiatry. "I've had enough of death and destruction. And burnout. It's patch-up work here. We resuscitate people, we save lives, then off they go to Intensive Care. The doctors upstairs get all the flowers."

Ron Lindzon walked into the Doctors' Lounge to begin his shift. He was in charge of Emergency overnight. He is a big man, in his early thirties, with square shoulders and dark, curly hair. He is a Torontonian who trained in emergency medicine in Denver, Colorado. The hospital in Denver where he worked straddled a tenuous boundary between the black and Hispanic sections of the city. It was a battleground. "I treated more gunshot wounds in one night in Denver than in three years in Emergency at Toronto General," he said.

At one o'clock in the morning, there was a call to Emergency from the Clarke Institute of Psychiatry. Gordon, a patient with a chronic personality disorder, was being sent over. Christopher Rubes, the doctor who received the call, recognized the name and groaned. "Not again," he said. "The man's a manipulator.

He's been coming here for ten years. He's the guy who takes thirty Tylenols a day."

Within the hour, two policemen and two ambulance attendants arrived with Gordon, who looked surprisingly well groomed, with a thin, professorial face. He wore expensive shaded glasses, a suit and tie, and a light pink shirt. His shoes were polished.

"Do you have our friend from the Clarke?" Rubes asked in a lilting voice.

"He's been Form-1'd," the first policeman announced.

A Form-1 is an order issued under the Mental Health Act that allows a hospital to detain a patient involuntarily for forty-eight hours. It often is used as a verb ("We better Form-1 him") or an adjective ("He's a Form-1 loony"). Gordon lighted a cigarette and said he had to go to the bathroom.

"C'mon, Gordon," Rubes told him, smiling, "you know where our bathrooms are."

Gordon walked quickly by the nursing station, by the big board, turned right and headed directly to the men's toilet. Rubes explained that taking thirty Tylenols a day over a long period can cause acute liver damage. "He probably likes the buzz he gets from the codeine, but it's not the codeine that does the damage," he said. "It's the acetaminophen, a mild analgesic." Rubes told the policemen he was not keen on having Gordon back again, but he would do a blood check on him.

When Gordon emerged from the bathroom, the policemen escorted him to one of the rooms at the back so that a doctor could get a blood sample. Gordon did not wish to co-operate. He refused to lie down on the bed. He lighted another cigarette and paced the room, keeping the bed between him and the policemen.

"Gordon, you'll have to put out that cigarette," a nurse said. "There's oxygen in here."

Gordon pretended not to hear.

"Put it out," one of the policemen told him.

"Why don't you just fuck off," Gordon replied, but in a whisper.

The policeman grimaced as Gordon dropped the cigarette on the floor and squashed it with his shoe. It soon became apparent that Gordon did not like policemen, but knew just how far to go without being actively belligerent. He finally submitted to the blood test, but as he did he softly interrogated the policemen on their work, their political views, their perception of the universe. The policemen struggled to maintain their composure, alternately looking down at the floor, at the equipment in the room, out the window at the nursing station. Gordon confided to the nurse that his IQ is in the top 2 per cent of the population. The nurse found the vein, inserted the needle.

"Do you know what your IQ is?" Gordon asked the policemen.

The question startled them. One clasped and unclasped his fingers, the other kneaded his knuckles.

"I'm curious," Gordon continued, as if he were conducting an undergraduate seminar. "I'd really like to know."

No reply.

"Let me guess, I'd say . . ."

Suddenly, one of the policemen wheeled and glared at Gordon.

"It must be higher than yours, fella," he shouted, his forehead red as a radish. "Because all you can say is, 'Fuck you!'"

Gordon looked pleased.

In the treatment rooms in Emergency there are framed instructions for various calamities. They are arrayed on the walls like ABCs and The Golden Rule in a kindergarten class. In one of the resuscitation rooms — they are called "Rees One" and "Rees Two" — there are instructions for managing snake bites, with illustrations of four poisonous snakes, the Timber Rattlesnake, Coral Snake, Eastern Cottonmouth, and Southern Copperhead. In the extremely unlikely event that a patient presents in Emergency with these snake-bite symptoms (the Timber Rattler is the only non-American snake of the four), here is what to do:

1. *Assess respiratory system.*
2. *Assess circulatory status.*
3. *Determine the extent of systemic reaction from the presence of hypotension; nausea, vomiting, sweating; weakness or neurotoxic symptoms such as dizziness, perioral paresthesia, ptosis, paralysis or muscle fasciculation.*
4. *Inspect the area of the bite, noting one or more fang marks (a Coral Snake may leave none).*
5. *Identify the snake if possible — most snake bites are from nonpoisonous snakes.*

There is nothing about cutting an X into the snake bite with your jackknife, sucking out the venom, and spitting it into the dust.

In an emergency operating room, more framed instructions, this time for patients who arrive with parts of their bodies cut off, including scalp, hands, feet, and nose. If the severed part is "a clean guillotine amputation," the sign advises, the part can be reimplanted if properly handled. The part should be thoroughly washed, preferably in a solution called Ringer's Lactate, then wrapped in sterile gauze, placed in a plastic bag and transported to hospital in an insulated cooling chest on crushed ice. It should *not* be frozen.

Ralph Manktelow, head of plastic surgery at Toronto General, is gaining a world reputation in the delicate, tedious procedure known as microvascular surgery. The operations usually last eight to ten hours, sometimes as long as twenty-four hours, with the surgeons going through three shifts of nurses. They can suture blood vessels and microscopic nerves and transfer tendons from one finger to another. Using microscopes that can make a nerve look as big as a garden hose and with sutures no thicker than a spider's silk, Manktelow and his team have rejoined severed fascicles — clusters of nerve fibres that carry messages to or from the brain — in order to bring motion and sensation to the transplanted part. The microsurgeons have found that a severed thumb can be replaced by a patient's big toe, with spectacular, if somewhat bulbous, results.

In January 1984, Manktelow performed Canada's first "living joint transplant" on a manual laborer who had had all four fingers of his left hand cut off in an industrial accident two years earlier. Manktelow's team removed the second joint from one of the man's toes and transplanted it to his index finger, giving him enough function to grasp a hammer or a screwdriver.

The challenge of microvascular surgery is limitless. Nancy McKee, a member of Manktelow's team who works across the street at Mount Sinai Hospital, once sewed a young man's penis back on after he had chopped it off in a fit of pique. The man, twenty-four years old, had done an admirable piece of work, using a razor knife, then tying off the exposed blood vessels with dental floss. As he was being driven to Emergency, he explained to the ambulance attendants, "My girlfriend left me and I didn't need it any more."

Shortly after two o'clock in the morning, Louie and Shirley walked in. Shirley had cut her left wrist badly on a piece of broken mirror. She might have been trying to kill herself, or maybe Louie had tried to kill her. It was hard to say. They were both drunk.

Shirley, a Canadian Indian, wore jeans and a black blouse and running shoes. She was pretty in a chubby sort of way, with long, teased black hair. Louie was short and wiry, with a thin gambler's moustache. He wore a black leather jacket, with a greasy plaid shirt open to his belt. He told Ron Lindzon, the doctor in charge after midnight, that he was Puerto Rican and was used to these things. He pushed up the sleeve of his jacket and showed Lindzon three deep purplish welts on his left forearm. He said, "Cut myself for thirty-one stitches there. Sewed it up myself. What do you think, doc?" Louie was a creep.

Lindzon asked Shirley to climb up on the table in the suture room and lie on her back. He reached for a hypodermic needle and novocaine and told her, "This will hurt a little. You'll feel a burning." Shirley rolled her head over, looked up at the doctor and said, "Thesh okay." It was a deep, ugly wound, with a flap of skin the size of a fifty-cent piece dangling from her wrist. Lindzon told her to look the other way while he injected the pain-killer. Louie, being helpful, diverted Shirley's attention by pointing out different-colored boxes of medication on one of the shelves in the suture room. He stroked her hair as he talked.

"See the yellow one . . ."

Lindzon sticks the needle directly into the wound.

"See the blue one . . ."

Lindzon sticks the needle at the top and bottom of the wound.

"See the green one . . ."

Lindzon sticks the needle at each side of the wound, then two more sticks inside the wound.

"Did you feel that, Shirley?"

Shirley rolled her head over and asked when he was going to start.

"Alcohol is a wonderful anesthetic," Lindzon said, reaching for iodine and a saline solution to wash the wound and flush out any stray fragments of mirror. "Have either of you ever had hepatitis?" he asked. Shirley and Louie looked at him blankly. Lindzon slipped on a pair of rubber gloves and a surgical mask. Louie began to ramble, talking in *non sequiturs*. "Water has no energy," he said. Lindzon sat on a stool by the bed and began sewing up the wound, starting at the top, nearest the heart, hoping to restore circulation to the dangling flap of skin.

"Thesh seven years' bad luck," Shirley said.

"What's that?" Lindzon asked, stitching, not looking up.

"The mirror," Shirley explained.

"Was it an accident?"

"No, I *purposefully* did it."

"I can explain it," Louie said. "She walked out on me. I found her like that and I said, 'That's too serious. You have to go to the hospital.'"

Lindzon continued to stitch and Louie began to smooch with Shirley, kissing her, rubbing her breasts. Then he stopped and said to Lindzon, "I don't believe in doctors. I'm Spanish. We can take pain." He pulled back the collar of his shirt and pointed to a scar on his neck. He said Shirley did it. "Pain doesn't bother us as much as you people . . ."

"We can take pain as much as you Puerto Ricans," Shirley said. She was getting angry.

"No . . ."

"If I wasn't Canadian, would you fuck me?"

Momentarily nonplussed, Louie pretended not to hear. He said to Lindzon, "I don't believe in doctors, doc. It's not you, I . . ."

"Why don't you just fuck off and get out of here, eh?" Shirley yelled, pulling her arm away from Lindzon, ripping out some of the stitches.

"Now *that* was a silly thing to do!" Lindzon shouted, jumping up off his stool. "I only had one more to go. Now I've got to start over again." He poured more saline solution over the wound as Louie, hurt and angry, began to make threats against Shirley. Lindzon walked to the door, towering over Louie, and ordered him out of the room.

"Where do I go?" Louie asked, petulantly.

"Down the hall! Turn right!"

With Louie gone, there was peace in the suture room. Shirley looked over and studied Lindzon as he weaved in the stitches, gently holding her arm as he worked. She smiled.

"I got mad because he said I hurt his neck," she said.

"Uh-huh."

"He really pisses me off."

"Uh-huh."

"I'm sorry, doc."

"That's okay."

When he finished sewing, Lindzon counted the stitches — eighteen. It had taken nearly an hour. Louie reappeared just as the doctor finished wrapping Shirley's arm in gauze. Louie walked to the side of the table and began kissing and hugging her, rubbing his hands over her legs. Then he told her, "There was some hassle in the lobby with two Toronto pigs. They said they were going to take me in. I told them they couldn't touch me because I'm from the United States. I told them, 'Arrest me!' They couldn't touch me. . . ."

"Shhh," Shirley said.

Lindzon helped Shirley off the table, then she and Louie walked down the hallway toward the lobby, where Louie pointed out a nurse who had been talking to a policeman earlier.

"That's the broad who kissed the pig," he said.

"Isn't he delightful?" the nurse remarked.

"Kissed a pig!"

"Don't be so fucking stupid," Shirley said.

Louie took Shirley by the arm and said, "C'mon, let's go home."

"I don't want this guy around me," Shirley said, pulling away from Louie as they reached the lobby.

Louie stomped out of the hospital through the automatic doors, waited in the driveway a few minutes, then walked across the street and got into a taxi. Just before he got in, Shirley went to the doors and shouted, "Thanks for stabbing me!"

At ten minutes after three o'clock in the morning, a well-dressed, middle-aged man entered Emergency and headed straight across to the three-bed room. Cathy Ryan followed him and they talked awhile, then she emerged from the room, picked up the blue marker-pencil and wrote on the big board:

Retention

"He's a nice man," she said. "He comes in about every three months. We'll get him a catheter because he's all stopped up. He hasn't had a whiz in twenty-three hours."

At ten minutes to four o'clock in the morning, a Code 50, which means "multiple trauma," usually an automobile accident. Two ambulance attendants wheeled the bed through the doors, followed by two policemen.

"Hit a telephone pole at sixty miles an hour on the Danforth, near Coxwell," one of the policemen explained. "The block ended up in the front seat."

The attendants pushed the bed straight through to the emergency operating room at the back, where Lindzon took charge.

In minutes, there were ten medicos in the room — doctors, nurses, paramedics, a radiology technician, a respiratory therapist. A Code 50 is heard throughout the hospital, as is a Code 99, which means cardiac arrest. The man was nearly unconscious, from the collision and from drink. One of the ambulance attendants stood at the front of the operating table and held the man's head straight while the other used heavy-duty scissors to cut away the sleeves of his jacket. Two nurses pulled off his shoes and socks, unbuckled his belt, unzipped his fly — and a cockroach walked out.

"*Yech!*"

"Put on cardiac monitor and a 100 per cent O_2, please," Lindzon said.

The man moaned, "Oh, my back. Oh, my back. Oh, my back."

"Make sure he gets a tetanus shot, please," Lindzon said.

The man moaned, "I'm finished. I'm finished. I'm finished."

Lindzon turned to the radiology technician and said, "Get ready for a CT-scan, please." One of the nurses stepped to the table to insert a yellow Dacron catheter into the man's penis. "Just pee," she told him. "Just let it go." The man began to cry. "I'm finished," he sobbed. And then he said, "My daughter!" And then, "My life — finished."

"Where are you right now?" Lindzon asked.

"I want to go home."

"What place are you in?"

In Emergency, one never assumes anything apart from the obvious. It is important to get information from the patient — where it hurts, how it hurts, what he feels — then determine if the patient is in any condition to provide good information. Lindzon continued with the basics, trying to confirm that the man at least was cognizant. The man was Chinese, which is unusual for someone so intoxicated.

"HOW OLD ARE YOU, MR. WONG?" Lindzon asked.

In a soft, slow voice, the man replied, "Between . . . forty-one . . . and forty-three."

"WHAT IS THE DATE TODAY?"

A pause, then, "March 10?"

"Well, that's close," Lindzon smiled. It was March 12.

"WERE YOU DRINKING?"

"Little."

"DID YOU TAKE ANY DRUGS, MR. WONG?"

"Don't . . . think . . . so."

An hour later, after the X-rays, it was determined that the man had suffered only a fractured rib. He was kept in hospital overnight. "He was probably pretty relaxed when he hit the telephone pole," Cathy Ryan said.

Lorne Greenspan, deputy director of Emergency, is a slight, gentle man, a natural teacher. He likes to remind newcomers to Emergency of the first principle of medicine: *Primum nil nocere*. "First do no harm," he translated. He is a storyteller and during the seven years he has worked at Toronto General he has kept a journal of some of the odd happenings.

Late one evening, Greenspan was called to the psychiatry room, where he met two policemen with their guns drawn. They had brought in a man they considered extremely dangerous. He was a power-lifter and a martial arts expert. Greenspan looked in the room and saw an enormous man sitting in a chair, next to a rather meek-looking male companion. The policemen seemed to have great admiration for the big man. One of them told Greenspan that the hulking patient could bench-press 485 pounds.

"Why don't you guys go in?" Greenspan asked.

"No, you go in. We'll protect you."

Greenspan entered the room and his first impression was that the man looked like a block of granite — *chiselled* — and he was extremely agitated. Greenspan sat across from him on a wooden bench and the man rambled on about his life, his sexuality, and then he glared at Greenspan and said, "You're reading my thoughts."

"Nooo, no," Greenspan assured him.

The man continued, this time telling Greenspan intimate details of relations with his wife, then he stopped and glared at Greenspan again.

"You're *controlling* my thoughts."

"Nooo, no," Greenspan said. "I'm just trying to understand."

The man told Greenspan he was going to be the new chief of police, then spun a long, tangled story of his career in the police force. As he talked, off in a world of his own, his docile companion told Greenspan of an incident when they were driving to town that morning. "He noticed this man standing at a bus stop, holding an attaché case. He stopped the car, got out, walked to the bus stop and told him, 'I've never met you, but I know you in spirit.' The man at the bus stop sort of blinked, then my friend told him he was going to be the new chief of police by nightfall. The man at the bus stop nodded and smiled, then my guy grabbed him in a bear hug, lifted him off the ground and kissed him — *on the lips*. The guy at the bus stop dropped his attaché case and fainted."

Suddenly, the power-lifter, aware that Greenspan was listening to his companion, leaped up from his chair, lunged toward Greenspan and unloaded a thunderous karate chop at the doctor, missing his head by inches and crashing into the bench he was sitting on. "It was the scariest moment of my life," Greenspan said. "I think I sh — well, it was the scariest moment of my life."

At twenty-five minutes past six o'clock in the morning, the big board read:

Abd. pain
Retention
NFW
Vomiting

The emergency room was quiet. Morning had broken. The situation was under control.

CHAPTER 8

I Won't Hire
Someone Who
Can't Cry

THERE USED TO BE a little game in some of the operating rooms, one of those occasional amusements at the expense of a new nurse who arrived wide-eyed and anxious to please. When the patient was safely asleep, a doctor — usually the anesthetist, though orthopedic surgeons were always ready for fun — crept behind the nurse, yanked the drawstring on her OR uniform, tugged it from her shoulders, and unhooked her brassiere.

"My, my . . ."

"Welcome to our OR, dear."

Bev McParland arrived at the Coronary Care Unit at seven-thirty in the morning, dressed in a bright red coat over a paddy green skirt and sweater. She is an attractive woman, with inquisitive blue eyes, but she downplays her looks. She keeps her dark brown hair short and unstyled — functional. She does not wear make-up. Her figure could be described, not unkindly, as unfashionably voluptuous. She attends exercise classes as often as she can in the gymnasium at the nurses' residence, which is connected by tunnel to the hospital. She is thirty-seven years old, married to a Toronto policeman.

McParland is head nurse of the Coronary Care Unit, known as the CCU. The position had recently been redefined, upgraded to "Manager, Nursing Practice," which makes McParland one of the top nurses of nearly a thousand nurses at the hospital (nearly thirteen hundred including part-time nurses). She is also chairman of a committee of 150 middle managers at the hospital, an elected position. That day she stayed at the hospital until well past the supper hour, another twelve-hour day —

her ninth in a row. Two of them were sixteen-hour days. Her official hours are from eight to four, and she is not paid overtime. She earns $32,000 a year, the highest salary at Toronto General for a nurse.

The mood is sombre in the CCU. You feel it as you push through the dark blue RESTRICTED ENTRY doors. You do not enter frivolously. It is scrupulously clean, but, apart from a splash of light over the nursing station, not as bright as other parts of the hospital, even early in the morning with sunlight through the east-facing windows. The patient-rooms are spread around the perimeter of the unit. The lighting in the rooms is subdued, restful. The patient-rooms have windows to the inside, facing the nursing station. The windows have thin venetian blinds.

The rooms are crammed with technology, like a sound studio — levers, switches, dials, gauges, buttons, tubes, wires — and almost always they are occupied by older patients whose bodies have broken down and betrayed them. They look frightened, chastened, as if they have encountered a horror. It is almost a surprise to see young patients here, patients in their twenties or thirties.

On the night shift, the CCU is even more sombre, more subdued. Sounds that were inconsequential on the day shift are magnified in the dark, reverent hush that settles after midnight. There are more deaths on night shift, and nobody knows exactly why. Perhaps it is somehow the felicitous time to go. The monitors in a line under the counter at the nursing station — one for each of the beds — record in squiggly, luminescent green lines the sleeping heartbeats, each as individual as a fingerprint.

The sickest patients in the hospital stay in the CCU, and in the other intensive care units — medical, surgical, neurosurgical, cardiovascular — down the long hallway on the second floor of the Eaton Wing. They are recovering from surgery, or waiting for surgery, or they've been wheeled up from Emergency in the taut, monstrous grip of a heart attack. Day and night, relatives pace the hallway or sprawl on chairs and couches in the waiting room next to stacks of magazines and boxes of Kleenex. All heads turn to the doorway when anyone in a white lab coat approaches.

The glamor event here is the Code 99, meaning a cardiac arrest, when someone's heart has stopped. When this happens, the piped-in FM music is interrupted. "Code 99, Coronary Care . . . Code 99, Coronary Care . . ." Changing in seconds from the most somnolent routine, the floor becomes action central. Doors fly open, medicos in wrinkled greens and Nikes, some with faces still asleep, come running to the CCU from all directions, knees belt high, stethoscopes flapping over their shoulders as if their wearers had been lassoed in some aseptic rodeo. "Don't ever get in their way," McParland advised. "They'll run over you."

At the first sign of arrest, the CCU nurse runs to the patient's room, pushing the "crash cart" in with her. This is the trolley equipped with the clear green plastic Ambu-bag to supply oxygen, with the defibrillator paddles, with the sterile syringes and jellies and cardiac drugs and medications. In the room, the nurse punches the blue button at the head of the bed, which triggers the Code 99. (If there is another arrest somewhere else in the hospital, it will be a Code 100; a third arrest will be a Code 101. The highest number anyone can remember at Toronto General is Code 103, which meant five cardiac arrests were happening all at once.) The nurse thumps the patient's sternum violently, with the bottom of her fist, which sometimes gets the heart going again. As she does this, she fumbles in the crash cart for the rubber tracheal tube, inserts it down the patient's windpipe, and squeezes the bulky Ambu-bag to push oxygen down the airway. If none of this works, and if the arrest team still hasn't arrived, the nurse reaches for the defibrillator paddles, holds one against the sternum, the other to the left side of the chest, and zaps a jolt of electricity through the heart, jerking the patient from the bed as if levitated by an impatient sorcerer. When the arrest team arrives at bedside, the CCU nurse may already have saved the patient's life.

The rush and the clamor are most distressing for relatives who have chosen to spend the night with loved ones. When there is a code, McParland said, "they just plaster themselves to the walls."

Nurses who have worked in the CCU a long time develop an uncanny, premonitory sense of when someone is about to have an arrest. They can tell, even without watching the monitors. There is the constant scribble of the read-out on the cardiac graph behind them, which makes an infinitesimally different scratching when a heart goes awry, like the tiniest nibble on a line at the bottom of a lake before the fish hits. But it is more than that. "It is an intuitive thing, and women *are* better at it than men," McParland said. "Sometimes when a nurse comes on duty at night she'll say, 'We're going to have a code tonight.' She'll even drag the crash cart across the floor and put it outside the room where it's going to happen. And she's usually right."

When McParland arrived in the morning, all eight beds in the CCU were filled and a patient in Emergency was on the urgent waiting list.

A young man just up from Emergency, in the early stages of a heart attack, was on streptokinase, a drug administered to dissolve the blood clot obstructing a coronary artery. If the drug works, the patient may not need open-heart surgery, perhaps not even the newer procedure called PTCA — Percutaneous Transluminal Coronary Angioplasty — which involves inserting a catheter to the plugged-up area and inflating a tiny balloon that squeezes open the artery from the inside to restore circulation to the heart. In theory, PTCA is simplicity itself — one of those brilliant medical eurekas — but in practice it is a delicate, painstaking procedure done in the Coronary Catheter Lab one floor down. The patient usually remains awake, and may be watching a television screen as the catheter pokes its way along from an incision in the groin or the arm all the way to the innermost recesses of the heart. Whenever a PTCA is performed, an operating room is put on alert in case the artery bursts and open-heart bypass surgery is required. Most hospitals are not equipped to do PTCAs. Toronto General does about three hundred a year.

Another patient was in heart block. McParland explained, "What it means is that the top part of his heart, the generating station, is not talking to the bottom part. His atrium is doing one thing and his ventricle another. He's getting only twenty-eight beats a minute."

The staff anesthetist entered the unit and shouted at the nurses because they had not prepared a woman patient who was due in the operating room at eight o'clock. The nurses had thought her operation was at noon, but they were not unduly alarmed because most of the pre-operative nursing work can only be done ten minutes before the operation. "Anesthetists are methodical and like to have things done their way," McParland said. "They have to be like that because if they're not, very major accidents can happen that you read about in lawsuits. They tend to be isolationist. There are some nice ones, but as a group they're a distant lot, not what you'd call 'people' people. Radiologists aren't either, or pathologists. So the nurses got yelled at this morning. It's normal. My pulse didn't even go up."

As a nursing manager, McParland oversees the operating budget for the CCU, which is $925,000. "And that's just my *operating* costs, not capital costs. It just pays my salaries and supplies. It doesn't cover doctors' salaries, or diagnostic tests, or food and linen. Three months ago, I signed a $250,000 contract to put new monitors in our unit. I had to go before the capital budget committee, and before that I had to lobby a bunch of people, including Bill Anderson, the vice-president for medical affairs. But it got me eight new monitors."

So intent is McParland on keeping costs down, meeting her budget, that she sticks price tags on some items to remind doctors how expensive they are. The heart-block patient required a pacing catheter, which costs $385. When McParland arrived at work, the senior resident who had used the pacing catheter approached her and explained, almost apologetically, why he *really* needed it.

Another patient in CCU was on Vancomycin, an antibiotic that may be used for extremely resistant infections. "I'm watching it like a hawk," McParland said. "It costs $83 a bottle."

Even more expensive is bretylium, a cardiac drug used to control ventricular arrhythmias — dangerously irregular heartbeats. "When it arrived at the hospital two years ago, from France, I had the only supply in Toronto. I keep it locked in a cupboard and ration it out. It costs $250 a bottle."

An I-Med Pump, used to run drugs into patients in intensive care units, cost $2,700. A new ECG machine costs between $10,000 and $12,000 — "the price of a new compact car." A regular intra-aortic balloon pump costs $35,000 and the portable model costs $45,000.

"A lot of nurses, a lot of women, are not comfortable with the money thing — with balancing a budget. Five, six years ago, a head nurse wouldn't have known what the budget was. She'd never have seen a budget report. And she'd never have reminded a doctor what X-rays or blood gases cost."

McParland keeps track of all the controlled drugs, the narcotics and barbiturates, the analgesics and hypnotics and sedatives, which are locked in a drawer in a small cupboard-room behind the nursing station — codeine, morphine, Demerol, Nembutal, Seconal, phenobarbital, Tuinal. Soon the locked drawer may contain heroin, which has been approved for hospital use in Canada by the federal government, creating more security problems on the floors.

On the day shift, nurse Bev Carlyle carries the key to the drawer on a long red cord, which she wears around her neck.

When called from the unit, or on a break, Carlyle gives the key to another nurse, but never to a doctor — even if he asks. "We're the ones responsible for the drugs," McParland said. "We have to count them and double-sign for them at the end of every shift. If anything goes missing, the Mounties visit *us.*"

She takes night courses at the University of Toronto, working toward a degree in political science. On a shelf above her desk are nursing and medical textbooks, drug catalogues, and books with titles such as *Stress Management, The Joy of Stress, The Nurse as Executive, The Financial Management of Hospitals, Management, Political Ideologies*. Many times a well-meaning doctor has asked McParland why she does not go to medical school to become a doctor. "It used to cross my mind, but it doesn't any more," she said. "Now I think going to medical school would be a cop-out. When doctors ask me why I don't go to medical school, I take it as an insult. I say to them, 'Because I'm a nurse. It's more important.'"

For McParland, this is not empty rhetoric. She believes, with passion, that nursing has a clear, distinctive role, one that is becoming increasingly difficult to define, but that is no less crucial in health care.

"Medicine's over there," she said, gesticulating with a sweep of her arm to some massive sweep of hospital in the distance. "Then there are all the technicians moving in, taking a patch here, a patch there. What are we going to claim for ourselves? The cynics say bedpans and bedbaths." She grimaced, rolled her eyes into her forehead. "Do you know what we do? We are *there*. We do the people part. We look at you as a person, as someone who relates to *us* as a person, who lives in a family and has a job and a past and a future. We are there — twenty-four hours a day, seven days a week. That's our strong point. Everybody else looks at you as a piece."

For several weeks, McParland had been interviewing nurses on her staff, having them fill out questionnaires on job satisfaction. The replies showed that the nurses were most concerned with conflict, assertiveness, and ethical issues. "Burnout was in vogue three years ago," McParland said. "We're tired of it now. Burnout is just one of the symptoms of not having enough power and recognition. Every questionnaire coming in shows the nurses are unhappy about the recognition they get from their peers. And do you know who they call their peers? *Doctors*! You can be sure doctors don't perceive nurses as peers."

As she spoke, Bev Carlyle emerged, red cord around her neck, from one of the patient-rooms and entered another. "There's an incredibly talented, intelligent young nurse," McParland said. "She can run rings around some of our learning physicians in terms of patient assessment and ECG interpretation, but every day she must swallow hard in front of a junior doctor and give him signs and symptoms. She can't say what she thinks the diagnosis is because she'll upset his ego. It just burns her."

McParland turned and walked into her small, windowless office in a corner of the CCU, behind the nursing station. She sat at her desk for a moment, then swivelled around and said, "Most doctors would not have survived their medical education without nurses. The smart intern caters to the nurses — buys them bagels on Saturday morning. I've watched doctors freeze at the foot of the bed during a cardiac arrest. We've all seen it. We've defibrillated patients and run full resuscitations with a junior doctor limping along behind. When it was over he'd sign the papers and get credit for it. What do you do? You know what you do? You say, 'Oh well, another day in the salt mine.'"

The nurses in the CCU, and in any of the other intensive care units, and in Emergency, are the most experienced, knowledgeable nurses in the hospital. They consider themselves an élite, on the front lines, and they enjoy considerable status among nurses at the hospital. They are tough, diligent, confident, and outspoken, which McParland encourages by arranging assertiveness-training classes for them. "Everyone in the hospital knows my nurses. A lot of the doctors tell me my nurses are too mouthy, but what they don't appreciate is that's the nicest thing they could say to me."

Nurses talk about an "age dynamic" among doctors that affects relationships between doctors and nurses. They seldom have problems with very young doctors, or older doctors. "We don't have problems with most students, interns, or young residents," McParland said. "We hear them talking about diaper services and complaining about how the baby kept them up all night. And the older ones, like Griff Pearson and Joel Cooper, the ones who know who they are, they're secure. Cooper may have a world reputation, and he can be quirky as hell, but nurses love working with him. He can be like a three-year-old kid — sometimes you want to tell him to take a Valium — but he always wants to help. He'll help us make beds. Once

I was joking and asked him to go brush one of the patient's teeth. And he did."

Doctors who give nurses the most problems are between thirty and forty-five years old. "The Big Chill generation," McParland said. "They were the teenagers of the 1960s, and they don't have the perks of doctordom that they expect — you know, life in the suburbs, two kids and a dog and a station wagon . . . dinner on, martinis made. No, they find they've got a wife who's gone out and got a degree, maybe an MBA, and has a good job. So, they've still got one group of women stereotyped in their minds as submissive, compliant, willing to care and nurture — nurses. And then, *wham*! The last bastion falls."

What McParland does not always tell doctors who ask why she doesn't go to medical school is that she has other plans. In 1977, she ran in the provincial election as a New Democratic Party candidate for the rural riding of Lanark. She lost, but she emerged with a taste for the rough-and-tumble of politics — hospital politics, party politics, doesn't matter. As for long-range plans? She mused aloud, "I probably could be a much better advocate of nursing as Minister of Health."

In the early Christian era, nurses were deaconesses of the Church. They brought food, herbs, and medicine to patients in their homes. They did bedside chores and ministered to the spiritual needs of the sick and dying. They were highly motivated, from the upper classes, and some were so good at their work that they came to be regarded as physicians.

By the sixteenth century, with the Reformation, many church properties in Great Britain were confiscated, Roman Catholic religious orders were suppressed, and nurses were drawn from the ignorant and illiterate, many of them prostitutes. In the seventeenth century, St. Vincent de Paul encouraged women to study nursing, but it was not until 1846 that a hospital school for nurses was established in Kaiserswerth, Germany, where Florence Nightingale trained. She became a legend during the Crimean War, when she organized a unit of thirty-eight woman nurses and set up model hospitals at Scutari and Balaklava. She was the Lady with the Lamp, the founder of modern nursing. She fought for sanitary conditions, for better working conditions, for more money. It was Nightingale who established the first school designed primarily to train nurses, at St. Thomas's Hospital in London, and in 1852 she wrote to her father to say, "Now that I have come into possession of myself, you must consider me . . . as a son."

Toward the end of the nineteenth century, nursing had come to be regarded as a branch of applied science that promised to be as important to the health care system as physicians and surgeons. Then, something happened. Gradually, inevitably, as the medical system became more complex and demanding, nurses came to be regarded more as helpmeets than as professionals. Only men were allowed to be doctors, and they were not anxious for nurses to keep up with them.

In 1897, the Canadian Sir William Osler, who was the most famous physician in the English-speaking world in his time, delivered the commencement address to graduating nurses at Johns Hopkins Hospital in Baltimore. He told the nurses, "You have made the practice of medicine easier to the profession. There is no higher mission in life than nursing God's poor. In so doing, a woman may not reach the ideals of her soul, fall short of the ideals of her head, but she will satiate those longings in her heart from which no woman can escape."

In 1906, an article in *The Journal of the American Medical Association*, commenting on "Nursing Schools and the Illegal Practice of Medicine," advised, in point form:

(1) Every attempt at initiative on the part of nurses . . . should be reproved by the physicians. (2) The programs of nursing schools . . . should be limited strictly to the indispensable matters of instruction for those in their position. (3) The professional instruction of nurses should be entrusted exclusively to the physicians who only can judge what is necessary for them to know. (4) The physician, charged with this instruction, should . . . insist on the possible dangers . . . of nurses inconsiderately stepping out from their proper sphere.

By the 1940s, doctors were making three times as much as nurses — $4,600 a year for doctors, $1,200 a year for nurses — but by the 1980s, the disparity had grown to three, four, five times as much. In her book *The Female Eunuch*, feminist author Germaine Greer complained, "The most depressing phenomenon in the pattern of women's work is the plight of the nurse. . . . That nurses can be victimized by the essentialness of their work into accepting a shameful remuneration is an indictment of our society, which is daring them to abandon the sick and dying, knowing that they will not do it."

Nurses are by far the largest single group in the hospital, but it has been traditional for them to be kept in check, fragmented, and far from the inner circles of power. The handmaiden-with-bedpan image persists, and it has become a cliché to say that nurses are their own worst enemies. There has been recent and significant progress, but the cliché remains sadly true. Nurses have always been timid risk-takers, and the most poorly organized, most fragmented, most politically apathetic group in the hospital.

Because of the nature of the work, nursing has always attracted generous, warm-hearted care-givers — one does not take up nursing for money and power — and for generations nursing schools have rewarded deference and penalized assertiveness, inadvertently weeding out any bright hotheads who might change the system. Nurses remain a minority in a minority in a minority: women in a male-dominated society, nurses in doctor-dominated hospitals, nurturers in an age of technology and narcissism.

The nurses at Toronto General know the groups within the hospital that they can depend on for support and the groups who are either openly against them or causing them trouble. They call them "enemies" and "allies." High on the list of allies is W. Vickery Stoughton, the president.

Almost from the day he arrived, Stoughton, sometimes publicly, sometimes covertly, has supported the nurses. One of his first bold moves was to recommend that Dorothy Wylie, the hospital's vice-president of nursing, be put on the executive committee of the hospital's powerful Medical Advisory Board. Then he had the head nurses reclassified as "nursing managers," giving them a beach-head in management, which meant control of operating budgets.

Under the old system, the budgets were controlled at the administrative level, under the scrutiny of Dorothy Wylie. It was a chaotic system, with two dozen administrative co-ordinators roaming around trying to check on spending and costs and replacements and the hiring and firing of nursing staff. Even Wylie admits that the new system, which has a nursing manager with hands-on control, is infinitely more efficient.

"Now, each nursing unit has a nursing manager, which puts her on a par with physicians," Stoughton said. "She has an equal say. She can raise issues. And because she has management responsibilities, in some cases that puts her *over* physicians."

Stoughton pushed for the head nurses, now nursing managers, to be included in the middle managers. There were groups in the hospital who strongly resented nurses' being included in the middle-management group, fearing that by the sheer weight of their numbers they would start taking over. Soon after, Bev McParland, who knows how to fight a campaign, was elected chairman of the middle managers.

Stoughton also streamlined nursing's chain of command, which used to be cumbersome and tortuous, leaving nurses stranded and politically impotent within the hospital. Now, every nursing manager reports to one of four nursing directors, who in turn report to Dorothy Wylie. And every Friday morning Stoughton goes on "nursing rounds," which means once a week he visits several of the forty-three nursing units in the hospital. He spends about an hour asking questions, listening, and generally chatting up the troops. It has had a tremendous impact on nursing morale. Wylie, the tough, wise administrator — she was educated at New York University and Columbia University — was impressed. "I've never seen any hospital president do that," she said.

The nurses still have a long way to go, however, and Wylie, for one, is not always optimistic. "We kill *ourselves*," she said. "And sometimes I think it's getting worse. For every three steps forward, we take four steps back. And being women, we have a lot of self-esteem problems." Two groups on a collision course are the traditional bedside nurses and the Young Turks, the feisty, university-educated, politically aware nurses who are impatient for change and progress. The stated position of the Registered Nurses Association of Ontario — the nurses' professional organization — is that by the year 2000 every nurse should have a degree in nursing to work in a hospital. Wylie considers this an unrealistic goal, as only 10 per cent of nurses have degrees now and there are only nine institutions in the province that award nursing degrees. Most of the nurses in the hospital trained at community colleges and have nursing diplomas, which the progressives hope will be obsolete by the year 2000. Wylie wants more university-trained nurses, but she thinks 30 per cent by the end of the century would be a more realistic goal. "If we achieve that, we'll be doing well," she said. "Maybe they'll all have degrees by the year 2060."

University-educated nurses represent more than a public relations effort, more than cosmetics. The campus environment itself allows nurses to jostle with other disciplines and build self-confidence and a broader base of knowledge. At many hospital meetings and forums, Wylie watches in dismay as nurses — easily the largest single group in the hospital — watch passively, rarely speaking out to push their opinions. "Nurses have *tons* of information," she said. "They're with patients day and night. They work with the doctors, the technicians, the social workers. They see everything, but they don't *use* that information."

Stoughton, ever aware of changing times, shrewdly sees nurses as a new and powerful force in hospitals — a sleeping giant. For every hour doctors spend with patients, nurses spend fifty; and they are in an ideal position to be both patient advocates and budget watchdogs. More important, they are the only other group in the hospital with the potential to balance the power and influence of the doctors. They are the group closest to the doctors and closest to the patients; they are the perfect intermediary between them. More than one senior administrator at the hospital has admitted, often reluctantly, "Nurses *are* the hospital." By championing the nurses and giving them more authority, Stoughton has found a way to neutralize the doctors, most of whom are not even hospital employees. As the nurses get stronger, more and more they are standing up to the doctors — and Stoughton watches from the sidelines.

At Quincey's Steak House, a restaurant a block from the hospital, McParland ordered a glass of white wine and Atlantic salmon. "I don't want to give any more business to our cardiovascular unit," she told the waiter.

McParland's most recent campaign at the hospital involved the Respiratory Therapists. Officially, they are called Registered Respiratory Therapists, but they are known around the hospital simply as "RTs." they used to be called Registered Respiratory Technologists, but "therapists" sounded more professional, so the name was changed. The RTs work out of a crowded room across the hallway from the intensive care units, but their headquarters is in the basement of the Norman Urquhart Wing where they are supervised by manager Len Brautigan, who sits at a desk in a glassed-in cubicle at one end of the room like a dispatcher in a busy warehouse. The RTs fan out from their basement war room to cover the hospital, whenever someone needs help breathing. They are the technicians of the airway, bringers of oxygen, guardians of the ventilators, masters of the bronchoscope — a fibre-optic instrument that enters the lung via the endo-tracheal tube. When the RTs are not out saving lives, helping people breathe, they are working at their basement benches with saws, wrenches, and screwdrivers, cleaning and repairing equipment. Unlike nurses, RTs are divided almost equally between the sexes with about 60 per cent of them women. They wear uniforms similar to surgical linens, but a darker, military shade of green. Nothing pleases them more than to be mistaken for a doctor, though the job requires only two years' training at a community college. They are an enthusiastic bunch.

For the nurses, the RTs are "enemies." Unwitting enemies, perhaps, but enemies. They represent the latest invasion of nursing's fiefdom, following along after the lab technicians, the blood technologists, the radiology technicians. As a group, the RTs were the most vocal opponents of nurses' becoming part of the middle-management group in the hospital.

"We have a technician for everything now," McParland said. "We have a technician who draws blood, who does IVs, who runs the gamma camera in X-ray. They've all been trained in community colleges and they're coming out with expectations that they are health care professionals, with power and control. They expect to be at least equal to nurses, if not a cut above them — nothing less. They're paid the same pay as nurses. Right now, there's a major confrontation going on between young RTs and nurses with five, ten years' experience. They're always telling the nurses, 'Don't touch our machines!' They think we're a bunch of dumb females."

For months McParland had been trying to negotiate a workable *rapprochement* with the RTs. It is an uphill struggle.

Over dinner, McParland talked of her upbringing on a farm near Perth, southwest of Ottawa in the rocky, hilly, Irish countryside of eastern Ontario. She was the oldest of eight children, growing up in a warm, loving, hard-working family. When she was twelve years old, the bull on the farm badly gored her father and she helped run the farm that summer. The next January, her youngest brother, then only a year old, took sick and had to spend six months in hospital. Then her mother was hospitalized, and one of her sisters required an appendectomy. These were pre-medicare days, when hospital costs were crushing, especially for farm families. She remembers how violently the doctors opposed the new public health insurance system.

When she was sixteen, she worked on a nearby vegetable farm to earn enough money for nursing school in Kingston.

She made $150, of which she spent $120 for tuition and books and $10 for a second-hand nursing cape, which left her with $20 for the school year. Throughout her three years of training she lived in residence and earned money babysitting doctors' children. "I wanted to be a university history teacher," she said. "I wanted to specialize in Elizabethan English history, but after grade twelve I went into nursing. I'm a nurse because of the doctors."

The early days were exciting, especially in Intensive Care and Emergency. McParland has always preferred critical care nursing. "You never know what tomorrow's going to bring," she said. "Nurses in critical care never want to work in a safe ward. They like the action. There's a certain mystique to it. It has a status among nurses. They'll grumble a lot, but the grumbling really starts when things get too quiet."

One shift in Emergency she will never forget was on a summer weekend when she had been a nurse only a few years. "In one night, we lost five patients, and they were all under thirty. All in less than six hours. There were two burn victims, a car accident, a boating accident, a young coronary, and a 'cause unknown.' The chaplain was going nuts. By the end of the shift, the resident broke down and cried at his desk because he could not tell one more parent that his child had been killed — that was the nineteen-year-old girl killed in a boat explosion."

There were the suicides, and the strange, pleading, lonely calls to Emergency at three o'clock in the morning. There was the elderly lady ignored by her family on Christmas Eve who drank a can of Drāno and took a taxi to Emergency, where she knew she would be cheerfully received. The suicides on farms always were more brutal than the overdoses and carbon monoxides in the city, which seemed genteel by comparison.

McParland quickly became "hospital-smart," recognizing the malingerers and manipulators. Anyone who has worked in Emergency is familiar with the ersatz "renal colic" patient, who knows what symptoms to fake for a hit of Demerol. He walks into Emergency groaning, bent over. Someone asks where it hurts. He knows better than even to hint at the agony of a kidney stone. Manipulators know the jargon of anatomy, often too well, and it is a dead giveaway to say, "Right flank pain." Instead, he clutches his lower right side and falls to his knees. He is asked to provide a urine specimen, so he takes the vial to the bathroom, pricks a finger under his nail, plops a few drops of blood into the urine, then staggers out with proof he is in a desperate condition. He gets the Demerol, and most often he is admitted to hospital, which means more Demerol and a bed and food for three days. Later he will try another hospital. If he is in the mood for amphetamines, "uppers," he may decide to be a "narcoleptic," a pitiable, yawning fellow with uncontrollable attacks of sleep.

As a critical care nurse, McParland has many times stayed at a bedside well past quitting time, until dawn, holding a patient's hand because it was all she could do and all the patient wanted her to do. These are the sad but satisfying times, when nurses feel they are nurses, when they are touching the human spirit. There was the lady with the basket of gladioli in her room who laughed with the nurse and said, "Now *who* would send a dying woman purple flowers?" Many times she has had to wrestle with imponderables, like the young father back from surgery who opened a conversation by telling her, "They said it was inoperable. . . ."

She knows how to have fun as a nurse, too. At Toronto General, she has worked as a medical consultant for various movies filmed at the hospital, including *Heartsounds*, when she worked with Mary Tyler Moore and James Garner. Often it meant working eight hours with the film crew, being on hand to correct medical imbecilities, then reporting for work in the Intensive Care Unit. (Several Hollywood movies have been shot at Toronto General and it is a thoroughly discombobulating experience for a patient or visitor who gets off an elevator on the wrong floor and encounters Moore or Garner or Donald Sutherland or Jack Lemmon — they have all performed at the hospital — wearing surgical greens and intently discussing infarcts and CT-scans.)

A week earlier, at the end of a shift, David Allen of public relations called McParland at the CCU and asked if she would like to go to Acapulco.

"When?" she asked.

"Tonight."

It turned out that four young Canadians on a Mexican vacation had been injured when a jeep overturned. One of the families called the hospital and asked if someone could fly down in a chartered jet and bring their daughter back to Toronto. McParland barely had time to dash home and pack a bag before heading to the airport, boarding the jet, and flying off to Mexico in the night. She brought the daughter back the next evening — and two of the other Canadians. "It was pretty busy," she said. "I didn't even have time for a margarita."

An incident the year before was even more dramatic; Allen called McParland and told her a limousine would be waiting for her at the Emergency entrance to take her to the Four Seasons Hotel. He asked her to bring one of the hospital's portable defibrillators with her.

"Why not an ambulance?" she asked.

"It's all rather hush-hush," Allen told her. "Sort of an undercover assignment."

Actor Robert Young was in town and his wife had taken sick in their hotel room. McParland would not divulge all details of her clandestine mission — nurses see and hear a lot and much of the nurse-patient relationship must be confidential — but when she arrived at the hotel she knew Mrs. Young was in serious condition. Robert Young did not want an ambulance, did not want his wife treated at a local hospital. He did not want to risk any press attention, so McParland took directions over the telephone from the Youngs' doctor in California. When Mrs. Young was stable enough, they drove to the airport and boarded a chartered jet for California. "I was having trouble protecting her airway on the plane," McParland said. "When we arrived, there was another limo waiting, which took us to this huge California home. In the driveway, in the back of the limo, Mrs. Young had a respiratory attack. She went cyanotic — blue from lack of oxygen — then she had a grand mal seizure. She wasn't getting enough oxygen to the brain. We did a code right there — called the fire department, the paramedics. There was a small hospital nearby, but no one on duty could handle the situation. We were on some street in Pasadena when she stopped breathing. I did a precordial thump, then full resuscitation — mouth to mouth."

Weeks later, Robert Young, Marcus Welby himself, sent McParland a long, handwritten letter, thanking her effusively for saving his wife. He called her "an angel of mercy" and invited her to visit them at their home any time. He said she could stay as long as she wanted.

The next day in the CCU was quiet, exceptionally quiet. No Code 99s overnight, patients in stable condition, nothing urgent down in Emergency. The nurses looked restless. McParland had a morning meeting with William Louth, one of the hospital vice-presidents, to discuss budgetary matters. A drug company provided lunch, a huge smorgasbord in the Medical Students' Lounge, after a film and talk in the Main Lecture Theatre on a new drug-distribution system for the hospital. After that, a saleswoman from a medical supply firm arrived to try to sell McParland a new gizmo for monitoring patients in intensive care. The saleswoman was a nurse herself. More medical supply firms are hiring nurses to design and sell equipment because they know the language and frustrations of nurses who must use the equipment, which for too many years had been designed by people who have never been in an intensive care unit.

McParland examined the plastic monitoring device closely, her glasses pushed back over her hair. She attached it to her left wrist, then rolled her wrist over, as a patient might do while sleeping. "Uh, oh," McParland said. "See that?" The plastic tubing pinched shut when she rolled her wrist on the desk. The saleswoman, who wore a long string of pearls, patent-leather heels, and mauve mascara over her eyes, produced a more expensive version. McParland tried it on, rolled her wrist on the desk again. "Much better," she said. "It's nursing-friendly. How much?"

The saleswoman said a year's supply would cost $14,780.

"That's more than a third of a nurse's salary," McParland said.

The saleswoman stared down at the equipment, perplexed.

"Look," McParland said, "I'll pitch for it at the budget committee next week. We may not swing it this time, but it's a crack in the door."

When the saleswoman left, McParland walked to the nursing station, where she said, "Want to see good nursing?" She motioned to one of the patient-rooms, where a small nurse stood talking to an elderly male patient sitting on the edge of his bed. "She doesn't have to be here. He's had his surgery and she's finished her shift. And she's from the cardiovascular unit. She just wants to see how he's doing."

The Nurses' Lounge in the CCU is equipped with a television, a microwave oven, a toaster, and a popcorn machine. A large poster on the wall says, "Remind government that when it comes to health care, nurses know, nurses care . . . nurses vote." The latest political brouhaha involved the issue of doctors "opting out" of the public health care system to protect their right to charge more than the stipulated minimum set down in the government fee schedule. The newly elected provincial government had come out against opting out, which enraged most of the doctors. There had been talk of doctor slowdowns, even doctor strikes. Where did the nurses stand?

"We're against extra-billing," McParland said. "And we're against it *publicly*." She explained that the Registered Nurses Association of Ontario has a position paper against the doctors' opting out. One of the most stalwart advocates of the doctors' freedom to opt out is Hugh Scully, an esteemed heart surgeon at Toronto General and a powerful member of the hospital's Board of Trustees. Some of Scully's patients are treated in McParland's CCU unit. "Oh, yes, Hugh and I have *lovely* chats in the hallways these days," McParland said.

Nurses and doctors are not always and automatically on opposite sides of the fence, but they often see the same things differently at the hospital. Many nurses resent transplants, the glamor medicine of the 1980s. Many nurses, and many physicians, resent the prodigious amounts of money lavished on transplants, which help only a few people a year. They would prefer that the money be spent on more prosaic, day-to-day health care and preventive medicine. Also, transplants raise ethical issues, which add to the stress of nurses, who are more likely to sympathize with the donor than with the recipient. They work in both operating rooms. They watch as eyes, kidneys, hearts, lungs, livers, and bones are cut from the lifeless victim, usually someone young, like them, who died tragically, or who snuffed out his life in a horrible moment of despair, which nurses understand. Often it was someone they knew by name in an intensive care unit. It disturbs the nurses, deeply, but the surgeons are caught up in the excitement of the transplant. They see things differently.

McParland has mixed feelings about transplants. "Sometimes you have to ask — Why? If we don't stay on the frontier, how will we ever learn? If we weren't on the frontier twenty-five years ago, with kidney transplants, they'd never have become commonplace. It's a lot cheaper now to do a kidney transplant than to leave someone on hemo-dialysis for the rest of his life. They also attract research funds, and really good staff. If Joel Cooper wasn't who he is, the whole world wouldn't be clamoring to come here and work with him."

Starting on June 30, 1980, and ending on March 22, 1981, a terrible and tragic — and still unexplained — series of baby deaths occurred in the cardiac ward at the world-famous Hospital for Sick Children, directly across the street from Toronto General. There were thirty-six deaths in all, supposedly related to an improper use of the heart drug digoxin. Many still believe some of the deaths were murders.

One of the nurses on the hospital's cardiac ward, Susan Nelles, actually was arrested and charged with murder, though the charge was later dropped at the preliminary hearing. That was not the end of it, however. The deaths and nursing procedures at the hospital were investigated by the police, by the Atlanta Centers for Disease Control, by Mr. Justice Charles Dubin of the Ontario Supreme Court, and, most thoroughly, by a Royal Commission of Inquiry headed by Mr. Justice Samuel Grange of the Ontario Supreme Court. For the nurses at Toronto General, and at hospitals throughout the country, the various investigations were nothing less than "a witch hunt against nurses." That was the exact phrase used at the Grange Inquiry by lawyer Francis Kiteley, representing the Registered Nurses Association of Ontario. For this outburst, Kiteley was severely reprimanded by Mr. Justice Grange. He came close to citing her for contempt of court.

Alice J. Baumgart, professor and dean of nursing at Queen's University, writing in *The Canadian Nurse* in January 1985, described the treatment of nurses at the Grange Inquiry as "nurse-bashing." She continued, "The Grange Inquiry is the highest-priced, tax-supported sexual harassment exercise that we've ever witnessed. Many people think one of the reasons nurses have been put on the executioner's stand in public is that they've been feeling their oats too much. This is a way for the system to say, 'You better know your place. Down, girl!'" In her article, Baumgart noted that lawyers at the inquiry, when questioning a doctor, invariably phrased their questions in terms of what the doctors *knew*. "When nurses were on the stand," she said, "the question was, 'Based on your *experience* . . .' Experience in our society is considered second-class compared to knowledge. Nurses should not know."

Perhaps nurses *were* beginning to feel their oats at the time of the Grange Inquiry. There had been a recent and well-publicized malpractice case involving an anesthetist at Oshawa General Hospital, whose actions in the operating room were found to have contributed to a patient's permanent brain-damage and physical handicap. Some of the most telling testimony in the malpractice case came from one of the operating-room nurses, Jackie Coatrup. At one point, the plaintiff's lawyer asked Coatrup what the anesthetist was doing when something appeared to be going wrong during the operation.

"He resumed his ventilating the patient with his left hand

and pulled the chart . . . to his lap with the right hand," she said.

"Did you see the chart?" the lawyer asked.

"Yes."

"Did you see — first of all, was the chart on a clipboard of some kind?"

"No, in a three-ring binder."

"Was there anything else on the chart?"

"There was a piece of newspaper slipped to the top of the chart."

"What was that newspaper clipping?"

"It was a crossword puzzle."

Coatrup testified that when things went seriously wrong during the operation the anesthetist tore the crossword puzzle to pieces. The Supreme Court of Ontario later awarded the victim damages and compensation of more than $1 million.

Arthur Schafer, director of the Centre for Professional and Applied Ethics at the University of Manitoba, said Nurse Coatrup's testimony was of "decisive importance" in the malpractice suit. "Nurse Coatrup's action should not be seen as an isolated event," Schafer wrote in an article in *The Globe and Mail* . "Increasingly, over the past two decades, the nursing profession has come to see its role as including patient advocacy, even when this means 'blowing the whistle' on doctors or hospitals or other members of the health-care team." Indeed, Schafer noted that the newly promulgated Code of Ethics of the Canadian Nurses Associaton makes no mention of "loyalty to doctors," or "unquestioning obedience." No longer were nurses prepared to "obey and grieve," once a motto that governed the nurse-doctor relationship. Schafer wrote, "There has been a quiet revolution in nursing ethics, and some members of the medical profession are beginning to look anxiously over their shoulders."

At Toronto General, McParland said Coatrup's testimony helped to unite nurses and make them more aware of their patient-advocacy role. "Five years ago, we would have been much more likely to knuckle under to doctors, but now we are saying we will not tolerate our patients' being treated this way. We have an equal role in health care, an equal say, and you will *not* treat *our* patients this way."

It was the Grange Inquiry, however, that angered nurses the most, that scraped nerves raw and somehow galvanized the nurses into action.

"At first, nursing drew back and did not support Susan Nelles," McParland said. "We did our typical knee-jerk thing and assumed she must be guilty because the police thought she was. Then, nursing felt very guilty — and still does — because we did not stand beside a colleague. Had it been a doctor, the entire Ontario Medical Association would have been down there at the police station. We went through a horrendous guilt complex. Yes, I felt guilty — and ashamed. But the next thing we felt was a whole lot of anger. We were the ones blamed for everything. We were the scapegoats. But it was a turning point, and the anger spread across the country. Nurses in Vancouver sent money toward Nelles's defence fund. We're learning how to fight back. What we have to learn is how to fight clean, without whining."

McParland was asked if she would hire Susan Nelles to work for her in the CCU at Toronto General.

"Sure I would," she replied. "The only person I wouldn't hire is someone who can't cry."

The doctors in the operating rooms don't play the game with the new nurses any more. They say the nurses are getting uppity.

CHAPTER 9

Normand
Love and AIDS

A THURSDAY morning late in June on Amelia Street in Toronto's Cabbagetown. Pots of freshly watered geraniums and touch-me-nots lined front steps and hung from porches. Years ago, the neighborhood had been fashionable; then it had fallen on bad times; then, in the 1960s and 1970s, young professionals and creative folk moved in to restore the dilapidated Victorian mansions and cottages, making them fashionable again with stained-glass windows, sidewalks of interlocking brick, gas lamps, and cobblestone patios. One of those early-summer mornings when the leaves smell of tree juice and it feels good to be alive, an irony not lost as one pushed open the small wrought-iron gate and walked to the narrow, red-brick house on the north side of the street.

Normand lived here, about a mile from Toronto General Hospital, east of the downtown core. He taught at Gabrielle Roy Public School and, part-time, at Jarvis Collegiate Institute, both a short walk away. "No trouble finding the place?" he asked, as he led the way through the tastefully but sparsely furnished house. He brought a mug of coffee from the kitchen to a round patio table in the backyard and sat in a chair with a yellow cloth back. His brown hair was cut short, almost army style, and his Vandyke beard was flecked with grey. He smiled easily and managed to look neat, presentable, in a white undershirt and khaki shorts. He was thirty-six years old, with a trim, athletic physique. He lived with David, who was a year older and worked as an executive in a bank in downtown Toronto. They were homosexual lovers.

For three months, Normand had known that he was dying of AIDS, the acronym for Acquired Immune Deficiency Syndrome. That morning, however, Normand was cheerful, for he had been in temporary remission for several weeks and it was the start of summer holidays. He looked fit enough to run a marathon.

Normand had first heard of AIDS three years earlier, in 1982, when word of a dreaded "gay plague" trickled northward from the United States, from San Francisco, Los Angeles, New York, and other cities with large homosexual populations. It quickly became the topic in Toronto's homosexual community and was beginning to appear more frequently in magazines and newspapers. In May 1983, Normand began to suspect that a friend, one of his sexual partners, had developed AIDS. He also worried about some disturbing symptoms of his own, swollen lymph glands, a skin infection slow to heal, but he thought they might be carry-overs from an attack of rubella he had suffered the previous summer. He reported this to his doctor, who in turn referred him to Mary Fanning, a staff physician in the Infectious Diseases Unit at Toronto General Hospital.

At the hospital, Normand went through a series of tests, which showed that, while there was nothing immediately serious, things were not what they should be. The tests showed the existence of antibodies to fight the virus, which meant he had been exposed to it, but did not indicate a life-threatening condition.

On and off, but for weeks at a stretch during the year that followed, he suffered high fevers, night sweats, and diarrhea. He lost weight and tired quickly. He continued to report to the hospital regularly and in December a blood test showed that his Helper T cells, a family of white blood cells, also called lymphocytes, that play a major role in the body's immune system, were abnormal.

To use a military analogy not uncommon in medicine, especially among immunologists, the immune system resembles guerrilla warfare. In Normand's case, the virus had not yet launched a full-scale attack, but it had gained a beach-head and was trying to disrupt communications in the body's immune defence system. The virus's battle plan is basically to cause insurrection. It turns the body's Helper T cells into traitors, then anarchists. The Helper T cells begin to replicate the virus itself and attack the bloodstream wildly, destroying other cells in their path, including the original virus. The virus is thus more kamikaze than guerrilla. Eventually, both the Helper T cells and the virus disappear, by which time it is too late — the state has fallen.

The results of the tests in December did not confirm that Normand had AIDS, but with all the other persistent symptoms, they classified him as a person with AIDS-related complex, known by the acronym ARC. Normand had a 5 to 10 per cent chance of developing AIDS. The insurrection had begun. "It turned out my friend was healthy as could be. He had been living in New York and for a time just wasn't feeling well, so he returned to his home in Victoria. It was just a rumor he had AIDS. He never got it. I did."

Sitting at the patio table, as a breeze wafted into the yard, Normand sipped his coffee and told his story.

He was born and raised in Sudbury, in a French-Canadian family, all devout Catholics. Mostly, he remembers wanting to get out of Sudbury, though not because of his family and friends, or because Sudbury was an unpretty place. "I've been gay as long as I can remember. As a child, I had curiosities aimed at both sexes, but certainly as an adolescent my interests definitely were geared to men. I dated girls and a couple of times I even came close to getting engaged, but that was because I had a very strong sex drive and what was most available were girls."

When he finished his studies at Laurentian University, he decided to go on to teachers' college with some of his friends. He loved it. He felt he was a natural teacher, with a gift for simplifying and communicating. "I liked working with kids and when it came time to do eight weeks of practice teaching, I taught grade seven and grade eight. I enjoyed it, I was good at it, and when I finished teachers' college I signed a contract to teach elementary school for two years in St. Catharines. I really didn't want to go to Toronto. I wanted to live in a small place near Toronto. It was a Catholic French school. I was a home-room teacher and taught everything, but I began to specialize in library work and guidance counselling. It was during my second year in St. Catharines that I discovered the life in Toronto and soon I was heading to Toronto five nights a week, then driving back to St. Catharines in the morning."

After his two years in St. Catharines, he moved to Toronto and worked as a teacher with the Catholic school board, then, in 1974, left to teach at the new Gabrielle Roy Public School on Pembroke Street. "I had to get out of the Catholic system.

I was brought up a Catholic, but I haven't practised since I was eighteen. I believe in God. I believe in life after death. I just didn't believe in the church, basically because I was gay. I wasn't allowed to participate, to take the sacraments, so I thought — screw you! For a gay person, a Catholic school is not the place to be, though I never tried to hide anything. Everyone knew I lived with a man. I attended all the staff parties, but I never came with a girlfriend."

Inside the house, in the kitchen, a telephone rang and Normand left the patio to answer it. When he returned he said it was the hospital calling to check on how he was feeling. The two doctors he was seeing regularly at Toronto General were both women, Mary Fanning, a senior doctor-scientist in the Infectious Diseases Unit, and Anne Phillips, a young resident doctor who was studying Hodgkin's disease and who worked under Mary. His own doctor was also a woman. Normand and many other homosexuals prefer woman doctors to men doctors because, as a group, they believe women doctors show more concern and compassion and seem to be more comfortable not just with sexuality and homosexuality but with illness itself.

There were a few exceptions, one or two, but nearly all the men doctors Normand encountered in hospital seemed to stand back, refusing to touch him, and invariably they were masked, gloved, and gowned as if Normand were radioactive. Most of the men doctors could not accept a male couple in an emotional situation being indiscreet about showing physical affection — hugging and kissing. And they asked questions like traffic cops. When did you last have sex with a man? Where did you do it? What did you do? Normand sensed that when the men doctors left the room they made snide remarks and told jokes.

"I have had many contacts. I have always been a very promiscuous person. For about five years, between 1972 and 1977, I had a lover and for the most part I was very faithful, with few indiscretions. When I finally split with this lover, I went, I think, wild — made up for all the lost time. I've had my share. I've certainly gone to bed with more than a thousand guys over my lifetime, mostly between 1977 and 1982 or 1983, which coincided with the dangerous period for AIDS. But I have no idea who I got it from.

"When I found out I had AIDS-related complex, I wanted to know, what next? And, should I stop doing anything? Mary Fanning's an impressive woman — absolutely honest, straight-forward, non-judgmental — so I explained to her that even though I'm in a relationship, it's an open one. It's the kind of relationship I wanted. I could not have lived in another monogamous relationship. David and I established at the beginning that we wouldn't run around behind each other's backs and the other person should be able to accept this. She said she couldn't tell me what not to do, because she didn't know whether I was transmitting anything. She said if she knew for sure I was transmitting something, she'd say don't do it. So I'm hearing what I wanted to hear, and I kept playing around.

"I presume I could have passed it on to someone else, but in the six months up to last April, all of last winter, I was not very sexually active. I was tired and didn't feel like going out, so probably I was developing this pneumonia. Whether I was passing something on six months before that, I don't know. I was fairly active last summer." Despite the diagnosis, he continued having sexual relations, including anal intercourse, though much less frequently, and with condoms.

Because of the AIDS scare, some homosexuals say their relationships are tested. Sometimes they are strengthened and develop a stronger emotional base, and sometimes they are ruined by the discovery that sex was all the partners shared. For Normand and David it made no difference at all. "Our relationship didn't get any deeper. It was always deep. It couldn't get any deeper." With AIDS on the scene today, he says, the pendulum has begun to swing toward a more restrained sexual lifestyle. The bath houses mostly are empty, desolate places. "I really do think things went too far in the 1960s and 1970s," Normand says, and he refers to fast-track sexuality itself, not just homosexuality. "I've been to New York, to some of the parties and clubs where the straights go and, boy, that was *something*."

Late in March, Normand and David were preparing for a trip to Arizona to help David's parents who holidayed there. Normand and David would fly to Arizona and drive the family car home, so David's parents could fly back. It was about this time that Normand developed what he thought was a bad cold, with a hacking cough.

Two weeks earlier, the biggest snowstorm of the winter had hit Toronto and it had taken Normand an hour and a half to walk home from school. When he got home, he had had to shovel his way in to the front door. That probably was when the pneumonia set in.

The cough worsened and soon he realized he had no ordinary cold. At first the cough came from low in his chest, nearly from his stomach, then it moved up in his chest and felt as if it was coming from the bottom of his throat. One night late in March he woke up feeling he was suffocating. He couldn't move without coughing and he burned with such a fever that he drenched the bed in perspiration. The next morning, for the first time that school year, Normand did not go to work. He went to see his own doctor, who thought at first he might have whooping cough. She told him to take a deep breath, which made him cough so violently he could hardly stay on his feet. She advised him immediately to check into a hospital.

That was on a Monday. He didn't bother calling the hospital Tuesday, hoping he would feel better after a good sleep, but the coughing and the night sweats continued, so on Wednesday he called Toronto General and was told to report for tests at two o'clock that afternoon. He was given a chest X-ray, which indicated something abnormal in his lungs. The doctors knew of Normand's AIDS-related complex and they were suspicious that the disease might have moved to the next stage. The next day, they ordered a bronchoscopy, which consists of a fibre-optic tube worked down through the nose all the way to the lungs to allow examination of the lungs from the inside. It is an uncomfortable, choking procedure, performed while the patient is conscious, and it is not without some risk, for it has been known to collapse a lung. The doctors could see nothing wrong through the bronchoscope, but they did a biopsy of the lung and sent a specimen to the lab. Normand waited for the results in a private room on the seventh floor of the Bell Wing.

Mary Fanning was away from the hospital that day, a Thursday, so she had delegated Anne Phillips, the young resident who was working with her in the Infectious Diseases Unit, to meet with Normand. He liked her immediately.

The results came in later that night, shortly after nine o'clock. Normand was diagnosed as having *pneumocystis carinii* pneumonia, one of the most common "opportunistic infections" of someone whose immune system is severely weakened. It is an air-borne organism that sometimes strikes frail cancer patients treated with radiotherapy, or transplant patients on drugs to suppress the immune system's natural instinct to reject a foreign organ. It rarely infects young, healthy people, who are able to fight it off routinely. For Normand, the fact that his immune system was no longer fighting off the infection meant he had crossed over the line from AIDS-related complex to AIDS.

Phillips telephoned David at home around ten o'clock that evening to tell him the results. She talked to him for a long time, nearly an hour, explaining as best she could what the disease was and what it wasn't and what treatment was available. All that can be done, she said, is to treat the symptoms. There might be a remission, perhaps several remissions, but these periods would get shorter and shorter as the disease progressed. There would be more opportunistic infections, more pneumonias, possibly neurological disorders and rare cancers such as Kaposi's sarcoma, which causes dime-sized, purplish-brown lesions on the skin. (Kaposi's sarcoma is a cancer previously found only in Africans and elderly Mediterranean men, but in AIDS victims it has become a mystifying but telltale signal of the disease.) Normand might live another three years, another eighteen months, a year, maybe not that long. Nothing could be done for the AIDS itself, Phillips emphasized. There is no cure.

The news stunned Normand, who had clung to the belief that the odds were strongly in his favor; that AIDS was a disease other gays contracted. He had always been an optimist, but he believed in certain signs — luck, coincidence, the weather — as if they were omens, tangible portents of good or bad. The night Normand heard that he had AIDS, he felt flattened, as if he had been punched in the stomach.

Mary Fanning was eating lunch at her desk, Swiss cheese in a kaiser on a paper plate and strawberry yogurt spooned from a plastic cup. Her office is on the ground floor of the Eaton Wing, a small, cluttered room with few luxuries. She is freckle-faced, with short hair clipped behind one ear with a barrette. She was dressed for comfort in a grey jumpsuit-smock. She was six months pregnant. AIDS, she said, is a "terrifying" disease, mainly because it appears to be new, and so little is known about it. When asked what questions *she* had about AIDS, she thought for a time, then looked up from her desk and said, "I don't have any questions that anyone can answer."

Fanning is a physician, an assistant professor, an infectious diseases scientist, and one of seven members of a Special Advisory Committee on AIDS appointed by the provincial government. The committee was created in 1983, when 1,641 cases had been reported in the United States. At the time, only 24 cases had been recognized in Canada, 7 of them in Ontario, but the medical community feared the worst. Fanning prepared a short, jargon-free paper on the subject, the first paragraph of which states:

Health planners today are frequently confronted with issues such as diminishing resources in the face of increasing needs, shifts in disease patterns in the community requiring re-allocation of health care resources or periodic short-lived epidemics with an identifiable control measure. However, the problem of the emergence of a new disease which is lethal, utilizes tremendous health care resources and is spreading in uncontrolled epidemic proportions with no known treatment or cure is seldom faced today.

The paper chilled the most phlegmatic medicos, who are not used to reading about disease in such stark, unvarnished prose. Fanning compared the outbreak of AIDS in the United States with outbreaks of polio, cholera, and plague. The paper continued: "The response of the community to newly emergent epidemic diseases is no different today than it was in the 1800s when cholera swept across Canada. . . ."

The great Asiatic cholera epidemic of the early 1800s spread from India to Indo-China and Japan and within ten years it had reached Moscow — it would kill more than a million Russians in 1848 alone — then the port cities of England. As with AIDS in the early 1980s, Canada a century and a half ago was warned of what was coming and tried to prepare for it.

Toronto, then the Town of York, had a population of about five thousand, with another forty thousand living in the surrounding countryside. On the evening of June 21, 1832, the steamship *Great Britain* dropped anchor in the harbor, bringing to York the first of eleven thousand immigrants that would arrive over the summer. With them came the cholera, which within three months attacked one in four of the townspeople, killing nearly five hundred of them before the first wave of the disease abated in the cooler early autumn weather. Thousands more died in Toronto in the years that followed, especially in 1847, when 3,876 patients were admitted to hospital, of whom 863 died. Death usually came within hours of the first symptoms of nausea and diarrhea. An editorial in the *Christian Guardian* called the disease a "public evil" and went on to say with no exaggeration: "Many actively engaged in business and in health one day have been buried the next and the hand that now writes may, before the sun sets, be cold in death."

The cholera epidemic strained hospital budgets and facilities. The infamous "cholera sheds" were constructed and to accommodate still more an addition was built at the rear of Toronto General Hospital, then further east of its present location, increasing the hospital's capacity to a hundred beds. Some medical people objected to admitting cholera patients because they feared the contagion would spread through the hospital. The epidemic provoked bitterness and hostility because it was regarded as a lethal and costly scourge brought on by the boatloads of new immigrants, a downtrodden, dirty and easily recognized group, nearly as readily blamed in their day as the homosexuals who bear the brunt of the blame for the AIDS epidemic of the 1980s.

The first case of AIDS in North America was recognized in 1979, Fanning's paper noted.

It had unknown etiology, was transmitted in incompletely understood ways, affected young people, was invariably fatal, and was spreading in epidemic proportions among groups against which racial or social discrimination were possible. These features are not unlike those which influenced the response to cholera. In March, 1983, while the first cases were being diagnosed in Ontario, the sudden emergence of sensational and repeated press coverage about this disease and its course in the United States sparked fear and panic in both the general and medical communities.

There were many theories at the beginning, when the disease first was detected among young homosexuals in San Francisco, Los Angeles, and New York City. One of the early theories linked AIDS to the recreational use of amyl nitrite and butyl nitrite, liquid inhalants called "poppers," which many promiscuous homosexuals use to enhance sexual pleasure. Amyl nitrite in particular has been known to produce immune suppression. Another explanation was that repeated anal intercourse introduced sperm into the bloodstream, which might also cause profound immune suppression. And there was the "immune-overload theory," which hypothesized that homosexuals, especially those who were promiscuous, with many partners, suffered from an accumulation of sexually transmitted diseases — syphilis, gonorrhea, intestinal parasites, hepatitis B, herpes — which escalated and combined to become such a burden on the immune system that it simply quit.

The questions raised are as interesting and varied as the theories. If AIDS is a virus, like hepatitis B, is it an old virus or a new one? If it is an old virus, why is it suddenly attacking so many people? If new, where did it come from? If it is a mutation of some sort, from what did it mutate? Why should the attack be aimed primarily at homosexuals, who have been with us from time immemorial? And, more intriguing for medical detectives, why does it sometimes veer off to attack heterosexuals, children, old people? Why are Haitians peculiarly susceptible to it? Why does it attack male and female heterosexuals almost equally in Africa?

The media, of course, had a field day. *Time* magazine visited the laboratory of Dr. Michael Gottlieb of the University of Southern California, one of the first physicians in the United States to detect symptoms of the virus. Over a period of three months, Gottlieb had treated four patients with *pneumocystis carinii* pneumonia, a lung infection that usually infects older, frail patients. Gottlieb's four patients were under thirty, and had enjoyed excellent health, but they were all homosexuals and three of them had been promiscuous. It was the third case that convinced Gottlieb he was seeing something new. When a fourth turned up so quickly, he told *Time*, "I knew I was witnessing medical history. . . ."

Dr. William Hasletine, an investigator with the Dana-Farber Cancer Institute at Harvard University, was as puzzled as everyone else by the questions that remained unanswered. In the summer of 1985, when AIDS killed Hollywood screen idol Rock Hudson, he admitted to a *Time* reporter that "we have moved from being explorers in a canoe to explorers with a small sail on the vast sea of what we do not know."

Not only *Time* and other popular journals reacted with confusion and alarm. In February 1985, an article in the influential *New England Journal of Medicine* described AIDS as a "catastrophic and ultimately fatal illness" and said "the implications of the presence of this virus in a community are staggering."

A controversial but comprehensive article on AIDS appeared in *Rolling Stone* magazine in April 1985, written by David Black, an author who not only specializes in medical stories but also writes award-winning mystery novels; he is thus uniquely qualified to tackle the subject. Black begins by stating that the search for a cure for AIDS is complicated "by a collision of different worlds: straight versus gay, scientific versus hedonistic." This is exemplified, he continues, by a clash of opinion between "single-agent theories" and "multifactorial theories," which has been a constant theme in the history of medicine. Those who believed AIDS was caused by a single agent, a new and lethal virus, "betrayed a mind that was, at its extreme, amoral: the virus hit you like a bolt from the blue; what you did had nothing to do with it." Those who believed in the multifactorial theory, that AIDS was caused by several interrelated factors, "betrayed a mind that was, at its extreme, moralistic: the disease was a direct result of how you were living your life — going to the baths, being sexually promiscuous. . . ."

A champion of the single-factor theory is Robert C. Gallo of the National Cancer Institute in Bethesda, Maryland, who had reported in 1983 on a retrovirus he called HTLV-1 (for *human T-cell leukemia virus*) that he believed was responsible for a human cancer. Gallo suspected it might also be the cause of AIDS. At about the same time, at the esteemed Pasteur Institute in Paris, a French team led by Luc Montagnier reported on a virus he thought caused AIDS, one he called LAV (for *lymphadenopathy-associated virus*).

Competition in medical research is intense, especially at the highest levels, so the Americans and French jostled each other to get to the head of the line. On the same day the French announced their findings, Gallo announced to the media that he had identified a virus he called HTLV-3.

The man who most vociferously espoused the multifactorial theory, and who thus betrayed what Black called a moralistic mind, was Joseph Sonnabend, a doctor-scientist who had been treating AIDS patients and who had launched a journal called *AIDS Research*. Tenants in Sonnabend's co-op apartment building in New York, worried that his work in AIDS research and therapy might infect them, managed to have him evicted. One more indication of AIDS-induced fear. Sonnabend alienated others, too, among them mainstream scientists who rejected his view that AIDS might be caused by something other than a single agent, and by homosexuals who reacted bitterly to suggestions that AIDS might be the result of sexual promiscuity. Sonnabend told Black: "Since I've been watching the disease in this city, it never occurred to me, never seemed possible, that this disease could be a specific syndrome, a new infectious agent. The patients getting sick had been exposed to an extremely complicated biological environment." This environment, he said, was the fast-track, homosexual lifestyle, which in the late 1970s had become widespread and socially acceptable, especially in the big cities. For Sonnabend, this development *was* new. "There has never been such a concentration of homosexual men, because only recently have there been cities this large."

Few would argue that AIDS began with homosexuality, but few would deny that homosexuality transmits and spreads it. Anal intercourse often causes ruptures that enable virus-infected semen to enter the bloodstream. This does not happen nearly so easily in vaginal intercourse because of natural lubrication in the vagina that prevents such ruptures. Sonnabend himself believes unhygienic conditions and poor nutrition may be as much to blame. This is borne out by statistics that show a higher incidence of AIDS among intravenous drug-users who share needles, and in slums and certain Third World countries.

There are researchers who believe that the AIDS virus originated in Africa, where it affects men and women in equal numbers in the central African countries of Zaire, Rwanda, and Burundi. The African green monkey has been singled out as a carrier and hence a possible villain. Virologists sampled the blood of two hundred green monkeys and found 70 per cent infected with a virus similar to the AIDS virus in humans. The monkeys have been known frequently to bite humans.

Whatever the cause and no matter who was to blame, Fanning, at Toronto General, sensed a panic taking root when the first AIDS cases were diagnosed in Toronto. She feared an emotional backlash directed against homosexuals. "There were all sorts of wild stories. In Australia, there were reports of people threatening to shoot AIDS victims who wanted to volunteer their blood. The real worry was that it would spread to the heterosexual community." A delegation from the Special Advisory Committee on AIDS met with Canadian newspaper editors to bring them up to date on AIDS, to discuss some articles that had been written, and to recommend strongly that each newspaper assign a reporter to cover the ongoing AIDS story. Fanning thought this an enlightened move that would keep the public informed in a consistent, intelligent manner. However, the editors rejected the proposal, saying they didn't work that way. Fanning was puzzled that the same newspapers regularly assigned reporters to cover the Blue Jays baseball and the Maple Leafs hockey teams.

When Anne Phillips finished explaining the results to David on the telephone, she asked him to visit Normand in hospital.

She had told the nursing station that he was to have unlimited visiting hours and that, if he wished, he could spend the night in Normand's room in the Bell Wing. Phillips also assigned a psychologist to Normand, Rosemary Barnes of the hospital's self-harm team, also called Project SHARE (Self-Harm Assessment, Research and Evaluation), a program aimed at potential suicides. Her role was to do what she could to help him accept the situation and to make sure he had support at home, from family and friends, when — if — he left the hospital. Normand assured her that he had lots of support and lots of loving. "I think I'm more fortunate than most people that way," he said.

David went to the hospital every day, sometimes on his way to work, or on his lunch hour, and he stayed most evenings with Normand in his private room. There are regulations for isolated patients and one is that visitors must wear gowns. Most of the nurses did not insist that David do so, figuring if he was going to get infected he would already have been infected, but occasionally a new nurse came on duty and would storm in and scold him for not being properly attired. When the nurse arrived to take blood samples from Normand, she wore two sets of gloves to protect her from needlestick injuries.

Normand stayed on oxygen for three days, during which time he was given Septra and Pentamidine, two drugs shown to be effective, temporarily, in treating *pneumocystis carinii* pneumonia. He responded quickly to the drug therapy, which began on the weekend, and by the following Friday he was well enough to go home. He had lost fifteen pounds in ten days, but by the end of April he had regained his normal weight and felt healthy as ever, though he knew the prognosis was a lifespan of twelve to eighteen months. He kept telling David he expected to see at least one more spring.

Normand wanted to show David around France that summer. It was one of two goals he set for himself before he died, the other being a trip to New York City with his parents to see the sights and catch some Broadway shows. At the table on his Cabbagetown patio, he gushed with enthusiasm at the prospect of the trip overseas. "I don't think we'll even spend time in Paris. We just want to relax and eat and drink. My best memories are of holidays in Europe — the cafés. I lived that with my first lover. I've never done that kind of holiday with David and I want to leave him with that memory."

He was not angry at what had happened to him because, he said, it was his own fault. "The warnings were there. I just didn't pay attention." When he turned twenty, he promised himself that when he died he would die a contented man. "It's not that I *thought* I'd die young, but that I would accept it if I *had* to die young. I never wanted to wait until I retired to have a good time." Here Normand stopped and stared off into the backyard, as if an echo of his words were coming back to him and they sounded melancholy and lugubrious, not the impression he wished to convey.

"You know, we've never had a major argument, never any serious misunderstandings. There are very few things I want to do now because I've only got a few years to go. I've been happy, happy, happy for the past five years. The worst thing David's ever complained about is I'm on the phone too long."

They were to leave on July 26, a Friday. David had doubts that they would make the trip and a week before their departure he noticed that Normand was becoming short of breath. He did not say anything at first, but when it got worse, he asked Normand about it and Normand admitted he was not feeling terrific. At the hospital, further X-rays showed a spot on the lung. The *pneumocystis carinii* had struck again. That was the Tuesday before they were to leave, but Normand insisted to David that they would leave for France on Friday. All the arrangements had been made, the hotels and even some of the restaurants had been booked. Anne Phillips said there was a chance, maybe fifty-fifty, that they had caught the pneumonia in time and Normand would be all right by Friday. The flight to Paris was scheduled to depart at five o'clock Friday afternoon. The drugs for the *pneumocystis carinii* take three days to take effect, so they were just beginning to kick in early Friday morning. "We didn't make the decision not to go until quarter to two on Friday," David said. "We came that close to going."

Cancellation of the trip was another emotional blow for Normand, another of the bad signs, but by the end of the day, having made the decision not to go, he was relieved. He had been denying his sickness, trying too hard not to be sick, and over the weekend he became deathly ill — vomiting, fever, sweats, diarrhea — then on Monday he snapped out of it. He dropped ten pounds to a hundred and fifteen pounds, twenty pounds below his normal weight, but he recovered so quickly during the next few days that he and David decided to take a short holiday and drive to the east coast.

They motored through New Hampshire, Vermont, and Maine, then on to Halifax. Then Normand got sick again. He was still on medication for the pneumonia — up to thirty pills a day — but the symptoms returned. When they reached the Atlantic, David suggested that Normand fly back to Toronto and he would drive the car home. Normand refused. They made it back to Toronto in two days, arriving home on a Sunday, and the next day Normand was admitted to hospital again. He stayed two weeks, then recovered enough to go home.

He decided not to teach that fall, one of the hardest decisions he had ever made, and probably the worst sign of all. Soon the fever returned, with all the other symptoms. He tried desperately to maintain his weight, because he had convinced himself that keeping up his weight was the key to health, even if he hated eating and even if he was only trying to look healthier. He stocked the shelves in his kitchen with high-calorie foods, including tiny jars of baby food, which is high in calories and easily digested. His fever would run to a hundred and four degrees, and David would bring it down with alcohol baths and Tylenol; then three hours later it would soar again. Throughout the night he would alternately drip with perspiration and shiver uncontrollably.

Early on Sunday, September 22, after another bad night, Normand went to the bathroom upstairs to weigh himself, the morning ritual. David was downstairs reading the newspaper when he heard a loud cry, and then sobbing. Normand's weight had dropped below a hundred and ten pounds, a psychological Rubicon. It was futile. He wept in anger and frustration. There would be no more springs.

Normand was supposed to go to a cancer clinic at the hospital on Tuesday afternoon because he had developed a small spot of Kaposi's sarcoma on his arm. David came home from work at noon and found him "sick as a dog." He cancelled his appointment and called Fanning at the hospital, who told him to bring Normand in. David said he would try to bring his fever down first, then bring him in later that afternoon. They arrived at Emergency at four o'clock, where a male doctor asked Normand when had he last had sex with a man, and what sort of sex had it been? Normand stayed in Emergency until eleven o'clock that night, until a room was available in the Bell Wing.

The regimen of tests began again. Normand's hemoglobin was low, which made him weak. They gave him three units of blood, but he kept getting weaker. His liver was enlarged, which meant he might be developing hepatitis.

Normand had asked to see the Roman Catholic chaplain, an older man he had met and liked when he was in the hospital in April. The priest had impressed him when he said one must sin very grievously ever to go to hell. He took communion in his room on Wednesday. "Normand's funny this way," David explained. "He did not have much use for the Church, but he saw it as some sort of insurance package to get into heaven." David spent all Thursday at the hospital and in the evening, after Normand was given still another unit of blood, one of the doctors told David that he could expect to see a big improvement by morning.

When David arrived Friday morning, Normand looked dreadful. He could barely walk. He tried to shave himself in the bathroom but his knees kept buckling. David knelt on the floor and held his legs together to prevent him from falling over. Mary Fanning and Anne Phillips arrived and they, too, couldn't believe Normand had deteriorated so quickly overnight. Fanning turned to David and, choosing her words carefully, said, "He looks like a frail little robin." Phillips motioned David to leave the room and come downstairs to her office. There, she told him she did not think Normand would last another two weeks.

"What about the family?" she asked.

David knew that one of Normand's nieces was getting married in Sudbury the next day. It would be a big family event, but he knew he had to call the family that day to tell them about Normand. He advised them to try to get to Toronto to see Normand that night.

The family arrived shortly after supper, and at nine o'clock they agreed to take turns in Normand's room so someone would be with him throughout the night. At about ten, a nurse came in to administer the painkiller Demerol. David remembers it as an especially moving moment, but one that he had to keep to himself. He had been in the room many times when the same nurse arrived for blood tests and she had always been double-gloved because of the risk of needlestick contamination. It was standard hospital procedure. David never questioned it. This time, when she administered the Demerol, the nurse wore no gloves at all, and David knew she did it out of consideration for the family gathered at the bedside. He saw it as a small, courageous thing to do, "a lovely human touch."

David was still in the room at eleven when Normand suddenly began to breathe in gasps, as if running. Normand's sister, a nurse, recognized it immediately as Cheyne-Stokes breathing, when the heart pounds and the lungs claw for air in one last lunge at living. For David, who had never watched anyone die, it was an overwhelming experience. "His heart and lungs just couldn't keep up. I even knew what his last breath would be. I could count them — five, four, three, two, one — and I knew there would not be another one. It was moving more than frightening. I kept thinking, this must be what watching birth is like."

Work on AIDS continued in laboratories around the world. At Toronto General, Randall Coates, a young epidemiologist, headed an elaborate prospective study of men who had had sexual contact with partners diagnosed as having AIDS or ARC. Between July 1984 and July 1985, two hundred and forty-eight homosexual and bisexual men were recruited for the study. All the men appeared to be healthy, though nearly all had developed antibodies to the AIDS virus. All are considered to be at extremely high risk for developing AIDS. An early hypothesis was that in order to develop AIDS or an AIDS-related condition, the men must have had a depressed immune system to begin with. Early returns do not support this hypothesis.

The immune systems of the men in the study were much like everyone else's. Every three months the men report to the Infectious Diseases Unit in the Eaton Wing for a regimen of tests, requiring specimens of feces, urine, blood, saliva, and semen. At each quarterly visit, lymphocytes and serum are separated from blood samples and are frozen at minus seventy degrees Celsius and stored for future analysis. The men filled out questionnaires on their sexual histories, current sexual practices, drug use, and travel. The information would be monitored over a period of three years. The men ranged in age from nineteen to sixty, the average being thirty-two. A third of the men had university degrees and 70 per cent had completed some form of post-secondary education. "They all seem to be so young and bright," Coates said. "The study is very hard on the workers. It is an emotionally wrenching experience."

Mary Fanning referred to the disease as "maddening" and "elusive" because its characteristics keep changing, thwarting attempts to develop a vaccine. Some of the moralists regard it as divine retribution, except when it infiltrates blood banks and reaches hemophiliacs, mothers, and children. Cynics shrug and ask, why the fuss? AIDS might have killed two hundred Canadians, to be sure, but lung cancer, most of it self-inflicted through cigarette-smoking, kills about thirty-five thousand Canadians a year. That's missing the point, the realists reply, because AIDS is new, a medical mystery that is 100 per cent fatal. At the start of 1986, AIDS had become the biggest single killer of men in their thirties, surpassing motor vehicle accidents and suicides. Authorities predicted that newly diagnosed cases of AIDS in Canada would double every ten months, as it had in the United States.

The panic, when there was panic, was in the not knowing. It was as though it was a moving target, or a chameleon. The body produces an antibody to the virus, and the virus changes, and the body produces another antibody, and the virus changes again. "It keeps changing its coat," Fanning said one day in her office. "One day it wears a blue coat, another day a green coat." Despite intensive research and many small breakthroughs, so much remains unknown. The mystery of AIDS is what provokes a pervasive anxiety that often borders on hysteria. Can you get it from kissing? From swimming in a public pool? From a hot tub? Can it be spread by mosquitoes? Controversies have erupted over whether AIDS-infected children should be allowed to attend school, whether AIDS-infected waiters or chefs should work in restaurants, whether mortuary embalmers should be required to work on AIDS corpses. Inevitably, AIDS jokes emerged, callous and cruel as gallows humor can be.

Did you hear about the new form of AIDS you can get through your ears?

No!

From listening to too many assholes.

People with AIDS-related complex may carry it indefinitely. Some studies say as many as 20 per cent will develop AIDS. It had been suggested that every case of ARC could lead to AIDS, as the immune system, which is strongest in one's late twenties and early thirties, inevitably wears down and weakens with age. The body becomes increasingly susceptible to various other maladies as well as AIDS. Because the latency period seems to be extraordinarily long, the horrible possibility exists that AIDS could be transmitted unknowingly for years to countless victims until the full fury explodes in an indescribable, exponential devastation.

The possibility exists, of course, that because so many top-flight medical brains are at work in a concentrated field of research, especially in the exciting and promising new field of immunology, great breakthroughs could occur at any moment that might involve a vaccine for AIDS, perhaps a breakthrough in cancer. There are reputations, and money, to be made. "Everyone in the field is aware of what AIDS research could lead to," Fanning said.

A month after Normand died, David was awakened early one morning by a telephone call from a woman reporter at a Toronto television station. She asked all sorts of questions about Normand, which surprised David. Barely awake, he thought perhaps the television people wanted to do a nice story on Normand because he had been such a good teacher. The reporter said she would drop by to talk to him.

She arrived with a camera crew and told David she needed confirmation that Normand had worked as a teacher and guidance counsellor when he knew he had AIDS, thus posing a danger to all his students. She evidently saw the story as a scandal of the first order.

She added that the story was going to be aired that night whether David co-operated or not. She wanted to interview him, however, and suggested that his face could be hidden from view and his voice disguised if he wanted to do it that way. If he agreed to do this, she said, she promised *not* to use his name on television. David refused, thinking he was helping his friend's memory. The story was aired that evening as the first item on the evening news, and David was mentioned by name. Two months later, he quit his job at the bank.

At Gabrielle Roy Public School, where Normand was known by everyone as just another *M'sieur*, the students wanted to do something for him. Normand had been with the school since it was founded in 1974 and he was one of the most popular teachers. He could make things simple. Over the years he had worked to raise money for the playground and the library. He often served hot dogs at these fund-raising parties. He loved to read and he had devoted himself to building one of the finest school library collections in the city. The students persuaded the parent-teacher association to inaugurate an annual award in his name for the two graduating grade eight students who best exemplified leadership and good citizenship. The students held more hot-dog lunches to raise money to buy a tree in memory of Normand. They planted it in the playground, in the spring.

CHAPTER 1 0

Lorna, Felix, and Family
We Don't Quit Until They're Forty

"JUST WHEN we thought we were getting caught up," David Allen said to no one in particular in his Public Relations office on the ground floor of the Bell Wing. "We weren't even notified," he continued, stomping around his office and looking harried.

Shortly after dawn, precisely at sixteen minutes after seven o'clock, baby David Thomas Francis entered the world wriggling and howling and bringing joy to the hearts of his parents, Lorna and Felix, who had come to Canada from Uganda twelve years earlier. Over the past nine years, living in a comfortable home in the Toronto suburb of Scarborough, Lorna and Felix had tried and tried to have a baby. She had had four unsuccessful pregnancies, then, in desperation and as a last resort, they had turned to the hospital for help. What made it a public relations issue that morning was that, though the pregnancy went the usual nine months, and everything about the delivery was normal, it was slightly historical. David Thomas Francis was the hospital's first in-vitro fertilization baby. He was conceived late last March, in an obstetrics laboratory — in a dish.

"You'd think someone could have told us," Allen muttered, hovering over Jane MacGillivray, the Public Relations officer, who was composing a one-page press release. Carol Saunders, the secretary, stood by, ready to crank out copies on the official blue-and-white hospital letterhead, to be distributed to the horde of newspaper, radio, and television reporters expected to descend upon the hospital in three hours.

Allen erupted again. "That's the trouble. It's new to obstetrics. The heart-lung people have been through this sort of thing many times. They know it's important to notify us soon as they get a donor, when the operation's a go. It gives us time to get ready."

It was nearly eleven o'clock and Lorna and Felix were in her room in the Norman Urquhart Wing. There was a small statue of the Blessed Virgin Mary on her bedside table. The light in the room was subdued, filtered through the drawn curtains from the dim winter morning outside. The new mother was propped up on three pillows, resting in her institutional bed. She was a lovely brunette, in a pink floral gown. She seemed to glow with health, but she was not feeling well. Earlier, when she had got out of bed to try to make it to the bathroom, she had fainted with pain. The photo session and press conference were scheduled for two o'clock, in Room 131 on the ninth floor of the Norman Urquhart Wing, down the corridor from her room, past the nursing station. Lorna didn't think she felt well enough to make it.

"Look, I'll talk to the parents," Allen said. "Maybe we can bring her from her room in her bed. We'll just wheel it down the corridor, mother and baby and all."

Within an hour, it became apparent that the media were enthusiastic about the event and more reporters and cameramen were going to arrive than had been expected. One never can predict these things. Most days the hospital is lucky to get a call from a newspaper re-write desk. Man-bites-dog wasn't news this time. Motherhood was.

Allen decided to transfer the locale of the photo session and press conference from Room 131 in the Norman Urquhart Wing to the lobby on the ninth floor of the Eaton Wing, in an adjacent building. The lobby is rather impersonal, nothing more than a waiting room outside a dozen doctors' offices, with magazines stacked on end tables and strewn on chairs, but the area was large enough to accommodate the clattering scrum that soon would arrive.

"Someone could have told us," Allen said again. "Good God, the mother was in labor for ten hours!"

Giving birth at home used to be the thing to do. The doctor would arrive, order someone to boil the water, unbutton his vest, roll up his sleeves, and head to the bedroom for the big event. An hour or two later, after much pacing about in the parlor, the father would hear a distant, muffled slap, a wet cough, and then the wail of new life filling the house like lilacs, making people laugh and weep and shine beatific smiles upon one another. The home birth now is old-fashioned, or part of some well-intentioned back-to-earth chic for people who drink carrot juice and attach Kahlil Gibran's poetry to their refrigerators. Same with dying at home, which used to be as routine as roasting the Christmas turkey and hauling down the storm windows.

Then the hospital took over. Now, one of the few spokes left in the circle of life and death that hints of transcendence and is still consigned to the home is the magic of conception, the love act itself, but even that is being eyed covetously by the folks who brought you the Caesarean section. They are the new reproductive biologists and there is research to be done at the modern teaching hospital into the abstrusities of oligospermia, azoospermia, oocytes, nidation failures, karyotypic abnormalities, follicular fluids, zygotes, and gametes.

Don Layne is vice-president of research at Toronto General. He is also an influential member of the hospital's powerful ethics committee, which can approve, delay, or kill any research project it chooses. Layne works out of a large, comfortable office in the College Wing, the oldest part of the hospital. He is a tall, lanky man one can easily imagine with his arms draped over a ranch fence, twirling a stem of hay in his mouth. He has a lilting accent that sounds suspiciously Irish, but that is, in fact, Barbadian. He was born in Canada, in the Eastern Townships of Quebec, near Sherbrooke, but his parents moved to Barbados when he was a year old.

When he was eighteen, he returned to Canada to study at McGill University. Around the hospital, he is called Dr. Layne, though he is not a medical doctor. He studied agriculture biochemistry at McGill. Specifically, he studied the egg-laying of hens, a subject that fascinated him. "The hen," he said, "is the only animal bred over the ages for its reproductive activity. Early on, I got interested in the hormonal influence of egg-laying. Not many people around here realize that their vice-president of research is a farmer." After McGill, he continued his studies in England and Scotland, then headed to Massachusetts, where he worked with Gregory Pincus, the developer of the birth control pill.

Layne is enthusiastic about the hospital's reproductive-biology work and sees it as a field ripe for dramatic medical breakthroughs, and as a service many desperate couples need. "The difficulties of infertility put a huge strain on a relationship. The word 'barren' always has been a pejorative, a term of opprobrium that dates back to the Bible. But it's strictly a rich-country phenomenon today, an outgrowth of affluence. You won't see much of this in Ethiopia."

The cost of the in-vitro fertilization procedure is between $3,000 and $4,000, though the hospital charges less than half that much, about $1,200. It is considerably more expensive in other jurisdictions outside Canada, as much as $10,000, which makes it a substantial out-of-pocket expense for an infertile couple determined to have a child. Some couples have to borrow money or mortgage their homes to pay for it. At Toronto General, except for the cost of the actual birth and complications during the pregnancy, the procedure is not covered by the Ontario Health Insurance Plan. This is one of those quirks of the Canadian personality, which likes to reward misery and takes a dim view of joy.

"Another example involves cosmetic surgery," Layne said. "A woman who has an operation to increase the size of her breasts isn't covered by OHIP, but if the operation *decreases* the size of the breasts, she is. Sometimes a woman is embarrassed because she has breasts of different sizes, one noticeably larger than the other. Now, she could have the small one enlarged, or the large one reduced. If she has the large breast reduced, she's covered; if she has the small breast enlarged, she isn't. You figure it out."

Alan Shewchuk is the obstetrician-gynecologist in charge of the hospital's in-vitro fertilization program. He started a small reproductive-biology unit at the hospital in 1969, when it was considered highly experimental research. Sixteen years later, nearly six hundred patients were visiting Shewchuk's clinic every month.

Women are examined for disorders of ovulation, for mechanical abnormalities in the vagina, cervix, uterus, and fallopian tubes. One of the most common reasons for infertility in a woman is a blockage of the fallopian tubes, where fertilization normally takes place. The fallopian tube is a thin, flexible conduit through which the egg, a speck one four-thousandth of an inch thick, is conveyed from the ovary to the uterus.

Men come to the clinic, too. Infertility is no longer considered mainly a female problem. Many men have difficulty making, transporting, or depositing sperm.

Early on, Shewchuk added two microsurgeons to the clinic for the delicate work of repairing the fallopian tubes. When infertility is the result of blockage caused by minor scarring in the fallopian tubes, the microsurgeons enjoy a success rate of about 70 per cent. In recent years, their work has been enhanced by the use of laser surgery. When the blockage is severe, it is extremely difficult to repair, sometimes impossible. These women are candidates for the in-vitro fertilization process, to produce a so-called test-tube baby — a quaint misnomer, since the fertilization actually occurs on a small glass plate called a Petri dish.

The in-vitro fertilization process was developed in England, at a clinic housed in a splendid mansion called Bourn Hall, in Cambridgeshire. Here, in the 1970s, the world-renowned team of obstetrician Patrick Steptoe and reproductive physiologist Robert Edwards worked to refine the procedure, which resulted in the birth of the first baby ever conceived outside the womb. Her name was Louise Brown and she was born in 1978. Since then, hundreds of in-vitro clinics have opened in hospitals around the world and couples previously categorized as infertile have produced more than a thousand babies, including, incidentally, an unusually high number of twins, triplets, and quadruplets.

The standard procedure is to remove the woman's eggs, fertilize them with her husband's sperm, and place them back in the uterus. However, already there are variations. A wife's eggs may be removed and fertilized with another donor's sperm — not her husband's — and placed back in her uterus. Or a donor's egg — not the wife's — may be fertilized by the husband's sperm and re-implanted inside the wife. A couple may also contribute sperm and egg and ask a third party, another woman, to carry the resulting embryo until birth. In this brave new world, the variations seem limitless — as are the ethical, moral, and legal complications.

In England, the Royal College of Obstetricians and Gynaecologists produced a document on ethical constraints for clinicians and scientists working in the field of in-vitro fertilization. The paper began by tackling the issue of whether or not there was a risk of abnormal babies as a result of in-vitro fertilization. There was a risk, it concluded, but no more risk than would occur under the circumstances of normal fertilization. At the time of the report, March 1983, a hundred and thirty babies had been born through in-vitro fertilization, with only one abnormality — a cardiac aberration in one of twins born in Australia. The only way to avoid risks of this sort, the College said, would be abstinence.

The guidelines set down by the College were eminently calm and reasonable, such as on the matter of whether or not a single woman should be allowed to have a baby by in-vitro fertilization: "In a society where a variety of family forms now exist and where adoption by a single parent, though rare, is possible, it is felt that it would be wrong arbitrarily to exclude all single women from in-vitro fertilization and embryo replacement without consideration of their individual circumstances." It recommended strongly that in cases involving donor sperm or donor eggs, the anonymity of the donors be preserved at all costs, which ruled out well-intentioned siblings or friends as donors. The College also recommended against the use of a surrogate mother "who cannot possibly predict before the baby is born what her attitude will be towards the child which she has been carrying for nine months."

The questions raised are fascinating, and endless, for the art and science of reproductive biology have outdistanced law and language. For example, regarding the matter of surrogate mothers, whether by in-vitro fertilization or the now old-fashioned process of artificial insemination, is payment of a fee to the surrogate the same as buying a child?

There are more questions.

What should you call a woman who bears a child conceived by another woman (since the bearer cannot be "mother")?

Should lesbians and transsexuals be allowed to make use of in-vitro fertilization?

How long should an in-vitro fertilized embryo be allowed to exist outside a womb?

Is it proper to produce these embryos solely for the purposes of research?

Should children be eventually told that they were conceived in a Petri dish?

If not, how does one keep track of such children, to study the long-term physiological, mental, emotional, and genetic ramifications? (The reproductive-biology team at Toronto General told the hospital ethics committee: "It is possible that children conceived outside the body may feel different to others and suffer adverse psychological effects.")

At least one case has arisen that involves the rights of an in-vitro-fertilized embryo. Mario and Elsa Rios, a Los Angeles couple, agreed to the in-vitro procedure and in Australia in 1981, doctors removed several of the eggs from Mrs. Rios, fertilized them with sperm from an anonymous donor and re-implanted some of the embryos in the woman's uterus. The doctors held back two of the embryos and froze them. "You must keep them for me," Mrs. Rios told the doctors. The implant failed and soon after, on a trip to Chile, the couple died in an airplane crash. Question: Are the remaining embryos, kept frozen in the lab in Melbourne, legal heirs of the Rios estate?

Reproductive-biological procedures are much in demand as a hospital service, and Shewchuk's busy little clinic promises to get even busier. In a submission to the ethics committee, Shewchuk said there are about twenty-four thousand infertile couples in Toronto alone and if only 10 per cent of them sought out in-vitro fertilization as a therapy, it would mean having to treat twenty-four hundred couples a year. Since a recent expansion in late 1985, his clinic manages to handle five hundred couples a year.

Fewer babies are available for adoption, because of more abortions and an increasing social acceptance of single mothers. There is also a surprisingly high, and growing, incidence of infertility among modern couples in their child-bearing years. In the United States, a study by the National Center for Health Statistics reported that between 1965 and 1982, infertility among married women between the ages of twenty and twenty-four had increased by a hundred and seventy-seven per cent.

Shewchuk sees a similar situation at Toronto General. In a presentation to the ethics committee, he suggested that reasons for the increase in infertility may include changing societal values that encourage couples to delay having children, often until their late thirties, in order to pursue careers and material acquisitions.

Shewchuk had the figures at his fingertips. A woman under the age of twenty-five has a 94-per-cent chance of becoming pregnant in a six-month period. For women under thirty, the success rate drops to 84 per cent; under age thirty-five, 69 per cent; under age forty, 57 per cent. Also, the older a woman, the greater the chances of a miscarriage. For women under twenty-five years, the miscarriage rate is 8 per cent; over thirty years, 23 per cent; over thirty-five years, 29 per cent; over forty years, 40 per cent. "Those are the risks you take," Shewchuk says. "You've got all your life for a career. You don't have all your life to have babies."

Shewchuk runs his reproductive-biology clinic with understated humor and an easy charm. He is bright and soft-spoken, with a patrician face that belies a sometimes ribald appreciation of the absurdities of life. Late in the afternoon, on a break

from his consultations, he stole away to a little cubicle down
the corridor from his office on the sixth floor of the Eaton
Wing for a smoke. It was an odd place for an interview. These
are the little cubicles, linen rooms really, where in-vitro fathers-
to-be come to masturbate. The sperm is needed for testing,
for measuring and counting the urgent little tadpoles, or for
the big day itself. Sometimes there is a line-up outside, with
nurses checking their watches. There are no hospital rules
prohibiting *Playboy* or *Hustler* from being smuggled into the
tiny, private cubicles and it is entirely possible that an
unadorned Bo Derek or dimpled cheerleaders from Ohio State
might be called upon to inspire, on a moment's notice, the
father of a future prime minister of the country.

In cases involving artificial insemination, when the husband
is not the donor, there are stringent criteria for the acceptance
of donated sperm. At Toronto General, thorough medical histories, going back three generations, are required. Shewchuk
explained, "We always pick married men who have had at
least two children. And they must be literate. I won't take
a donor who's not a university graduate. I realize this does
not necessarily equate with IQ, but it is a way of determining
if a man has reasonable intellectual development. If you were
sterile and needed a donor, wouldn't you prefer a university
graduate with three healthy kids at home?" Male sperm donors
must not have high blood-sugar levels, or abnormally high levels
of cholesterol and triglycerides, or a history of coronary disease
in their families. "If your grandfather had a coronary when
he was seventy-one years old, you could be a donor," Shewchuk
said. "If he had one when he was sixty-one, you couldn't."
The list continues. The men must be at least five feet, ten
inches tall, with no male-pattern baldness.

"Why are we seeing more infertility?" Shewchuk asked,
rhetorically, flicking a light to his cigarette. "Because humans
are stupid. They start menstruating and ovulating around
thirteen or fourteen. That's when nature says, 'Get pregnant.'
Kids that age will get pregnant necking in the back seat of
a car. But what do we have today? We have social mores that
encourage women to pursue careers and acquisitions — and
delay childbearing. They'll get pregnant in their thirties, they
say, but there is a drop-off in fertility, fecundity, after the
age of twenty-three. That's the major reason, but there are
new factors today. There are all the forms of contraception
— the Pill, IUDs. Women are subjecting themselves to more
sexual experiences, which means their uteruses get knocked

around, which means more chances of tubal damage, ovulation disorders, more chances of sexually transmitted diseases."

He stubbed out his cigarette in the drain in the stainless steel sink behind him and plunged his hands into the pockets of his white coat, anxious to get back to his office. "Have to go," he apologized. "Got two students and a naked woman in my office."

One more question, as Shewchuk started down the corridor. What about Alvin Toffler, who says it is the wave of the future to have babies later in life, that older couples make better parents?

"That's a pile of horseshit," he replied, without turning around.

The consent form for in-vitro fertilization begins in the usual way: "We, the undersigned, hereby consent to our involvement in the procedures of in-vitro fertilization and embryo transfer." It continues: "We understand the possible risk of foetal malformation occurring in the event of pregnancy and are aware of the availability of tests to detect foetal malformation during pregnancy. We also accept the risks of multiple pregnancy and/ or a tubal pregnancy arising from these procedures." And, finally: "We are aware of our freedom to withdraw from the procedure at any stage."

The qualifications are in point form:

1. *The husband must be the sperm donor and the wife must be the recipient of the fertilized ovum.*
2. *The wife must be forty years of age or younger.*
3. *Preferably, the couple would have no other naturally born, non-adoptive children.*
4. *Only patients referred by physicians will be considered.*
5. *Only patients whose fallopian tubes are absent or blocked and not amenable to conventional surgical repair will be considered.*
6. *Patients must have a normal uterus and at least one normal and laparoscopically accessible ovary.*
7. *There must be no evidence of untreatable ovulation disorders.*

At the initial consultation, the process is carefully explained, the wife has a complete physical examination, and the husband provides a semen specimen. When the results are in, the in-vitro team decides if the couple is suitable for the program. If they are, they are put on an active waiting list. Usually the woman's pelvic region is examined to determine the accessibility of the ovaries, and the instrument of choice is a laparoscope, a telescopic device that is inserted through a small abdominal incision directly below the navel. Sometimes, depending on what the surgeons see inside, the problem is simple tubal damage that can be corrected by microsurgery, or laser surgery, and in-vitro fertilization is unnecessary.

Early on, the couple is advised not to discuss their situation with the media. There is nothing secret about the process, but it is intricate, delicate, and not a little miraculous. There are intangibles. The reproductive-biology team explained to the hospital ethics committee that "media contact . . . might result in unforeseen emotional stresses which may have a negative impact on the processes of ovulation and pregnancy."

The exact time for the in-vitro fertilization is determined by the woman's menstrual cycle, specifically by monitoring the blood estrogen concentration and, by ultrasound measuring, the size of the tiny follicles in the ovary that contain the eggs. On the third day of the menstrual cycle, tests of blood estrogen and follicle size are taken for baseline measurements. Between day three and day five, the woman is given hormonal stimulants, first Clomid, then Pergonal. Pergonal is administered daily for three to four days by injections in the hips or buttocks. It is a mixture of two pituitary hormones and produces multiple follicles, stimulating their development and making them ripen so that several eggs can be harvested.

Pregnancy can be achieved by fertilizing only one egg, but the chances are better with two, and much better with three or four. Shewchuk maintains his statistics assiduously. The chances of a pregnancy with only one egg are 6 to 8 per cent. With two eggs, the success rate rises to 12 to 14 per cent; with three eggs, to 18 per cent; with four eggs, to 25 per cent. There are slightly increased risks as well of a multiple birth, Shewchuk said, but they have been exaggerated over the years.

For the big day, the woman is brought to a special operating room adjacent to a laboratory, and given a general anesthetic for the laparoscopy incision. Another incision is made lower in the abdominal wall, in the pubic region, so that the surgeon can insert instruments to grasp and stabilize the ovary. Next, through a third incision and inside the woman's body the small, bluish follicles are punctured, releasing the eggs, which are sucked out in their fluids with a long, hollow needle.

The eggs are taken immediately to the lab, where they are washed, placed in Petri dishes containing nutrients, then put in an incubator for up to eight hours. During this time, the husband produces his sperm, which is washed to separate good sperm from defective sperm, then united with the woman's eggs. This washing procedure — discovered by reproductive-biology researchers at Toronto General — has meant that males previously considered infertile sometimes can impregnate a fertile female without resorting to the in-vitro process. "We monitor ovulation in the wife carefully, to get a very narrow 'window,' then we inseminate the eggs with the husband's sperm through the cervix," Shewchuk said. "We've learned how to triple-wash the sperm. We're the only people in the city doing it."

In the next twenty-four hours, there may be conception, and no matter what the wisecracking of the morning entails, it is always a happy and solemn moment. "When one sees, in the laboratory, a developing human embryo," Shewchuk told his peers on the ethics committee, "one's reverence for life and its creation increases." The woman is taken back to her room where she waits as the embryo grows in a softly lighted incubator in the lab, at body heat, for thirty-six to forty-eight hours, until the cells divide to the four-cell stage. At that time the woman is brought back to the operating room, where sometimes she is joined by her husband. She is fully awake, unanesthetized, as the doctors transfer the embryo in a plastic catheter from the Petri dish, through the vagina, into the uterus. There should be music, wine.

In a few hours, the woman goes home, where she rests for a day and then waits for the pregnancy to be confirmed. Most often, she is referred back to her own physician, for the pregnancy from here on is like any normal pregnancy. The procedure is successful about 30 per cent of the time. If it fails, the couple and the laboratory wait for another menstrual cycle to try again. "Once we take on a couple," Shewchuk said, "we don't quit until they're forty."

"Don't scare the baby!"

David Allen was lecturing the horde of reporters and cameramen on proper behavior as Lorna and her new son were wheeled into the lobby in her hospital bed for the photo session. Carol Saunders pushed along a trolley with a cake, freshly baked in the kitchen in the basement of the Bell Wing. The icing on top said "Congratulations." Felix, the new father, looked on as if he were witnessing the invasion of Normandy. A television cameraman, suddenly agitated by the lighting in the lobby, lunged forward and pushed aside the trolley carrying the cake, which nearly toppled against a wall. "It's a zoo," Allen snapped. Shewchuk, in a freshly laundered white lab coat, stood at the head of the bed next to the mother, who clutched his hand as he prepared to make an announcement. He spoke calmly, assuredly, idly running one of his fingers through the sparse hair on David Thomas Francis's head. "Ladies and gentlemen," he began, "this is the only perfect thing you'll ever see — a new baby."

Earlier, while he was waiting for the show to begin, Felix had wandered to the obstetrics ward in the Norman Urquhart Wing and gazed for a long time through the large window at the roomful of new babies, all looking like miniature Winston Churchills. It is a calming thing to do. When he was ready, Felix turned to the man beside him and asked, "Would you care for a cigar, sir?"

CHAPTER 11

Diane
The Little Woman
Who Wouldn't Die

JOEL COOPER was lying on his back on the floor in his office on the tenth floor of the Eaton Wing, his head on a pillow in front of his desk, his feet propped up on a couch by the window. There was an open jar of peanuts and a telephone on the floor beside him. His back had gone out — again.

He first injured his back when he was twenty years old. He was lifting the engine out of his car to do a valve job. "That's when I popped the disc," he said. "It bothered me all through medical school. Sometimes I'd have to stand with my back against the wall during lectures." This time it happened when he was on vacation with his family. "I was playing with the kids. It might have been the waterslide, or tennis. I'm not sure how it happened, but everyone seems to have a good reason why I deserve it."

It was late on a Monday afternoon and Cooper had been on his back on the floor all day, making telephone calls, checking his caseload, dictating letters, receiving visitors, briefing junior surgeons. The only time he had been on his feet at the hospital was to struggle down the corridor to the Norman Urquhart Wing to visit Diane, the twenty-eight-year-old woman from Quebec he had operated on six weeks earlier: a heart-lung transplant. "The nurses were complaining again," Cooper said. "She's so *demanding*. I admire her courage and her persistence, sure, but she's a manipulative little thing. I took away her telephone because reporters kept calling and she'd talk to them for hours. I restricted her boyfriend's visiting hours. I told her she has to concentrate on getting better. This isn't a joke!

She wanted to go out this weekend. That's the trouble, she wants *everything*."

Mostly, Diane wanted to live. She would stop at nothing. For three years, staying alive had become a desperate game for her, ever since the cardiologist in Montreal diagnosed her condition as primary pulmonary hypertension, a rare and usually fatal heart disease. Her heart could not pump enough blood through her lungs. The cardiologist told her she would not live more than two years. Her only hope was a heart-lung transplant.

She was tiny, only five feet, one inch, and normally she weighed just over a hundred pounds, but after the operation in November her weight had dropped to eighty-six pounds. Her face was as pretty as ever, but she looked shrivelled, skeletal. She needed splints on each leg, from knees to ankles, so she could get out of bed and walk down the corridor, past the nursing station, to the "treadmill room" for her twice-daily physiotherapy sessions. But, she had something — a sparkle. She had a smile that could turn lights on, that could shift in an instant from mischievous to coquettish. Her features were delicate, doll-like. Her eyes were deep brown and big as chestnuts. She photographed beautifully. In the newspaper clippings she kept hidden under her bed at the hospital, she looked like a glamorous actress — Genevieve Bujold, a young Jane Fonda — only pretending to be dying.

Her father was a carpenter. As a girl growing up in Chomedey, Quebec, Diane worked in a furniture store. She married and gave birth to a daughter, Isabelle, but the marriage ended when she got sick and it was decided it would be best for Isabelle to live with her father. Diane loved to bowl and play baseball and racquetball and music. She was a romantic. Two days before her operation in November, she played the organ at an evening service at Sacré Coeur Church in downtown Toronto, swaying rhythmically to the music, her face shining with devotion. Diane was irresistible that night, a valiant Joan of Arc, clinging to life through a thin plastic tube from an oxygen cylinder to her nostrils. When the service ended and the congregation filed out everyone was in tears. And on the operating-room table, just before she slipped into the bottomless sleep of anesthesia, she beckoned Cooper to her side and whispered to him her last thoughts. "Docteur," she said, "when you work on me, can you give my breasts a little lift?"

Diane was born with a heart ailment, a congenital defect in one of the heart valves. Doctors waited until she was six years old, then operated on her to replace the valve. She does not think it was a plastic valve. One afternoon when she was sitting on her hospital bed, she said with some conviction, "There is nothing artificial in me." She was able to live a normal life and it was not until she was twenty-five, married, and three months pregnant that she began to have difficulty breathing. She first noticed it playing baseball, when she had to run. As her breathing became more labored, she continued to play, but she could only pitch and hit. If she got on base, she asked someone else to run for her.

When the cardiologist diagnosed the primary pulmonary hypertension and told her she had two years to live, Diane refused to give up. The only thing that could save her was a double-lung and heart transplant, a procedure that was not being done in Quebec. Her case became a local *cause célèbre* — single mom, dying, won't quit — and Diane soon became a darling of the media. Service clubs raised $140,000 to send her off to Palo Alto, California, and the Stanford Medical Center, where surgeons were experienced in the heart-lung transplant operation. The Laval Optimist Club provided her with $1,500 a month living expenses and paid for medical expenses not covered by Quebec's public health insurance plan.

She had also found a new man in her life, a strapping young fellow named Yves. When she knew she was dying, she told Yves that he owed her no loyalty and did not have to stay with her. Her dying made no difference, Yves tried to assure her, but Diane insisted that he should think about it for a day. Yves agreed.

"He waited a day, then he came and told me he would stay and follow me to the end," she said.

In October 1983, brimming with optimism, Diane left for the Stanford Medical Center in Palo Alto, California. When she said goodbye to the reporters gathered around her, she told them, "If this works, I'll come back and dance for you all."

She waited two years at Stanford for a transplant. The surgeons there kept putting her off because they could not find a suitable donor. The problem was that Diane was too small. The surgeons also were reluctant to go ahead because of scar tissue left from the heart operation when she was six years old. She and Yves bought a Volkswagen camper and went on short trips, never straying too far from Palo Alto because word could come at any time that a suitable donor had been found. They shared an apartment in Palo Alto with another couple, one of whom was also waiting for a heart-lung transplant. While she waited, Diane edited a newsletter for transplant patients, which is how she heard of Joel Cooper at Toronto General. She read about his remarkable success with Tom Hall, the world's longest-surviving single-lung transplant patient, who set a new record for longevity every time he woke up in the morning. On an impulse one afternoon, she picked up the telephone, asked the operator for the number of Toronto General Hospital, and called Cooper at his office.

Cooper explained the procedure to her as best he could over the telephone. If she wanted a heart-lung transplant at Toronto General, he told her, she would be considered a candidate with all the others, which meant she would have to submit to the same examinations and tests. These would take about ten days. Only then could a decision be made. Cooper told her he could not promise she would be accepted. He often got queries from patients outside of Toronto, and often nothing more was heard from them. He thought that the call would be the end of it, but he knew nothing of Diane's determination. After she finished talking with Cooper, she made arrangements to fly to Toronto. She decided she would arrive at the hospital like a baby in a basket and announce herself as a candidate for a heart-lung transplant. On the day Diane's plane was to land in Toronto, David Allen of Public Relations got calls from reporters at *The Toronto Sun* and Global Television, both of whom said they were going to the airport to pick up Diane and drive her to the hospital. No one knew who tipped them off, but Allen was suspicious. He knew that Cooper loathed pre-operative publicity, so he assigned a team of respiratory therapists from the hospital to meet Diane. They hurried to the airport and arranged for Diane to be taken off the plane on the tarmac, from a rear exit. The medicos hustled her away from the reporters to the customs office, where one of the officers asked if she had anything to declare. Diane fumbled in her purse and held up a miniature bottle of liquor from the airplane.

"That's okay," the officer said.

"But I have *two*," Diane told him, smiling her wicked smile.

"That's okay."

The respiratory therapists drove Diane to Toronto General and by nightfall she had a room at the hospital and was on the waiting list for a transplant.

"What could we do?" Allen asked, exasperated. "We couldn't toss her out on the street."

"I guess you could say she inflicted herself on the system," Cooper shrugged.

"I waited two years in California," Diane said. "I decided if I was going to die, I wanted to die near my family."

Early in October, Diane was waiting for the operation in her private room on the tenth floor of the Norman Urquhart Wing. She sat up on her bed wearing little-girl pink pajamas, with booties attached. Pinned to her pajamas was a button that said, "Help Save a Life, Be an Organ Donor." Carol Fray, a nurse, walked into the room to remind her she had an appointment that afternoon for one of her tests and Diane told her that would be fine but she would have to be back in her room by four-thirty. Fray asked why. "The Young and The Restless," Diane said, referring to the popular afternoon soap opera. "I missed it yesterday afternoon and had to catch it on a rerun early this morning."

When Fray left, Diane said the nurses were keeping a close watch on her and on who went into her room because Cooper did not like her talking to reporters and the subsequent stories in the papers. "He is very strict about publicity," she said. "He scolded me for some stories in the newspapers since I arrived here." Cooper actually had done more than scold her; he had warned her that if she did not stop talking to the reporters he would cancel the operation. Diane put a finger to her lips, checked to make sure the door to her room was closed, then got down on her hands and knees on the floor and rummaged in a pile of personal belongings under the bed until she pulled out a thick scrapbook. She climbed back on her bed, opened the scrapbook on her knees, and showed page after page of newspaper stories and photographs of her odyssey from Quebec to Palo Alto. There were pictures of Diane in a Montreal hospital, in a wheelchair, in a bed at the Stanford Medical Center, with her daughter. There was a telegram from Marc Johnson, the newly elected leader of the Parti Québécois, wishing her good luck.

After Diane had replaced her scrapbook, Ian Waters, a hospital social worker, entered the room with a large map of the city. He spread it across the bed and pointed to an area of Toronto where Diane could rent an apartment after the operation, when she would have to visit the hospital every day for more tests and physiotherapy on the treadmill and exercise bicycle. He also showed her the area where her former husband and daughter would be staying when they came to visit her. When Waters left, Diane said she wanted to be with her daughter, who was five years old, but her daughter wanted to stay with her father. "She likes my Yves, but only as a friend. She wouldn't want to live with him instead of her own father." Diane sighed aloud, and then said, "My husband would like to remarry me, you know. He told me that when he left me he didn't know my sickness. There were fights. . . ." Her voice trailed off. "You know what my husband said? He said he will wait for me until the day my boyfriend leaves. Yves is hoping my husband doesn't romance me."

Cooper had doubts from the beginning about Diane. First there was all the publicity, which made him uncomfortable, and he suspected all along that her size would be a problem, as would the scarring from the heart operation when she was six years old. The truth, he admitted, was that he was getting a little bored. Tom Hall's operation had been a great success and had made medical history and Cooper had done several more single-lung and lung-heart transplants that had all gone superbly, without a hitch. He said, "I thought these heart-lungs were getting to be routine and perhaps we needed a little excitement. Well, I'll tell you — we got it."

Diane's operation, on November 26, lasted six and a half hours, from just before midnight Monday to the pre-dawn hours of Tuesday. The donor was a woman, thirty-four years old, who had been killed in an automobile accident earlier in the day. It looked like a promising match-up because the donor was small, only five feet, two inches, but during the operation it became evident that the woman was considerably thicker than Diane, and her heart was too large. It was one of a series of catastrophes and near-catastrophes that began soon after Cooper's first incision and continued unabated for several days.

First, the scar tissue.

"Once you open the chest cavity, you have to divide the lung from all the scarring," Cooper explained. "The lung gets stuck to the inside of the rib cage with this dense scar tissue, which you have to cut through. There are thousands of little vessels. It's not like something you can just tie off. It's a flat surface, like a sponge welling up at you. When you anticoagulate and go through a lot of scar tissue, often you can't stop the bleeding."

Cooper suspected that the scar tissue around the heart and lungs was as much a reason for the Stanford surgeons' not operating as Diane's diminutive size. "They've lost a lot of people on the table at Stanford and other places because of this. She had all the scar tissue that we worried about, but we were able to do something about it. We used less anticoagulation than we'd normally use. Some people consider this unsafe, but we've had a lot of experience with our membrane oxygenator, the artificial lung. We have all our heart-lungs on half the heparin, the blood thinner, that we'd normally use. There were fears of clotting off the pump, which would have been a disaster, but I kept saying, 'Look, we've got to prevent bleeding. I'll take the chance.'"

The next surprise was the condition of Diane's lungs. "We sent them off to pathology and twenty-four hours later we got a call saying they were full of tuberculosis," Cooper said. "I checked the X-rays and, sure enough, there was a cavity in the right upper lobe. In retrospect, knowing where to look and what to look for, I can say, yeah — there it is. But it wasn't ordinary TB microbacteria. It was atypical. She had probably had it only for a few months, because of her weakened condition, but there was some concern because people in the operating room had been exposed to it. But it wasn't Diane's problem any more; if you want a radical cure for tuberculosis, just take out both lungs."

Next, the donor's heart.

In the operating room, when the MORE workers brought in the new heart in a stainless-steel basin, Cooper turned to Griff Pearson, who had been working on the donor, and said, "Jeez, that's a very large heart." It was a normal heart, and it was functioning well, but there was a lot of fat. It's because the donor was a chubby woman. Also, when you preserve the heart, you flush the coronary arteries with a very cold solution, which chills the heart quickly, preserves it, but causes swelling. I didn't think any more about it, but when it came time to close, here's this heart sort of welling up above the chest. If we closed then, the blood pressure would just go to pot. If we squeezed the heart, it wouldn't work. We tried closing, but the blood pressure would drop, so we'd open her up again and the blood pressure'd come right back up. I tried making room for the heart by removing excess fat. And I thought if I opened up the abdomen a bit — drained off fluid so the diaphragm could go a bit lower — we could make more room in the chest. I opened her belly to see, but there was no fluid. We didn't gain *anything* there. We even considered taking part of the new lung, probably the lower lobe of the left lung adjacent to the heart, to make room. That would reduce the amount of lung, which is all right, but we'd have to divide the airway, the blood supply, which in the lungs is always very tenuous. We never know if it's going to heal properly or not, so I was reluctant to do that. Normally we concentrate on the lung size. That's the match. You can't put in big lungs because you'd squeeze them, and you can't put in too-small lungs, because they won't fill the space. The heart comes along and, I mean — what's the heart?"

Cooper was still lying on his back on his office floor as he talked, and at this point he reached up, grabbed the edge of his desk and hoisted himself to his feet. "Come on along with me," he said. "I want to show you something. I need the exercise anyway." He limped to a small anteroom at the rear of his office and riffled through several large envelopes, looking for Diane's and the donor's X-rays. When he found them he snapped them to the display screen and flicked on the lights behind them.

"See those lungs," he said, pointing to the donor's X-rays. "They're actually a little smaller than Diane's, which is great. We like them a *little* on the small side. And look at the heart. I mean, the heart looks all right; I wouldn't have thought twice." Cooper then snapped Diane's X-rays to the display screen. One showed a frontal view of Diane's chest cavity. It did not look much different than the donor's. Cooper pointed to her spine, to her breast bone, to her heart shadows. "Looking at the X-rays of Diane and the donor from the front, you'd say no problem — a perfect match. But, look here. . . ." He pointed to the second X-ray, which was a side view of Diane's chest cavity, which showed that the donor was a much thicker, stouter, woman than Diane. "See all that fat tissue between the rib cage and the skin. That's all fat. She was a very fat donor. If you look at Diane's X-ray from the side, you'll see there's very little space between her spine and her breast bone. There wasn't enough room for the donor heart."

In the operating room that night, momentarily stymied, Cooper conferred with one of the other surgeons, Richard Weisel, a cardiovascular surgeon. Weisel told him, "Look, Joel, we have this problem all the time when we do coronary bypass surgery." He explained that a cold solution is also used in bypass surgery to preserve the heart when it is not beating, and surgeons often find they cannot close the breastbone because of the swelling that has taken place. "We just close the *skin*. We let the bones sit and come back in a week. The bones will move a bit, and if she tries to breathe it will be a problem, but she's on a ventilator anyway. When we come back in a week, usually the swelling has gone down and we're able to close."

"So that's what we did," Cooper said. "We closed the skin and sent her to Intensive Care."

It did not work. An hour later, Diane had a cardiac arrest. "I have no doubt it was caused by compression of the heart," Cooper said. "Even with the breastbone open, it was tight. And the inevitable post-operative bleeding added to the pressure." Cooper quickly opened her up again, pulled apart the breastbone and massaged Diane's new heart, reviving it. When the heart was beating again, he kept the bones spread apart with a metal retractor, which he left in. This time he went a step further and did not sew her up at all, which meant Diane could look down into her chest and watch her own heart beating and her lungs expanding and contracting. "We covered her with clear plastic as a protection, to keep it from drying out. She wasn't awake, but any visitors, like her boyfriend, could see right inside her and watch her heart and lungs working."

Later, Diane's heart slowed down again, threatening to arrest. Ron Grossman, the physician on duty, noticed it first and he called upstairs to ask Alex Patterson, the surgeon on duty, for instructions. Patterson told him to cut through the covering and massage the heart. Grossman is a respirologist, not a surgeon, and he had never massaged a heart. He suggested that it might be better if the surgeon came down to do it. "That'll take ten minutes," Patterson told him. "She'll be dead by the time I get down there." Grossman had no choice. He opened the covering and massaged Diane's heart and saved her life. She had two more arrests, and each time Grossman rushed to her side, opened the covering, reached in and massaged the heart again. "He did a great job," Cooper said. "She would have been dead now if he didn't do what he did. But you should have seen him the next morning. He was *something*. You know, walking about the halls, muttering, 'With these hands . . .'"

There was a worry of infection with Diane's chest cavity open, even under the covering, so Cooper next devised a technique to stretch the chest cavity in order to make room for the heart. He installed metal struts in the chest cavity, which kept the bones apart and enabled him to bring the skin over the opening and sew her up. To do this, he had to lift the skin away from the muscle and stretch it so that it would cover the opening. The skin is like a thin elastic sheet, which would later re-attach itself to the muscle. Innovating as he went, Cooper then devised a system of bolts and nuts and pulleys and weights — he borrowed most of the equipment from Orthopedics — which tugged constantly at the breastbone while she lay in bed recovering. "We invented most of it on the spot," Cooper said. "It was all a jury-rigged device."

Gradually, the stretching permanently enlarged the chest cavity and eased the pressure on Diane's new heart. An ironic twist is that by stretching the skin away from the muscle in order to close, Cooper inadvertently fulfilled Diane's request just before the anesthetist put her to sleep at the start of the operation. Cooper explained, "By pulling the skin together on each side, we brought her breasts in and up. I teased her about it the next day, but there's no doubt she has better-looking breasts now."

The following March, the week before she left Toronto to return to Montreal, Diane worked out on the exercise bicycle in the treadmill room. She was trying to rebuild her strength and endurance and put on weight. She still weighed only eighty-six pounds. She wore leather pants and a T-shirt that said, "I Left My Heart and Lungs in Toronto." There was some fuzz on her cheeks and upper lip, the effects of the cyclosporin, but she looked as vivacious and determined as ever as she pedalled. She no longer had to be attached to an oxygen tank. "Before I used to feel like a dog on a leash," she said. "Now Yves can't keep up with me." She talked of her plans, which included writing a book on her experiences, and then she apologized for all the trouble she had caused at the hospital. "Cooper didn't like me very much because I talk too much," she said. "I guess I was the worst patient he ever had. I'm sorry about that, but I wanted to live." As she pedalled, she stared down at the digital timer on the bicycle to see how long she had to go, then she pulled herself up like a child riding a bike with no hands and she said, "When you see the docteur, tell him I love him."

CHAPTER 12

Bernice
Champagne
in the ICU

THE OTHER NIGHT, just before supper, we watched a man bleeding to death. He was stretched out on an operating-room table and a team of medical professionals, eight in all — doctors, nurses, radiology technicians, respiratory therapists — tried to keep him alive, or to determine at least what was causing his life to leave him.

A Sengstaken-Blakemore tube was inserted in the man's mouth, plunged down his gullet all the way to his stomach, where a balloon device had been inflated in an effort to control the bleeding. In less than three hours, four pints of blood had been fed through a vein, keeping him alive, but also spilling out of his mouth, nose, and rectum. Blood splattered everywhere — floor, walls, curtains, on most of the staff present. The radiologist inserted a catheter in the man's exposed jugular vein and fed it into the body, searching for a route through an anatomical wilderness between the middle hepatic vein and the left portal vein. The manoeuvre can be compared to sending a search party out into a blizzard to look for someone missing on the prairie, somewhere between Winnipeg and Saskatchewan. During all this, a breathing machine called a ventilator acted to inflate the man's lungs for him, keeping up a macabre *fump-whoosh-fump-whoosh* beat.

All useless in the end. The man was a wreck, a forty-nine-year-old alcoholic who had been in hospital for nearly a month. He was also huge, bloated, with spindly legs and white, blotchy skin. Five people struggled to lift him to the operating table, after the radiologist had counted, "Okay, one . . . two . . . THREE!" The man had an ulcer, massive internal bleeding, and cirrhosis of the liver, the drinking man's nemesis. On his "history sheet," an entry for one night three weeks earlier said the man would probably bleed to death before morning. He didn't, and the fight against death continued. Makes no difference if the patient is a wasted, forty-nine-year-old alcoholic or a high-school student struck down by a truck while walking home from basketball practice. This is as it should be. If doctors are to be God-like in the wielding of their skills, it is good that they should also be God-like in their objectivity.

When it was time to leave, we walked along a corridor toward the elevators and passed a small room where relatives wait for news of their loved ones. The mother of the man on the operating table waited in a wheelchair, her eyes red and wet with worry and grief. One hand clutched a ball of Kleenex, the other rested on the shoulder of a young girl, about ten years old, who was crying. It was startling for an outsider, sometimes even a surgeon, to be caught unawares like this, suddenly to come upon evidence that a patient is a son — or father, wife, daughter — not just a medical challenge in a well-lighted operating zone. The realization was profoundly depressing.

Next morning, back at the hospital, a wander up to the Obstetrics wing seemed in order. Nothing is healthier than a healthy pregnant woman, nothing more cheerful than a new father's nose pushed against a window, nothing more optimistic than a roomful of howling, wrinkled, bald babies, even when they are making strange at the world. It takes the chill out of a cold November morning, and it is a helpful antidote to the night before.

Bernice, a fifty-seven-year-old woman, has been a patient in the hospital longer than anyone, has been there longer even than most of the doctors and nurses. She has been living in the hospital for twenty-three years. She contracted polio when she was ten, recovered and finished high school, took a business course and worked as a government secretary, then was struck down again, this time by lung disease. By that time she knew just about everyone at the hospital. She is a tiny, stooped woman who speaks in a squeaky, Mickey Mouse voice, because she has to speak in reverse, enunciating as she breathes in. She has had to learn to speak all over again, and it took years. At first, she could barely whisper, and years later she can still only talk in bursts, gasps. If anyone needs perspective, Bernice often says, "Why don't you spend . . . a day in a wheelchair? It'll drive you . . . nuts but you'll know . . . what you have."

Many people on ventilators are able to live at home, but Bernice has a private room in the Medical Intensive Care Unit. She moved there in 1980 from a smaller private room in the Norman Urquhart Wing. On the door of her room, a cardboard sign says, "Please knock." It is a cozy room, with a television, a small library, an old-fashioned upright telephone, a comfortable armchair for visitors. The walls are a rich, dark green. Framed photographs line a bedside bureau, one of them an autographed picture of former Governor General Ed Schreyer and his wife, Lily, taken at the 1982 Queen's Plate. Bernice likes to gamble and often plays poker with the respiratory therapists. Having a tube in her windpipe connected to a ventilator, which keeps her alive, does not stop Bernice from going to the ballet, to restaurants for lunch, or to the races. At the races, she advises, "Always bet across the board."

She likes it here, even though the walls are thin and her desperately ill neighbors are regularly wheeled in — and out — sometimes forever. She prefers being in a private ICU room instead of what she disdainfully calls "the floors," the regular hospital rooms for ordinary patients with ordinary ailments. "The 'floors' are the . . . pits," she says. "You get better-quality . . . nurses here and it's . . . just more interesting."

Today, Bernice sat on the side of her bed, wearing a lime-green housecoat, her slippered feet dangling over the side. "There was a big commotion . . . here the other night early . . . in the evening and the man next . . . door had a heart attack. He fell out of his . . . chair and smashed his face . . . on the floor. I heard a nurse . . . yelling, 'Get me a bag! Get me a bag!' I thought it was funny. This poor fellow's having . . . a heart attack and . . . the nurse's yelling . . . 'Get me a bag!' I thought she wanted . . . a paper bag but she . . . meant one of those plastic . . . bags they use to pump . . . oxygen into a patient. Anyway I'm listening to . . . this commotion next door . . . and can't breathe! I thought, oh . . . jeez wouldn't you know . . . what a time for my ventilator . . . to get gummed up! I didn't want to summon . . . help with all the commotion . . . so I climbed out of bed . . . crawled across the room to . . . my walker and hooked myself . . . to the reserve tank."

Bernice seemed to be able to get her way, probably because she knew she had the hospital over a barrel. When she arrived in Emergency twenty-three years ago, unconscious, she was given a tracheotomy, hooked to a ventilator, and given oxygen, which she stayed on for two years. The old ventilators could not blend oxygen properly, so Bernice got "pure" oxygen, which actually is air containing about 85 per cent oxygen. Normal room air contains about 21 per cent oxygen and Bernice needed air with 42 per cent oxygen. The oxygen she got was too rich and scarred her lungs, ruining them, making her dependent on a ventilator for life.

When she went for a walk, she relied on an aluminum walker, which she pushed ahead of her like a shopping cart. Each tank of oxygen lasts an hour, and if she was away too long, she had to hurry back to her room to plug herself back into the hospital's central supply. Sometimes during an animated conversation, the tube dislodged from the stoma, or small opening, in her throat and she reattached it as casually as one might brush back a stray lock of hair. She even managed occasionally to visit her home town, Port McNicoll, by having a friend load fourteen oxygen tanks in the trunk of his automobile for the day-long trip.

Bernice was looking forward to New Year's Eve. She had become friends with many of the nurses and doctors and respiratory therapists, but every New Year's Eve one of the anesthetists, who knows a thing or two about pain and suffering, drops by her room for a short, celebratory visit. It has become a tradition. "He comes by with two bottles . . . of the best French champagne. We drink one bottle and he . . . leaves the other with me."

I Thought
Maybe
I Died

EARLY IN the afternoon of Sunday, November 6, 1983, Robert Smith settled in to watch a football game on television at his apartment in Toronto's east end. It was a bleak, overcast day, with a raw whiff of winter in the air and Smith welcomed the diversion of the football game. It had been a long, busy week at the hospital.

As transplant co-ordinator of the Multiple Organ Retrieval and Exchange program, Smith worked in a narrow, crowded office on the second floor of the Bell Wing, one floor up from David Allen's Public Relations operation. The two men met occasionally to compare notes and map strategy, Allen the smooth and seasoned pro, Smith the young, irrepressible whiz kid.

The Multiple Organ Retrieval and Exchange program began in 1976 as a "medical awareness" program and much of the early work indeed was public relations, trying to convince people that signing over their organs — mainly kidneys and corneas, though exciting work was being done with hearts, lungs, and livers — was not a ghoulish thing but an act of generosity and compassion, a dying person's last chance to help another human being. An early brochure explaining the MORE program reads like a script from *Sesame Street*: "One day you may be involved in a motor vehicle accident or suffer a brain hemorrhage and be brought into hospital for treatment. If, after fighting for your life for hours or perhaps even days, your attending medical team decides you are dead, even though a machine still keeps your heart beating, will your death be for nothing?"

Transplantable organs include kidneys, corneas, hearts, livers, lungs, bone, skin, pancreas, and knees and other joints. Eyes can be removed up to twelve hours after death and stored for four days and the success rate for corneal transplants is excellent, 95 per cent. Skin taken from the back, chest, thighs, and buttocks is used as temporary dressing for large open burn wounds until the patient is ready for skin grafting. Pituitary glands provide a growth hormone used to treat a type of dwarfism in children that prevents them from reaching full growth. The extracted hormones of one hundred and twenty pituitary glands administered to a child can add two or three inches a year to the patient's height.

Smith was twenty-seven years old, but with his long brown hair, sparse moustache, and mottled complexion he looked like a high-school senior. On the job, he preferred running shoes, open-necked shirts, and corduroy trousers, usually under a flapping, unbuttoned white lab coat. Smith was the man in charge, the one who called the shots during the bargaining and manoeuvring behind the scenes of a major transplant operation, as in Tom Hall's case. To everyone in the office and around the hospital, though, he was "Rob." His desk was squeezed alongside everyone else's, at the end of the room, with a large poster of Dave Stieb, the Toronto Blue Jays pitcher, tacked to the wall beside his chair. He started work at the hospital in 1980, the year he graduated from the University of Guelph as a biological engineer. He had considered going on to become a doctor — his father and grandfather were doctors — but he had grown weary of studying, writing examinations, and the penury of student life. He especially did not want to face all the memory work medical school required. The work at the hospital was challenging, the pay cheques were regular, and so the dream of going to medical school faded more and more.

"Sometimes it just goes *crazy* around here," Smith said, recalling a shift that involved procuring organs for a multiple-transplant operation that involved an international search. The seeking is a delicate, tense business, always a matter of life and death, and this time he manned the phones for twelve hours straight, co-ordinating efforts in Toronto, Kitchener, Hamilton, Pittsburgh, and Chicago. He made most of the calls from home and he remembered there was a full moon that night. "Over the years we've noticed that when there's a full moon the number of kidneys we get always picks up. It happens all the time. They're always talking in Emergency about the crazy things that happen in full moons."

The function of MORE no longer was a matter of mere medical awareness or public relations. It had become a crucial hospital operation, with Smith and his staff on call twenty-four hours a day, seven days a week. The MORE program extended beyond the walls of Toronto General to include three other transplant hospitals in Toronto and transplant hospitals in Hamilton, Ottawa, Kingston, and London. A rivalry has even developed between Toronto General and University Hospital in London over which should be the dominant transplant centre in the province, if not the entire country. For the most part the rivalry is keen and high-minded, but as each accuses the other of jealousies, trickeries, power-plays, and assorted political shenanigans, it threatens to degenerate into something ugly and dangerous.

The MORE program is connected by telephone and computer to a vast and complex transplant network encompassing the North American continent. On any given shift Smith could be negotiating for a human liver to be shipped that night from Toronto to Pennsylvania; or for a heart, from Chicago to Toronto; or for a brain-dead donor on life support to be flown in from Kirkland Lake or Thunder Bay or Alabama. Smith often is on the phone to several North American centres, performing like a harried commodities broker. *Hello Pittsburgh, we have a liver . . . male, thirty-four, five feet eight, hundred and fifty pounds . . . carbon monoxide suicide. . . .* He books operating rooms, usually for late at night, when he can obtain adjacent rooms, one for the donor, one for the recipient, with the scrub basins in between. He requests police escorts and hires helicopters and jets as easily as most of us order pizzas.

In the 1960s, the newspapers dutifully reported each medical miracle and the stories quickly yellowed with age as newer miracles occurred. The transplanted human heart gave way to the transplanted baboon heart, which gave way to the transplanted plastic heart, which will give way to God knows what other epochal breakthrough around the next corner. Medical miracles that used to take years to become unnewsworthy now take only months, weeks. The more successful the transplant, the more it becomes a reliable therapeutic procedure, the more likely it is to be relegated to an inside page, or not reported at all — which probably is good news. Between the lines, of course, and on an intensely personal level, the drama never changes. Miracles remain miracles. But it is no longer remarkable that the eyes of a boy who watched a truck career toward him in Ottawa this morning might see a husband's smile in Toronto at nightfall. It has been reported in some journals that organ recipients feel a vague, unsettling awareness of another psyche merged with theirs — something odd, transcendent. A child dies, a child lives. We race on with astonishing equanimity to an era when it may well be possible to replace every major organ of the body.

Minutes after the opening kickoff, Smith heard the *beep-beep-beep* of the pager he always carries with him when he is away from his office. He was officially off duty that afternoon, but when he left the hospital Friday his department had been put on an alert and he had half expected to be interrupted.

The call came from Montreal.

"Do you need a heart for transplant?" the Montreal caller asked. She told Smith that a thirteen-year-old boy and his father from Rosemont, Quebec, had been killed in an automobile accident the previous day. Routinely, she reported the details of the boy's blood type (A+) and cause of death (cerebral trauma). Smith jotted down the information and said he would get back to her.

He called University Hospital in London, Ontario, one of the eight Ontario hospitals participating in the MORE program, to ask if anyone there needed a heart. London told Smith no heart-transplant patients were on the active list. Smith called Montreal again, reported that no hearts were needed, then asked about the donor's size. "We might be interested in a lung," he said.

This was no ordinary request, for single-lung transplants were still considered a rarity. Only thirty-nine had been attempted in the twenty years since the first, by Dr. James D. Hardy, had been carried out at the University of Mississippi Medical Center in 1963. After experimenting for years on dogs, Dr. Hardy had selected as his first human candidate John Russell, a fifty-year-old convicted murderer. Russell had advanced kidney disease, emphysema, and progressive cancer of his left lung. Hardy implanted a lung in him from a man who had died of a heart attack. Although the graft appeared to work, other organs failed, and Russell died eighteen days after the operation. A brief flurry of lung transplants followed in the next few years, but the results were not good. Of the thirty-nine patients who had received new lungs, seven had died within twenty-four hours, twenty-nine others within a month. The longest-surviving lung-transplant patient had lasted only ten months. Surgeons eventually came to regard the combined heart-lung transplant as the preferred procedure.

Montreal called Smith back five minutes later to say the boy was five feet, six inches tall and weighed between a hundred and twenty and a hundred and thirty pounds. Smith checked this with Tom Hall's measurements and told Montreal that Toronto might want the boy as a lung donor. Montreal said a doctor at Maisonneuve Hospital would call back as soon as possible.

As the day unfolded, Smith kept track of events in a Donor Log:

1410: Maisonneuve Hospital describes donor's blood gases, says respirator set at twelve respirations a minute, asks if Toronto wants lung. Toronto says surgeon involved will call him back. Montreal says should be no problems getting consent for lung donation.

1415: Smith calls Joel Cooper, Toronto General chief thoracic surgeon, who is paged by the hospital and reached at skating rink.

1430: Cooper calls Smith, says he will call Montreal directly.

1450: Cooper calls Smith to say Montreal doctor is trying to get consent for organ donation.

1510: Montreal doctor tells Smith family has given consent for lung donation, arrangements being made to transport body to Toronto.

1525: Cooper calls Smith, says the operation will be performed, asks for team from Toronto to fly to Montreal to pick up donor.

1535: Smith requests pressurized Lear Jet for Montreal trip.

1550: Smith tells Toronto General resident doctor to arrange for a respiratory technician to accompany him on plane to Montreal.

1555: Smith tells Montreal doctor to have ambulance ready at Montreal airport in two hours, with copy of donor's X-rays. Montreal doctor says he wants kidneys and X-rays returned to Montreal after Toronto operation.

1715: Toronto doctor tells Smith he needs EEG readings on donor so he can officially pronounce death when body arrives at Toronto General. Smith says he'll try to have them shipped with body.

1730: Smith checks airport, told plane leaving in five minutes, arriving in Montreal within the hour. Arranges for twin-engine plane to transfer body back to Montreal after lung operation.

2030: Smith calls Montreal doctor. Where's the body? Told body left for Toronto fifteen minutes ago.

2300: Donor body arrives at Toronto General.

Tom Hall arrived at Toronto General shortly before six o'clock that evening.

He thought it would be best to stay calm and maintain some sort of routine, so before he left for the hospital he finished peeling the apples for the apple pie and told Barbara to put the roast in the oven, drive him to the hospital, then get back home in time for dinner. "Everyone was getting antsy," Tom said. "They were all hot to trot to get my bag and coat, shouting, 'C'mon, Dad! Gotta get going!' I knew we had two or three hours, that they had to fly the other fella in from Quebec. . . . "

He had made tentative funeral arrangements for himself. He had selected the minister and made some suggestions for the service. He had organized his worldly affairs as best he could and put all the important documents in an envelope and told his oldest son, Donald, who was twenty-two, to give it to Barbara immediately if anything went wrong. He had spoken many times to all his children about the operation and the risks involved. He and Tammy Lee, his oldest daughter, who was twenty-four, had gone on a vacation together so he could be alone with her for a time.

"I didn't want anyone to misunderstand how serious this was. I didn't want any of them to think I was being sort of cavalier — throwing my life away. I told them if I didn't have the operation I was only going to last a year or so. And that it might be a hell of a year, because if my breathing went down I'd be a total invalid. I didn't want to live that way, I told them that too. I'd rather die than be an invalid. All I was gambling was a portion of a year of life and I told them I wasn't being all that brave."

As he waited in his room, members of the transplant team walked in, one by one, to say hello and talk about how historic the night would be. They gave him progress reports on when the plane left for Montreal and when it was expected back. Cooper dropped by and he and Tom chatted, then he patted Tom on the leg and gave him a thumbs-up. Minutes before the operation, Carolyn, Tom's youngest daughter, broke down and cried. She was seventeen years old. "We're very close,"

Tom said. "I told her to be strong, that if she broke down I'd probably break down too, and the whole family'd fall apart. So she pulled herself together, but soon as she heard I was going in, she broke down again."

When Cooper left Hall's room, he took an elevator to the operating rooms on the second floor of the Eaton Wing, inspected the two adjacent operating rooms and talked to members of the transplant team who were beginning the routine preparatory work for major surgery. Then he went for a nap. He knew it would be a long night. He was anxious to start because he had something to prove, to himself and to the rest of the world.

Cooper knew he had the right match-ups between donor and recipient. In his late fifties Hall was older than Cooper would have preferred, but the man's attitude was excellent, and he had undergone weeks of physical and nutrition therapy to prepare for the trauma of surgery and the ordeal of recovery.

Hall also had been given his first, pre-operative dose of cyclosporin, the new immunosuppressive agent. Cyclosporin had been discovered only seven years earlier, developed from fungus grown in the soils of Norway and Wisconsin, but already it has come to be regarded as a wonder drug. It works by suppressing the body's mechanisms to repel an invader, in this case the foreign tissue of a transplanted organ. More important, cyclosporin works its magic selectively, allowing the body's immune system to remain on alert against infection, a leading cause of death among transplant patients. In recent years, cyclosporin has been used in a world-wide flurry of transplant operations, with astonishing success, but this time it would be used for a lung transplant, and Cooper knew better than anyone that lungs are different.

He had performed a lung transplant the year before on James Franzen, a young man from Marietta, Georgia, whose lungs had been ruined by Paraquat, the potent weed-killer. Franzen had owned a tree farm in Tennessee and two nurseries in Georgia and he had been using Paraquat for ten years, usually with a hand sprayer and a tank strapped to his back. The last time out, however, he had used a ten-gallon power sprayer and had got soaked in the chemical, which seeped through his clothes into his body, causing irreversible lung damage.

Franzen clung to life in hospital on a respirator, but his doctor knew that the Paraquat poisoning was relentlessly fatal and that the only hope was a lung transplant. The Georgia doctor knew Stanford Medical Center in California had a heart-lung transplant program, but when he called he was told Franzen didn't qualify because the Stanford program was biased toward heart disease, not lung disease. Also, Franzen was on a ventilator, which kept him alive only as long as there was some lung function. His time was running out rapidly. When his lungs failed utterly, as they inevitably would with Paraquat poisoning, he would require a membrane oxygenator, really an artificial lung that enriches the blood with oxygen and recirculates it back to the body, working in much the same way as a kidney dialysis machine operates. Stanford did not have Toronto General's expertise with oxygenators.

The Georgia doctor next called New York and spoke to a surgeon who he knew was doing lung-transplantation work. The New York doctor agreed to take Franzen, but then had to decline because he did not have access to a membrane oxygenator and there was no way to keep the patient alive while waiting for a donor. The Georgia doctor then tried Massachusetts General Hospital, which did have a membrane oxygenator but no one to do the lung transplant. Cooper had trained at Massachusetts General and someone there remembered him and told the Georgia doctor to try him at Toronto General.

"We happened to be the only people in the world with a combined interest in lung transplants and membrane oxygenators," Cooper said. "They called me and I said, sure, we'll take him. I was rather naïve then, knowing so little about Paraquat, but I thought here's a young healthy fellow and we'll put in a lung. He's going to die anyway, so what's to lose?"

Franzen was flown to Toronto by air ambulance and arrived at the hospital at ten o'clock in the evening of August 24, 1982, breathing with his own lungs, but straining, and assisted by a ventilator. Cooper did not want news of the operation to get out, not just yet, but the story leaked in Atlanta and soon queries trickled in from all over.

"It hit the wire services before he even entered Canadian air space," Cooper said with some chagrin, as if outpointed again by the media horde. "We denied it. I asked David Allen to say we were bringing him up here so he could be put on our membrane oxygenator, not for a transplant. They kept feeding news of Franzen to the press down in Atlanta. Everyone was calling. There was a great deal of interest because up until then there had been only thirty-eight lung transplants done, world-wide, and of these only three people had lived more than a month. I didn't answer my telephone for three months, not here and not at home. Once a reporter from *Time* magazine called and asked if he could do an article on the operation. My secretary replied, 'He does *not* want an article in *Time* magazine.' And then, *Crash!* She hung up in his ear. He seemed shocked that we didn't want an article in *Time*."

Franzen was in terrible shape. His lungs were deteriorating quickly, and his liver and kidneys were damaged. The day after being admitted to Toronto General he was attached to the oxygenator, which pumped blood out of his body at a rate of six litres a minute, enriched it with oxygen and removed carbon dioxide, then pumped the blood back into the body. Franzen also was connected to a dialysis machine, an artificial kidney device, in an attempt to remove as much of the Paraquat as possible from the blood before the operation. He remained on both support systems for five days, until the MORE people found a donor, a young man in Atlanta who had been shot in the head. Ironically the man was shot the day before Franzen was flown to Toronto.

Cooper and his team, which included surgeons from Grady Memorial Hospital in Atlanta, transplanted a new right lung into Franzen in an operation that began before midnight on a Saturday and finished at dawn Sunday morning. Cooper was happy with the results, but two days later the Paraquat level in Franzen's blood rose unexpectedly and dramatically to five times what it had been at the time of the operation, a lethal level. No one could explain it, not Cooper nor anyone on the transplant team, not even the toxicology experts at the Chevron Company of California, where samples of Franzen's blood were sent every day for analysis. The explanation came later.

"We now know that the muscles can store very high concentrations of Paraquat," Cooper said. "After the transplant, when Franzen started moving around, we think the stuff poured out of his muscles into his blood and began to attack and damage the new lung. We had to put him back on the membrane oxygenator, this time for another seventeen days. The longest anyone has ever been kept alive on a membrane oxygenator was fourteen days, also at Toronto General."

Cooper discussed his next step with Franzen's family — a second lung transplant less than a month after the first, a measure he described as "heroic" and "a Star Wars bailout." The family consented. Besides going back on the membrane oxygenator, Franzen again was hooked to a kidney dialysis machine in order to lower the Paraquat level in his blood before the operation. Another call went to the MORE people for a donor, and after failing to find one in Canada, they extended the search across all of North America. In what turned out to be a remarkable coincidence, again they found a donor in Atlanta. The body was flown by air charter to Toronto with a medical team aboard to keep it functioning.

With lungs, time is of the essence. The organ must be transplanted quickly, unlike a kidney, which can be preserved on ice for up to twenty-four hours, or up to seventy-two hours on a perfusion machine that pumps a cold plasma solution through the kidney to maintain hypothermia and provide nutrients.

This time Cooper replaced Franzen's left lung, which had been rendered useless by the Paraquat, leaving the transplanted right lung in the body. The right lung was in bad shape, and by itself it could not keep Franzen alive; but it showed some function, however minimal. It was still better than his original right lung. Cooper also felt that for technical reasons it would be better to do a fresh transplant on the left side than to re-operate on the right side, which had been opened and closed only twenty-two days earlier. The new left lung worked splendidly almost immediately, and Franzen was taken off the membrane oxgenator. "By this time," Cooper remarked, "he was three people in one body. I don't think that's ever happened before."

While his lungs were fine, the rest of Franzen's body continued to deteriorate. His kidneys never recovered, so he remained on daily dialysis, and after the second transplant his muscles, ravaged by Paraquat, continued to erode and weaken. He could not sit up by himself or even raise one leg off the bed. He managed to breathe on his own for only thirty-six hours, then had to be hooked up to a ventilator because his body simply wasn't strong enough to use the new lungs. He remained dependent on a ventilator until the day, two months later, when he died in the Intensive Care room in what the autopsy report lists as an "extensive right cerebrovascular accident." The tube connecting the ventilator to the windpipe wore through the windpipe and broke through a major blood vessel, causing a massive hemorrhage. "It's one of those rare but well-recognized complications of being on a ventilator too long," Cooper said. "He stroked, and it killed him, but both lungs were working fine when he died."

The extraordinary measures to save Franzen cost about $400,000 — four times what a lung transplant would have cost if it had been performed on a Canadian patient. The amount was covered entirely by private medical insurance in the United States, where such heroic operations are considerably more expensive than in Canada's state-run medical plan. In fact, Toronto General made money on the Franzen case, and used it to subsidize the transplantation program.

At least with Hall, Cooper thought a year later, there was no Paraquat complication. His kidneys and liver were functioning normally. The preparatory work had been done. Apart from his diseased lungs, Hall was as healthy as a man in his late fifties could expect to be. It would be simply a matter of taking a lung from one man and installing it in the body of another, which was challenge enough, but Cooper had a trick up his sleeve and he was anxious to try it.

He napped for two hours. By four-thirty in the morning he was in the operating room, scrubbed and gowned, ready to begin.

The cyclosporin had been administered to Hall several hours before he was anesthetized. Cooper knew this would give him a huge advantage over other transplant patients, many of whom had died because of rejection, or, more often, because of infection. Infection is more troublesome with lung transplants than with other organ transplants. The immunosuppressive agent most often used before cyclosporin was prednisone, which interferes with wound healing as well as infection defences and thus promotes infection. In reviewing the many lung-transplant failures, Cooper detected a pattern: a patient would be doing well for about three weeks, then would suddenly die, almost always because of a disruption in the patient's airway, what Cooper calls "the bronchus connection." It is the crucial point of the trachea, the windpipe, slightly bigger than a thumb. It is where the cut is made for a lung transplant, and where the new lung is reconnected.

"We spent several years working out the process," Cooper said. "We weren't sure if the problem with the bronchus was rejection or something else. We went back to the dog labs where we'd take out a lung and put it back in the same dog. Now, there's no possibility of rejection here, because it's the animal's own lung, but the technical problems are the same — the connections, the disruption of blood supply. We gave the dogs drugs they would have been given if they'd been truly transplanted, in the same doses that would have been used to prevent rejection. What happened is we produced in the dogs the same type of bronchial problems that had been seen in the human transplant patients.

"We linked it to the prednisone. We had this problem with the airway, which is automatically open to the air and therefore subject to infection more than the connections of other organ transplants, which usually are deep in the body and therefore not as exposed to infection. Then we added prednisone, which interferes with wound healing, and so looking back it isn't surprising there were so many failures. When cyclosporin came along we found it was a good rejection drug and does not interfere with wound healing. It allowed us to avoid prednisone in the early post-operative period, about three weeks, until the wounds healed.

"I keep saying the lung is different, and one of the ways it is different is that the major artery to the lung brings in blood with little oxygen. It is not a nourishing artery. At this crucial point, at the bronchus connection, the blood supply is poor. When you cut these little vessels it may take two weeks for them to regrow and meantime there is no oxygenated blood reaching this tissue of the lung. That was the Achilles' heel of the ones that didn't work, the ones that died."

With Hall, Cooper tried a new surgical technique, really a corollary of an old trick surgeons have used elsewhere in the body for decades with little acclaim. He stretched Hall's omentum, a fatty appendage from the abdomen, and wrapped it around the bronchus connection. In the laboratory dogs, he had found that the omentum caused new blood vessels to grow through the suture line, enough to restore circulation to the bronchus connection in three or four days. The omentum is a jack-of-all-trades of the innards, with no specific function, though Cooper seems to have affection for it, and like generations of surgeons before him calls it "the policeman of the abdomen." It has a fatty, greasy texture, like chicken fat, and it can be stretched and pulled to just about anywhere in the body. Long before the coronary bypass, surgeons would haul up the omentum and wrap it around the heart in an early form of revascularization. It seals, mops up infection, and restores blood supply. People's lives have been saved by the humble omentum when they've suffered a perforated ulcer and couldn't make it to a hospital, or when they've been stabbed and left in an alley.

Hall's operation went smoothly. It took ten hours, but compared to Franzen's a year earlier, with all the complications arising from the Paraquat poisoning, it was a cinch.

"I remember coming around and I thought maybe I died," Hall said, when he recalled the afternoon after the operation, when he woke up in an Intensive Care room feeling weak and disoriented. "They let my family in two at a time and I had tubes down my throat and more valves and things on my arms and I was pointing at my wrist, trying to find out the time. It was all kind of hazy, dreamy, but I knew they were thinking I was trying to pull these things out of my arm. I could hear them. They were saying, 'He's trying to pull the tubes out. He must be hurting.' Then the next two came in and I tried to find out again what time it was. I was under so many drugs I didn't know if it was real or if I was dreaming or if I was dead. Everything was misty and out of proportion, and I thought maybe this is it, maybe I died and this is how it is, seeing your wife and kids coming into the room, two by two. I have a neighbor who sells coffee to hospitals and he had left his card in the room and I noticed it on the table beside me — Club Coffee. That's when I knew I was in the living world. I couldn't dream that one up."

While recovering, Hall made his own contribution to the storehouse of medical knowledge. Late one afternoon he became convinced he was experiencing a form of organ rejection, but the doctors wouldn't believe him. It is difficult to diagnose rejection in a lung transplant without doing an open-lung biopsy, a serious procedure that can't be done every time someone has a hunch that rejection is happening.

"There were about seven doctors in my room, all high-powered guys, and I was trying to tell them I was having trouble breathing. They kept telling me that the tests showed everything was all right and that I should be able to breathe fine. Tests, tests — *tests*! So I said, 'Look, you've all had your shot, could I have a crack too? Why not give me a shot, knock me out, and see if my breathing returns to normal. If it does, I've got no control over it — it's all in my head. If it doesn't, then we've got a physical problem.' They said, 'Hey, good idea!' So they did just that and they could see I was having difficulty. It was one of two small rejection bouts I had after the operation. What's interesting is that they concluded the patient might feel the symptoms of rejection and it would be good policy to listen to him."

Hall experienced some of his post-operative breathing difficulties because he was still getting signals from the old lung, which was still part of him, hollering for more air. He continued to pant, heeding the commands of the old lung, and only after some time and a considerable act of will was he able to relax, take deep breaths, and attain a new breathing rhythm that eventually became natural.

Hall remained in Intensive Care only a week, then, five weeks later, he left the hospital, walking, after a little party in a room on Joel Cooper's Floor in the Norman Urquhart Wing. The transplant team reassembled to say goodbye over cakes, cookies, coffee, and tea. Cooper, haughty and ham-handed as usual when it comes to public relations, had insisted that the story be given exclusively to *The Globe and Mail*. This caused a lot of grief for David Allen, whose job was to maintain good working relationships with all three Toronto dailies as well as television and radio. Cooper remained adamant. He liked and trusted Joan Hollobon, *The Globe and Mail*'s long-time medical reporter, so she would have the story first. As it turned out, Hollobon had been assigned to city desk and the Tom Hall story went to another reporter. It appeared the next day, but it was tucked well inside the newspaper.

A year later, at his office out by the airport, Hall looked healthy, vigorous, clear-skinned and — yes, it was obvious — thick-haired. Hirsuteness is one of the unexpected side effects of cyclosporin, and, though Hall's hair remained silver, it definitely was thicker, more lustrous, and the small bald spot at the back of his head was now fully covered over. "It's grown new hair all over my back too," Hall said, running his hands over the sides of his head. "The hair on my body used to be all grey, but now it's black and long and sort of shiny. I've got to shave every day now. I didn't used to." Some in the business of raising money for hospitals actually have explored ways of marketing cyclosporin as a baldness cure, figuring it might do for Toronto General what Pablum did for the Hospital for Sick Children across the street. Hall continued, "Cooper says it might be a cure for baldness. He says he might get out of the surgery business and start making some real money."

Hall keeps the cyclosporin in a bottle in a desk drawer at the office and twice a day he measures his dosage into a graduated tube, pours it into a glass, mixes it with milk, and drinks it. The dosage has been lowered twice since the operation, but Hall knows he will remain on the drug for the rest of his life. "It's not that bad tasting, kind of spicy, oily. It's supposed to be the price of gold but because it's still considered experimental I'm only charged a nominal fee, five dollars a fill-up. A bottle lasts me three weeks." (A 50-ml bottle of cyclosporin costs the hospital $172.40, and in a seven-month period from April to November in 1985 it used 1,288 bottles, or $222,051.20 worth.)

Hall had thought about the donor as someone generous and anonymous who one day had left life at his doorstep and walked away. He was shocked and saddened when he heard that the lung had come from a thirteen-year-old boy out for a Saturday morning drive with his father. "I could have coped with it better if I knew it had been an older person. I don't know if I should try to contact the mother. Maybe she's put it all in the past and buried it, or maybe she'd be happy to know what it's done for me, what her son contributed. You're not supposed to communicate directly with a donor. My wife wrote a beautiful letter to her, care of MORE, but we never heard back. I guess she could find me easier than I could find her."

Rob Smith had worked on co-ordinating Tom Hall's transplant around the clock and stayed on his feet twenty-six hours, which is not unusual. "The adrenalin keeps pumping like mad," he said. There was a slight complication getting the donor body back to Montreal. When he called the air ambulance people who had transported the body to Toronto, they said they were not allowed to transport a dead body. "What do you mean?" Smith asked, angrily. "You did it before. You flew the body here." The air ambulance people told him that the body may have been dead, but it had been on a life-support system. Under the Ambulance Act, they could not transport a dead body to Montreal. Smith called the coroner to check on this and he repeated what the air ambulance people had said — the dead body could not be transported back to Montreal. In desperation, Smith called several body-transferring services, and they all told him of a multitude of requirements for a body being shipped out of the province, including one that the body be embalmed. The doctor at Maisonneuve Hospital had promised the boy's mother that the body would be returned within ten hours and the deadline was approaching. Finally, a man at one of the body-transferring services said he'd do it and wait for the repercussions.

The last item in the log says the pilot picked up the body at the hospital's emergency department at 7:45 Monday morning, drove it to the Toronto Island Airport, rented a plane, took off at 8:30, and got the body back to the Montreal hospital by 10:30, missing the deadline by four hours. The delay distressed Smith and everyone else at MORE, but a lot had happened in between.

CHAPTER 14

Hospital Junkies, the Drug Vault, and Gypsies in the Foyer

NORMA BUTLER, the supervisor in Admitting, opened a small brass-plated case and pulled out a cigarette. It was nine-thirty on a warm April morning and the Admitting office was busy. Busier than usual, Butler thought, reaching for a sheet of paper to check admissions and discharges for the weekend. "Ah, there, you see," she said, in a mild Scottish accent, "a hundred and thirty-seven admissions, sixty-five discharges. That's why we're having difficulty finding beds."

Computerized sheets wide as a broadsheet newspaper list everyone admitted by name, age, and ailment, with time of admission, the admitting doctor's name, and with special codes such as "C2HS" and "NUOR" and "GW3E." These are the abbreviations for the different wards in the different wings on the different floors (C2HS means College Wing, H-south ward, second floor). Butler, in a well-tailored skirt and sweater, with primly coiffed grey hair, looked like a young Beatrice Arthur of the television sitcom *Golden Girls*.

Even though renovators were at work ripping down old walls, hammering up new ones, a process which often required an entire ward to be relocated from one wing to another, Butler knows the hospital as well as her own house. Obstetrics and the nursery had always been on the ninth floor of the Norman Urquhart Wing, for example, but they had been temporarily relocated to the second floor of the College Wing. "It's a bit more miserable, being an older building," Butler said. The tenth floor of the Eaton Wing is for Chest Medicine, the eleventh for Neurology and Hematology, the twelfth for Cardiology, the thirteenth and fourteenth for General Medicine. The fifth, sixth, and seventh floors of the Bell Wing are also for General Medicine, which encompasses general malaise — fever, cramps, aches, nausea, anything Emergency would list as NFW — worrisome enough for a person to be admitted. The eighth, ninth, and tenth floors of Eaton South are for General Surgery, things like gallbladders and appendices. Neurosurgery is on the tenth floor of the Eaton Wing, Gynecology on the sixth. The second floor of the Bell Wing is for Urology, the third and fourth floors are for Orthopedics, the seventh is for patients dying of AIDS (Acquired Immune Deficiency Syndrome). Endocrinology is in the basement of the College Wing. Gastroenterology is on the third floor of the Gerrard Wing.

The Admitting office opened at seven and the worst of the morning rush was now over. Outside Butler's office, a few people sat on the chairs and couches in the lobby, suitcases on the floor at their feet, waiting for a bed to become available. There had been only one brief altercation, about thirty minutes earlier, when two men who seemed to be brothers stepped out of a blue van in the driveway and entered the lobby. One of the men wore a three-piece suit and appeared to be on his way to his office; the other had a day's growth of beard and wore dusty jeans and a plaid lumberjack shirt, with one sleeve nearly torn off.

"You've got to go through with this," the well-dressed man said, plunking himself down on a couch beside the other man.

"Why don't you just bugger off?" his companion said.

"Look, George, I promised I'd bring you here and . . ."

"*Bugger off!*"

"What I'm . . ."

Bam! The man in the lumberjack shirt backhanded the man in the three-piece suit, knocking his glasses off, then jumped up, stomped out of the lobby, climbed into the van, and drove away, burning rubber. The man in the suit retrieved his glasses, sat holding his head in his hands and said, "Well, shit."

Some of the patients waiting in the lobby had known for weeks, months, that they would be checking in on this Tuesday morning. They had been referred to the hospital by their physicians for elective surgery — a gallbladder, a lung tumor, a heart bypass, a hernia, a hysterectomy. The admitting supervisor's job is very like that of the manager of a large downtown hotel in a questionable neighborhood of Lourdes, with buses arriving every morning with a new cargo of tourists, most of whom look as if they'd been into the gin the night before. It would be a hotel that always operates at 90 per cent capacity, seven days a week, fifty-two weeks a year. And the guests always arrive sick, often perilously sick. The manager has to contend with at least a dozen or so deaths a week. And foul-ups — reservations that can't be honored, elective surgery postponed, someone assigned to the wrong room, a non-smoker bunked in with a pack-a-day man, a guest who heaved a room-service breakfast at the wall, another who pinches the cleaners' bums.

Butler explained the room rates charged to OHIP, the provincial health insurance scheme. The standard four-bed ward was listed at $436 a day, a two-bed semi-private was $466, a private $486, a large private $491. "We have only a few of the large privates, maybe a dozen," Butler said. "Some patients like them so they can do business in the hospital. Some bring their secretaries in to take dictation." Patients from outside the country are charged about twice as much, $925 a day for a standard-ward bed. "If it's an emergency patient with no money and no hospital insurance he'll still be admitted. If we ever collect, it's a plus."

The worst times in Admitting are when patients arrive for elective surgery and have to be told their operations have been postponed. They have arranged for time off from work, hired babysitters. Some might have visited their lawyers, or priests, to make sure other matters were in order. There are patients who arrive having made hospitalization payments for years, thinking it guaranteed them a private or semi-private room, but are told only ward-beds are available.

"I really feel sorry for people who've been paying for private coverage and we have to put them in a four-bed room," Butler said. "It means all that private coverage has been wasted."

There are no guarantees in the hospital, but some patients work the system better than others. "Oh yes," Butler said, smiling, "you can break into a semi-private room. It means taking someone else out and putting him in a four-bed room — or even a private room. Let's say we have a semi-private male bed available and there's another man at the end of the hall in a private room. Then, say, we have a lady in Emergency who requires a room on that floor, but there are no lady beds. We never put men and women in the same room, except in Intensive Care, where they're so sick it doesn't make any difference. What we'd do is ask the man in the private room to go to the semi-private, which opens the private for the lady.

"Then there are the obstreperous patients who always manage to wangle a semi-private or private. They're assigned to a four-bed room, but they start acting loud and obnoxious, disturbing their roommates, and we have no choice but to move them out into a semi-private or private. It's dreadful to give in on a principle, especially when we know we're being manipulated. Sometimes I'm tempted to say, 'No! You're staying put!' But you have to think of the other patients. It's the same all over, eh? The squeaky wheel gets the oil."

There are patients who loathe being in hospital. They leave as soon as they can, sometimes climbing into their clothes in the middle of the night and exiting without bothering to say goodbye — or to check out. And there are patients Butler calls "hospital junkies." They love hospitals. They make lifelong friends with other patients. They joke with the nurses and orderlies. They rave about the food. They stroll the corridors as if they were recuperating at a private spa. When they are discharged, they walk around shaking hands and hugging people. Some of them later send cards and letters to the staff, or return to ask if they can work somewhere in the hospital as volunteers, answering phone calls, watering flowers in the boutique.

"Really, there aren't many foul-ups, not for a place this huge," Butler said. "There's the odd typing error and an incoming patient winds up in the wrong wing or the wrong ward, but it's usually discovered quickly and corrected." There are times, however, when a foul-up is so horrendous that all you can do is laugh — or weep. When Susan MacKay went to check out after having delivered her baby in March 1986, the clerk handed her husband, William, an invoice for the amount owed. According to Invoice No. 185000032723, which the MacKays now have framed in the baby's room, the full amount for Susan's five-day stay came to $1,329,901. The computer in the admissions office had listed her as having checked in on March 7, 1907.

Jack Kugelmass is manager of Social Work at the hospital. His office is on the eighth floor of the Bell Wing, a floor that looks more like a storeroom or a warehouse attic than a hospital, though Ophthalmology is right next door. "Did you know that ophthalmologists have one of the highest rates of mental breakdown?" Kugelmass asked. "They're right up there with psychiatrists."

Kugelmass is bright and articulate, a thoughtful and gregarious manager with a doctorate in social work. When he allows his hair to grow long, he looks like a first violinist in a symphony orchestra, but his usual greeting is, "Boy, have I got a deal for you." This is because he is always getting donations of underwear, socks, shirts, sweaters, hats, coats, jackets, shampoo, soap, and other items from well-intentioned altruists who want to help needy patients. Many of the items are manufacturers' rejects, such as a recent shipment of boxes and boxes of Colgate toothpaste that were perfectly acceptable except that the tubes were not sufficiently filled and therefore could not be sold over the counter. There is more than enough stuff for the needy patients, so Kugelmass often tries to make trades, such as a carton of improperly stitched Harvey Woods knickers for a box of floppy discs for his Apple computer.

Kugelmass gets around. He and his twenty social workers cover all parts of the hospital. On a moment's notice, one of them might be sent down to Emergency to investigate an indigent arrival, or to sort out a disagreement in Admitting, or to explain hospital procedures to someone waiting for an organ transplant.

A lot of social work business comes from the nurses, who know patients better than anyone. One day there may be a patient with cancer, the next day a teenager who's had a leg amputated. The social worker tries to help the patient to cope, and works with parents and spouses. Often the worker's task is to sort out the nuts and bolts of welfare and unemployment payments, or subsidized housing, while the patient recuperates.

Kugelmass's most recent bit of social work involved an eighty-six-year-old woman who appeared in Emergency on a weekend. She lived alone and had fallen and cracked her pelvis. She stayed for a day at Toronto East General Hospital, then was discharged. Hospitals are not keen on old people seeking admission because they know once they are admitted, it is often difficult to get them out.

"Twenty-five per cent of the beds at East General are occupied by old people waiting for nursing homes," Kugelmass said. When the woman's pain persisted, she took herself to Toronto General's Emergency Department. There the senior doctor on duty, Lorne Greenspan, examined her and discovered the cracked pelvis and blood in her urine. He did not have to admit her, but he did, because she was eighty-six and because she lived alone — and because Kugelmass had championed her case.

It was what he called a "social admission." Most often these are old people who live alone, or who are not wanted by their offspring, or who can't pay their bills at a nursing home. They

are frail, confused, and often a nuisance, frequently soiling
their beds or peeing on the nursing-home carpets.

"There's a word for it," Kugelmass said. "It's called 'a dump.'
We have about fifty patients like this and some of them have
been here two years, some longer. There is no quota on them,
but the hospital's policy is the fewer the better.

"The problem is some people know how to use the system.
If you come in and say grandma is on her own and has nowhere
to go, most doctors will say they can't take her in. But, if
you bring grandma to Emergency and say she fell and is bleeding
from the rectum, or she keeps setting fire to herself, they might
let her in. Sometimes knowing the system is knowing who's
on duty. Older doctors usually are more experienced, and can
act more independently, and often they're more compassionate.
The key is to get her *admitted*. Once you've gained access,
it's hard to turf someone out. It's actually against the law
to put people who can't look after themselves on the street."

The hospital likes patients to be obedient and submissive.
These people are called "good patients," but it does not mean
they get better treatment; probably they will get worse treatment, because they are easier to ignore. The difficult, snarly,
querulous patient is more likely to get what he needs, minimize
mistakes, and emerge from the hospital intact. But for this
he will be labelled a "non-compliant" patient.

"Non-compliant is a word that's big around here, but I see
it as a strength," Kugelmass said. "When doctors come in as
patients they're certainly not compliant. I know I'd be a terrible
patient. But one thing I would do is tell the doctor that he's
off the hook. I'd say, 'Listen, doc, I don't really want you to
cure me. You're off the hook. Just tell me what's wrong so
I can make up my own mind.' The trouble is, most people
worship the doctor as some sort of pseudo priest *and he responds
to it that way*."

Social workers and doctors tend to be natural adversaries
in a hospital. Social workers sometimes make pests of themselves by reminding patients of their rights. They might
comment to a number of patients suffering from the same
disease, perhaps a group on dialysis, that they should get
together and talk about their problems. Doctors are never happy
when this happens. It means the patients might compare notes
and detect disparities in their treatments, even errors, which
might make the doctors look bad or raise the awful spectre
of a lawsuit. The patients might also form a coalition, a power

base, against the doctors, or against the hospital itself. It makes life difficult.

Most of Kugelmass's social workers are women, which heightens the adversarial relationship with the doctors, most of whom are men. "A lot of the clashes in a hospital are between the sexes," Kugelmass said. "The nurses talk of how doctors never say good morning or thank you, and the doctors tend to lump female social workers in with the nurses. If the social workers are men, the doctors think they're bleeding hearts. Most doctors don't take social workers seriously. They call them 'sociable workers.' If you want to survive around doctors, you should know two things. Doctors trust people who have expertise, and, more important, people who will go to bat for them.

"Doctors really aren't a bad lot. They're called sons of bitches and uncaring bastards, but I've never really met an uncaring son of a bitch of a doctor. They're myopic about a lot of things, but they've given up a lot — especially in Canada, with medicare. It's not just all the years in medical school, then interning and being a resident. It takes time to become a good lawyer too, or a good journalist. What doctors have given up is a lot of power and prestige. The bright kids today don't want to be doctors. They want MBAs so they can get into the take-over business. I know I wouldn't want to spend my days looking up somebody's asshole."

George Tsallas, manager of Pharmaceutical Services, has a cramped, windowless office in the basement of the Eaton Wing in an area where windows and doorways are protected by steel bars and an elaborate alarm system. Tsallas oversees the hospital's supply of narcotics and other restricted drugs, which are kept in a high-security bank vault. Anyone entering this area without knowing what codes to punch, or after hours, sets off an alarm that automatically alerts the hospital switchboard, which contacts the nearest police station.

Toronto General buys drugs and medications on a weekly basis from around the world. The hospital has teamed up with other hospitals in order to negotiate better deals, which helps the smaller Canadian hospitals that don't have Toronto General's bargaining muscle. The hospital spends about $15 million a year on drugs, medications, and various intravenous solutions, all of which are Tsallas's responsibility.

There are thousands of items, from acetaminophen — a non-narcotic analgesic such as Tylenol — to zinc sulphate. There are controlled drugs, restricted drugs, and experimental drugs. There are antidotes such as "tear gas exposure decontamination solution for skin." There are hemorrhoidal balms, wild cherry syrup, and antifungals. There are serums and antitoxins that include gas gangrene antitoxin, hepatitis B immune globulin, and something called "Minnesota Antilymphoblast Globulin." There are antibiotics for anything from an abscessed tooth to syphilis. There are activated charcoal tablets for flatulence. There are tranquillizers, antidepressants, hypnotics and sedatives, and amphetamine stimulants. There are vaccines for cholera, diphtheria, measles, mumps, poliomyelitis, tetanus, typhoid, and the plague.

Tsallas must know them all, and must make sure all medication orders are correctly abbreviated. For example:

a.c. means "before meals"
b.i.d. means "twice daily"
c.c. means "with meals"
h.s. means "at bedtime"
O.D. means "in the right eye"
O.S. means "in the left eye"
p.o. means "by mouth"
q.i.d. means "four times daily"
stat. means "at once"

There can be no substitions. The abbreviation "o.d." has been used at some hospitals to mean "daily" but it is forbidden at Toronto General because it could easily be mistaken for "O.D.," which means "in the right eye." Any medication that is required daily is not abbreviated. It is listed as "Daily," as in:

Digoxin 0.25 mg Daily p.o.

The hospital was changing to a new system of distributing drugs within the hospital, called a "unit-dosage system," whereby drugs would be centrally and individually packaged before going to the various departments. It was designed to be a safeguard against staff people abusing drugs, a direct result of investigations at the Hospital for Sick Children, where thirty-six babies had died mysteriously, most from apparent overdoses of the heart drug digoxin.

Under the old system, there was a strict procedure for the disposal of any narcotics left over on a surgical tray. Years ago, they were supposed to be flushed down a drain by two people, each of whom signed a form to attest that the drugs had been properly disposed of; nothing could be done if the two people colluded to steal drugs from the hospital.

Tsallas's latest worry was heroin, which had recently been approved for use in Canadian hospitals. There was no supply of heroin in the pharmaceutical vault, but a special committee was examining guidelines for the drug and ways to bolster hospital security when the first shipment arrives. Nobody has ever broken into the vault at Toronto General and the hospital has been remarkably free of narcotic misadventures, but Tsallas was taking no chances.

"It has happened at other hospitals in Toronto," he said. "Thieves have broken into rear doors using crowbars, in broad daylight. Someone with a gun walked up to a wicket at a hospital in Alberta and ordered one of the pharmacy employees to take him to the vault."

A report Tsallas was preparing on the use and control of heroin in the hospital said a kilogram of heroin, obtained from a manufacturer in Europe, would cost about $3,000. "This is pure stuff," he said. "It can be diluted down many, many times. The street value of a kilogram of heroin would be about $3 million."

When approved for use at Toronto General, the heroin would be shipped by bonded couriers to the hospital, then delivered directly to Tsallas's pharmaceutical department.

"Sure I worry about it," he said. "Once it gets here, it's *our* problem. I'm responsible."

When Al Trupp reports for duty at the hospital, often as early as six-thirty in the morning, he shines his shoes. It is an old habit from his days with the Royal Canadian Mounted Police. The Mounties know that neatness counts, that it ranks up there with always getting their man. When bivouacked in some isolated rathole of the country, somewhere on the frozen canvas of the Barren Ground, nothing brings on the numb horror of *weltschmerz* like an unkempt room and muddy boots.

Al Trupp is head of security. His office is on the ground floor of the College Wing, in a small, bunker-like cubicle that could probably withstand mortar shells. Two brass hose-couplings sit on a board on the radiator as ornaments. The floor of Trupp's office is hard — a bathroom floor. Tangerine-colored curtains on the window nearly soften the view of the parking lot outside. There is a fire extinguisher on the floor in front of his desk. There is a Security-Officer-of-the-Month plaque on one wall and a portrait of the Queen on another.

Trupp's hair is white; he is balding slightly, and he has a moustache. This day he wore a gleaming white shirt and a blue tie with thin diagonal stripes. He sat at his desk talking on the telephone to someone about a shipment of material, which, in the military way, he pronounced "materi-EL."

When the phone call ended, Trupp got up from his desk and walked to the metal filing cabinet across the room. After rummaging for nearly five minutes, making loud crashing sounds, he pulled out a large manila folder and brought it to his desk. The folder contained applications for the job of security officer, which pays $17,971.20 the first year, rising to $18,948.80 the second year. "But there are all sorts of benefits working at a hospital," he said, without going into detail. He pulled out three of the applications, sorted them, then tapped a finger on the first one. "One has a bad stutter and the other is stupid," he said. "But I'm impressed by this third one." What impressed Trupp about the third one was that he had come from another country, was married with no children, but he mentioned in his application that he supported two illegitimate children back home. "That shows a sense of responsibility," Trupp said.

Trupp's twenty-two security officers patrol both Toronto General and Mount Sinai Hospital across the street. They move in "a crisscross pattern," he said, and their orders are to "keep their eyes open and their mouths shut." The officers carry two-way radios, but they do not carry guns. "I know, I know, there have been shootouts in some big hospitals in New York, Chicago, and Detroit, but I don't ever want to see the day when armed people are necessary in a Canadian hospital."

The hospital security guards are sworn in as special constables, which means they can write out parking tickets. They must have at least grade ten, and, though there are no height requirements, Trupp prefers tall officers. "Short men are challenged more than tall men," he said. There are no women officers, but Trupp would like at least one in case something nefarious was suspected in a women's locker room somewhere in the hospital.

Trupp was born on a farm near Russell, Manitoba. With his family the youngster moved to Windsor, Ontario, where his father worked in a Ford automobile factory. He tried working in the factory on school vacations, but it never appealed to him, so he joined the RCMP and went off to train in Saskatchewan. He worked for seven years in New Brunswick, then was stationed in Hanover, Germany, where his job was screen-

ing brides for Canadian servicemen. "It was important that
they didn't get involved with the wrong sort of women, for
security reasons," he said. He ended his career with the
Mounties in Ottawa, working in security and intelligence. He
started at Toronto General on January 1, 1971, as manager of
security and fire services. He loves the place.

"We have three duties, to protect patients, staff, and hospital
assets."

"Is fire the number-one threat?"

"No, our primary job is security against thieves and the
likes of that."

He walked to the filing cabinet again and after more crashing
and banging, returned to his desk with more manila folders,
all containing reports of incidents. "One thing we might be
expected to do is look after a principal witness who needs
protection. He may be in hospital with a gunshot wound and
there may be people who would rather that he not be alive.
What we have to do is move the fellow to another room so
they can't find him. We advise the information desk that if
someone comes looking for Mr. X to notify us and we'll
determine if the visitor is a legitimate relative. If he's not,
we call the police and ask them to interrogate the visitor to
see why he wants to see this patient. This is an extreme
example. It might come up maybe once a year."

He opened another folder. "Sometimes we'll get a husband
or a boyfriend who's not in accord with an abortion that's
taking place. They may come in making threats and causing
a big hoopla. Our duty is first to the patient. We tell them
if they have a beef there are legitimate avenues of grievance.
Sometimes we have to escort them out of the hospital and
tell them not to come back."

The next folder contained information on an incident across
the street at Mount Sinai Hospital a year earlier. One of the
security officers had encountered a band of gypsies camped
in the foyer. "There were about twenty of them and they were
determined to spend the night because one of their elders was
sick in an upstairs room. They had a spokesman who explained
that it is their custom to camp round the clock when one of
the elders is sick. They had bedrolls and tents and food. They
weren't violent, just a nuisance. We had to explain that it
is an unwritten policy not to have more than two visitors per
patient, but it took about two hours to resolve. We had to call
the police in. We come into these ethnic, cultural things often."

A security problem Trupp was keeping an eye on involved a man who used to work at the hospital as a lab technician. He retired five years ago, but he kept returning to the hospital, usually in the early hours of the morning, after midnight. He headed straight to the lab where he used to work and he would sit on his old stool and his old bench and smoke cigarettes. "There would be butts and ashes all over the place and we were concerned about a fire," Trupp said. "We usually just escorted him out and that would be the end of it. He always left quietly. We hadn't seen him for some time, but he was in again this morning, just before two o'clock. My men say he's becoming a little more aggressive. I'm not a prophet, but, judging from experience, he'll probably get worse and worse and we'll have to put him in the hands of psychiatry."

Trupp opened another folder, this one with information on a visitor to Emergency who had come to the hospital late at night the previous weekend and abused the receptionist. According to the receptionist, the man is a regular visitor who always comes in complaining of all sorts of pains but when he is examined there is nothing wrong with him. This time, the man "slammed things around . . . spit on the receptionist's computer terminal." Trupp seemed to be engrossed in the report. He read it in silence for a few minutes, then said, "This is interesting. She says in the report the man had a black beard and was crazy-looking."

The next folder told of an incident that involved two employees in Housekeeping, one of whom has worked at the hospital for twenty-two years. Trupp investigated it himself. "This is an example of what we call crisis-intervention. Apparently this woman — I can't give names because it's confidential — got so irate that she punched her supervisor in the mouth. When I arrived on the scene there was a whole bunch of people, all het up and screaming. I removed the woman and brought her to my office. I wrote out a letter directing her to leave the hospital for a while to allow for a cooling-off period, then she could go through a grievance procedure. That's not an everyday occurrence. We get something like that maybe once a month. This is a life-and-death institution. Stress builds up here, but you have to keep a cool head. We've had nurses kicked and bitten and their hair pulled by patients."

Trupp's secretary, Lita Vlassopoulos, had a call on the line, someone from Personnel who wanted to know about the applicants for the security officer job. Trupp excused himself and picked up the receiver. He listened for a few moments, then told the caller, "I don't want them if they're not bright. . . ." He listened a while more, saying, "Yes . . . yes . . . yes." Then he interrupted. "Stutters? What would he do on the radio then?" Trupp put his foot down. "I have sympathy for anyone who needs a job," he said, "but I think the time has come when we can't afford the halt, the lame, and the blind." When he finished, he got up from his desk and shut the door.

"We had a funny one yesterday," he said, opening another folder, which contained information on a small extortion ring in the hospital. Someone in Housekeeping had been telling job applicants that for $1,000 he could get them a job in the hospital. "This person has no influence at all in hiring," Trupp explained, "and he tells the people he can't *guarantee* them jobs, but for $1,000 — $500 now, $500 later — he would do his best. We were to monitor the situation and watch for money passing hands. It turned out that the person being extorted was not much interested in the job. He eventually got a job elsewhere, but while we were monitoring the situation we found there may be *ten* such cases."

Then there was the young man who worked in one of the labs, who walked across to the parkade at Mount Sinai Hospital nearly every day, at lunch hour, to expose himself. "He's our flasher," Trupp said. "We knew about him for a long time, but we only found out recently he worked here. He had the women frightened to death. These fellows are usually harmless. They don't really even want to touch women. But something went wrong with this fellow. Maybe he wasn't happy flashing any more, maybe the sensation was wearing off, because he started getting abusive, this time in *our* parkade, right across from the entrance to the Eaton Building. One lunch hour he exposed himself to a doctor's secretary who had gone to the parkade to fetch something from her car. He forced her down on the stairwell and masturbated all over her." Trupp was going to court in three days to testify at the man's trial.

"There was something about his eyes. All the women noticed his eyes. They never said much about his height or weight, only his eyes."

Next folder, theft of cocaine, possibly related to a plot to overthrow the government in Guyana. Cocaine has been used in hospitals for years as a local anesthetic, also to stop serious nosebleeds, but by the mid-1980s it had become the drug-of-choice in the streets. Trupp was careful with this one. The folder contained a long single-spaced report and newspaper clippings. "This was an outright theft of a shipment of cocaine from the loading dock," Trupp said, then he read: "Two hundred grams — that's quite a lot . . . August 19, 1963, mid-afternoon . . . purchase order 200387 . . . package received by registered mail, put on shelf, to be picked up by transportation to be brought to pharmacy, but pharmacy closed . . . package eight by six inches . . ."

Trupp looked up and explained, "That's about the size of a shoebox, maybe a breadbox."

He continued, this time reading from the newspaper clippings: "Five Canadians and an American pleaded guilty to conspiracy and weapons charges from a plot to overthrow Guyana . . . proceeds from sale of cocaine went to purchase weapons that went to South America. . . ." One of the five Canadians worked at the hospital, but was only "a small cog in a big wheel." He "fronted" for the group, got information about delivery of cocaine to the hospital. "He had a porter-type job, transporting material, taking specimens to the labs," Trupp said.

Drugs are a constant worry at the hospital. Twice recently staff members have been found stealing small amounts of morphine. A nurse was caught after she had taken small amounts of morphine from the hospital over a long period, passing it to her boyfriend. And there was an orderly who used to shoot himself up with morphine in a washroom, using a syringe from Emergency. Trupp walked to the metal filing cabinet and reached for a blood-spattered bag containing the evidence, which he brought to his desk. "With his experience, I'm surprised at how messy the guy was," Trupp said. "There was blood all over the place."

As for heroin being used in the hospital, Trupp said it has its place, especially for cancer patients, but as head of security he is "leery" of it. "I knew a man who got a bellyful of shrapnel in the war and he became addicted to heroin in hospital. I knew the man well, so I asked him what heroin withdrawal was like. He told me he'd kill for it. I stopped him there and I asked, 'You would *murder* someone?' He looked me in the eye and said, 'If I knew you had it and I needed it I would kill you.'"

Trupp works ten to twelve hours a day at the hospital during the winter. "I don't like working those hours in the summer, though. In the summer I like to get home early in the afternoon so I can work in my flower garden."

CHAPTER 15

Never Too Thin
The Scourge
of
Anorexia Nervosa

THE BOARD OF TRUSTEES meets on the second Tuesday of every month, at four o'clock in the afternoon, in the boardroom down the hall from W. Vickery Stoughton's office. This is a long, narrow room with grey walls and a grey rug, a room dominated by a huge, oblong, rosewood table on which are placed agendas for the thirty or so trustees who show up. Stoughton sits at the centre of one of the long sides of the table, facing anyone who enters. To his right is Alf Powis, the chairman, a legend of Canadian industry who chainsmokes through these sessions, to the chagrin of the medicos biased against carcinogenic pollutants. Sometimes, between smokes, Powis pops sugar lumps into his mouth and crunches on them while fabulous amounts of money are considered for new buildings, new equipment, renovations, medical supplies, and research programs. Careers can be launched here, and ended.

When the business is done, there is a medical presentation, something to remind members of what a hospital does. It might be an update on orthopedics, an explanation of the new immunosuppressive drugs, a slide presentation on the latest transplantation wizardry. On this second Tuesday of December, a bitterly cold day after the worst snowfall of the winter, Allan Kaplan, a young psychiatrist, and Niva Piran, an Israeli-born psychologist, had come to talk about eating disorders.

They arrived burdened with notes and slides to discuss anorexia nervosa, a frustrating illness that has bedevilled medical minds for centuries. In recent years, it has become a scourge among young women, owing as much to the dictates of fashion as to the study of psychopathology. Young Kaplan, dressed casually in a checked sports jacket, explained that anorexia nervosa dates back at least to the seventeenth century. "It used to be a medical curiosity," he said. "Now it is alarmingly common, affecting about one in every hundred university-age women, which is a *huge* number." Powis reached for a sugar lump, stopped, decided on a cigarette instead.

The reason for the presentation was the new Eating Disorders Centre, to be located in a renovated part of the old College Wing. It is one of Stoughton's pet projects, for he admires the work of Paul Garfinkel, the hospital's chief of psychiatry and an acknowledged world authority on anorexia nervosa. Stoughton loves to have world authorities under his wing. The presentation was important in Stoughton's mind because not all the trustees were convinced that anorexia nervosa should be given a priority in the hospital. It is regarded by some as a fashionable disease, the "golden girl syndrome," an affliction of affluent spoiled brats. The hospital is a jealous place and there are doctors who prefer that money be spent on more traditional, flesh-and-blood ailments, preferably ones covered by their specialties. Garfinkel is a member of the board of trustees, which makes him one of the anointed doctors at the hospital. Stoughton likes his style. Early on, Garfinkel suggested to Stoughton that the new Eating Disorders Centre be staffed by newcomers because, not knowing as much as he does, they would have a better chance to innovate and break new ground. The approach delighted Stoughton, who regards delegating as a new managerial art form. He quickly cleared away any obstacles to the Centre and as the Board of Trustees convened, the renovators already were at work.

When Kaplan had finished, it was Piran's turn. She wore a bulky coral sweater and was nervous, though she spoke competently and with conviction. With treatment, she told the trustees, about 40 per cent of anorexics recover, and another 30 per cent show some improvement. The rest deteriorate. The illness leads either to some sort of recovery, or to death. Piran explained the underside of the disorder, *bulimia*, which is a morbid hunger accompanied by a compulsion to regurgitate food as a method of extreme dieting. Many bulimics do this several times a day for years. Jane Fonda did it in order to look presentable in a bikini for a scene in the movie *On Golden Pond*. The new Eating Disorders Centre at TGH was to be a day clinic for out-patients. The average overall cost of treating an anorexic as an in-patient is \$22,000; as an out-patient at a day clinic it is cheaper, only \$9,000.

The lights in the boardroom dimmed and at one end of the long table a picture of an anorexic woman was flashed on a screen. She looked like a skeleton, clad only in loose panties, her back to the camera. "These people are hard to find," Piran said. "They don't tend to seek treatment for the anorexia itself, but for something else brought on by the illness."

The next slide was a close-up of the back of the woman's head, which showed enlarged and inflamed glands on each side of her neck, the result of months, years, of vomiting. Another slide was a close-up of the woman's right hand, which showed a callus on the top of her middle finger, roughened by the constant scraping against her upper incisors to induce vomiting. Piran told of a woman patient in her seventies who had been vomiting like this for sixty years. Early in her treatment, the woman pleaded: "Don't take this away from me."

"Why *shouldn't* we be treating these people?" Garfinkel asked, a week after the board meeting, in his office on the eighth floor of the Eaton Wing. He is thirty-nine years old, a tall, personable man in a brown suit. Psychiatrists and psychologists tend not to wear medical lab coats or walk the corridors with stethoscopes around their necks, as if this makes them look less medical and more like your Uncle Harry. Garfinkel's other concession to his calling is a dark, thick beard, a shrink's beard if ever there was one, something for the fingers to probe and curl while he listens to another lifetime of *Sturm und Drang*.

He continued, "We won't withhold treatment for other self-induced medical problems. The obese person who gets heart disease, the smoker who gets lung disease. And what about drinking drivers? These people need help as much as anybody else. I drink eight cups of coffee a day — *that* could be a self-induced problem." Anorexia nervosa may be a disease of the "haves," Garfinkel admits, but that does not make it any less serious.

It usually has innocent beginnings. A young woman, nudged by her family, well-intentioned friends, or the fashion of the day, decides to embark on a diet. She cuts out sweets, loses a few pounds. She is pleased with the results, and proud of herself. It is a discovery. For most young women, that is the end of it, but for young women with a psychological vulnerability, perhaps a propensity for excess, it triggers something that says, "If dropping three pounds feels good, how much better to lose ten pounds?"

The anorexic pursues thinness with a grim determination, until the pursuit becomes an end in itself. The time spent not eating is occupied with repetitive tasks, often long, aimless walks, all the better to burn off more calories. As the jogger becomes obsessed with distance — if a five-mile run is good, a ten-mile run is better — the anorexic becomes obsessed with weight, with thinness.

She becomes obsessed with food. She thinks and talks and dreams about food. She studies gourmet cookbooks. She watches television cooking shows, mesmerized by the paraphernalia and preparation of food. She may forage for food and hoard it. She may even become an accomplished cook — for others.

Probably she was a model child who grew up to be a perfectionist and her self-esteem is directly related to *things*, to accomplishments. Probably she has an above-average intelligence, and, because of an intense competitiveness, she may indeed be a super-achiever. In every major ballet company, for example, there are dancers who are "functional anorexics." Her weight loss is perceived as control, as palpable mastery over her body and thus over her life. She will deny she is hungry or tired — or too thin. She does not see the fuzz of hair growing on her face. She would accept utterly the Duchess of Windsor's dictum that a woman "can never be too rich or too slim." She may cheat and connive in her pursuit of thinness. She feeds her dinner to the dog, throws it out the window, buries it in a flower pot, flushes it down the toilet. She comes home and says she ate at a friend's house. If she is also bulimic, she excuses herself from the table and leaves the room to throw up. She may go on binges of eating, gulping down two dozen glazed doughnuts, an entire cake, a jar of honey, pastries still frozen. Then she will not eat for days, or will vomit, or will resort to laxatives to purge herself thin again. She feels better about herself, worthier, and nobody can tell her anything different.

"They have no sense of worth inside," Garfinkel said. "They tie their self-worth to things and they are devastated when things aren't perfect. If they get a B on a grade, it's terrible, a personal assault. It reflects on them as a person. They feel more in control when thinner, and it's often in spite of what they're perceived to look like. People might tell them they're too thin, boyfriends might say they find it unpleasant, but

they really are oblivious to how they look. They like to keep
checking the scale to find lower and lower weights. They get
a real thrill out of it."

On a personal level, as a man, Garfinkel is averse to the
cultural emphasis today on thinness. "It's not just on a clinical
level, though there's no doubt that clinically it does a lot of
damage," he said. "No, it's the woman who clearly should weigh
about a hundred and twenty pounds but who struggles to
maintain a weight of a hundred and five pounds. I see it as
nonsensical, and not just for medical reasons — for cosmetic
reasons. Women can be very competitive with other women
about weight and size."

Because women dress for other women?

"There's an element of that, yes. Maybe some day there'll
be a self-correction and fashion will bring back the Rubens
model, but now there's a whole generation of women who are
aspiring to this thinness in an unhealthy way. Many of them
will pay the price by becoming ill."

It is not a modern phenomenon, though it has never been
so pervasive, so massively embraced by all levels of society.
In pre-revolutionary China a thousand years ago, girls from
the high social classes submitted to footbinding in order to
achieve the feminine ideal of the dwarfed "lily-foot," a physical
deformity admired as much as thinness is today. Men regarded
clubbed feet as status symbols because they demonstrated that
their wives did not have to work. In the nineteenth century,
another deformity was achieved by the corset, which interfered
with digestion and was known sometimes to actually stab a
woman when one of the steel stays split. A woman uncorseted
was considered loose and wanton; thus footbinding and cor-
seting were each means of keeping women on the straight and
narrow, an effect achieved more unwittingly today by extreme
thinness. The anorexic woman loses interest in sex, and those
who must have sex do it perfunctorily, without joy. Garfinkel
uses the word "anhedonia" to describe the anorexic who strives
to remove the physical and live only through her mental being.

There is evidence that some female saints who have been
venerated through the ages for their piety and hair-shirt
penitential behavior may in fact have been clinical anorexics.
The subject is explored in a book titled *Holy Anorexia*, written
by Rudolph M. Bell, a Rutgers University history professor.
While doing research on the lives of Italian saints of the
Renaissance and Reformation, including the lives of 261 "holy
anorexics" from the thirteenth to the twentieth centuries in

Italy, Bell noticed distinct anorexic symptoms among many of the women saints. He was particularly fascinated by the lives of St. Clare and St. Catherine of Siena. He notes that many of the women were of noble birth, and as children they demonstrated a tenacious will and an obstinacy to both parental and ecclesiastical authority as they single-mindedly pursued their own type of holiness. In his book, Bell suggests that anorexia "is but one aspect of the struggle by females striving for autonomy in a patriarchal culture."

In the secular world, the debilitated, tubercular look was considered high fashion. Susan Sontag writes in *Illness as Metaphor* that in the nineteenth century the consumptive look was considered an "index of being genteel, delicate, sensitive." Women used whitening powders instead of rouge to achieve a sickly but fashionable pallor. The tubercular look indicated an artistic, romantic personality, and some suggested that when it fell out of fashion it brought about a decline in the arts. In his book *Anorexia Nervosa: A Multidimensional Perspective*, Garfinkel observes that "one has only to compare the full bodied women in Rubens' seventeenth century paintings with Modigliani's elongated women in the early twentieth century for examples of the shift as reflected through art." In poorer societies, where food is scarce, the reverse usually is true, and fleshy women are the ideal. Garfinkel continues, "When food is not abundantly available to all, overeating and obesity are viewed with admiration. It seems that only when food is plentiful can the luxury of dieting and slimness-consciousness develop."

Garfinkel and an associate, David Garner, studied a population of professional dance students and fashion models, two groups of women whose careers emphasize control over their body shapes and thus might be expected to show "anorexic behaviors." They compared the dancers and models with a group of patients with anorexia nervosa, a group of female university students, and a group of students at a music conservatory. The music students were included because they would have the same high-performance expectations as the dancers and models but without any pressure to control their body shapes.

The study showed that the dancers were most inclined to anorexic behaviors, the models slightly less so. Indeed, of sixty-nine dancers studied, Garfinkel detected twelve cases of anorexia nervosa. At the time of the study, some investigators suggested that the disorder may be induced by the extreme competitiveness of ballet training. For these reasons, too, Garfinkel included the music students, who were the same age as the dancers and equally competitive. Not a single case of anorexia nervosa was detected among them.

Anorexia nervosa is primarily a women's illness — Garfinkel uses the feminine pronoun throughout his book for all anorexics — but there are rare male examples. In the early 1980s, he studied male jockeys, but without much success. He found many jockeys who admitted they vomited to shed a few pounds, but it was always to make their weight for a race, not because they wanted to be thin. "They all said we should see this *other* guy who probably is anorexic, but it was always some fellow who would never agree to talk to us." Garfinkel has studied male homosexuals and discovered that bulimia is popular among them. "The gays value thinness in a way similar to women," he said. "We saw nine last year, which is quite a few."

Garfinkel vividly remembers his first anorexic patient who died. It happened in 1977, soon after he started practising. He was astonished at how quickly she became emaciated, how even her family was oblivious to her exteme weight loss in such a short time. The woman was hospitalized for a while, then sent home. Her blood pressure was extremely low, the result of starvation, and Garfinkel thinks that might have been what caused her to lose consciousness one afternoon when she was having a bath. She slid into the water and drowned.

The case fascinated Garfinkel because it involved the psychiatry he was always most interested in, psychiatry that dealt with the physical and emotional. He wanted to know about the biology of emotional problems. He was not interested in treating healthy people with minor neurotic problems. "I wanted to work with people who were really ill."

It was, as psychiatrists say, a "sequela" of anorexia nervosa. Anorexics do not die of anorexia nervosa. They die of all sorts of other things: heart failure, kidney disease, liver failure, blood disease, gastrointestinal complications, neurological breakdown. They die of depression, by killing themselves, and sometimes of an afternoon they slip under the water in the bathtub and drown.

The Eating Disorders Centre opened on March 15, 1985, appropriately with a small wine and cheese party. The first patients arrived two weeks later. The centre is an unhospital-looking corner of the hospital, with white-painted walls and ceilings, green plants, chairs covered in green and blue, and bright watercolors hanging in the spacious corridors. On the wall behind the main reception desk is a picture of penguins on an ice floe. Many of the rooms overlook a treed courtyard that was rediscovered during the renovations. The clinic has been designed not to look like a hospital, because anorexics tend to view hospitals as places of torture and humiliation.

The Centre can handle fifteen patients a day. They arrive at eleven o'clock in the morning, in time for lunch, and stay until six-thirty in the evening, when dinner is finished. The hospital's psychiatry department elsewhere in the hospital, has forty-two beds, four of which are for anorexic in-patients. Part of the therapy at the Eating Disorders Centre is for staff and patients to eat together. Many of the anorexics have bizarre table manners. Some cut their food into tiny pieces, which they push around their plates, sometimes off their plates to the table, or the floor. Some fear specific foods. If they fear butter, and many do, for it is a fatty food perceived as an enemy, they might eat it only because they are asked to. Anorexics do what they are told. But they won't spread it on bread. They will eat it out of a spoon, as if it were medicine. Some of them drink the salad dressing instead of spreading it on their salads. Some eat with their hands, pushing food into their mouths with their palms. Others insist on eating while standing, or in darkness.

"Those who end up here are the ones other professionals gave up on," Piran says. "There is no program like this anywhere in the world." She remembered Paula, who came to her eighteen months ago. She was thirty-two years old, single, the daughter of a Jewish family who had come to Canada from Poland. Both her parents had survived the Holocaust. She has a sister who is five years older, who works as a marketing consultant and is married, with children. Paula is one of the success stories.

When she first appeared in Piran's office, Paula looked boyish, with thin, closely cropped hair. She wore baggy jeans, a loose-fitting T-shirt, and odd, high-topped, black leather boots. They were not fashionable boots; there was nothing funky or punk about them. Piran thought they looked like the sort of booties a pre-schooler might wear. Paula could not have a bowel movement without laxatives. Her breasts were undeveloped, her nails dry and brittle. Paula had come to see Piran because her mother had insisted, not because she thought she had an eating disorder. She had been to specialists for her constipation and because she was not menstruating, but they could not help her.

At the first session, Paula spoke carefully, deliberately, anxious not to betray her feelings. She nodded at everything Piran said. Piran studied her as they talked and thought, "She's hooked. Everything I say is right." She saw encouraging signs. Paula was back living with her family, but she had lived on her own for two years, evidence of what psychologists call "ego-strength." She also could analyze herself, look at herself critically and objectively, evidence of what psychologists call "ego-observance." She had had a romantic involvement, including a sexual relationship, which indicated she could trust someone. Paula's age, too, was in her favor. Any woman who can survive to the age of thirty-two with the baggage she carried probably had strength enough to change.

After two sessions, Piran had a clearer picture of Paula's life. Her parents were survivors who wanted Paula to achieve what the horrors of war had prevented them from achieving. They wanted to live their lives through Paula, their youngest daughter, the bright, active girl who could make them happy and help them forget the past. Paula was not aware of this, but she felt confined and oppressed by her parents. She wanted to break from them. She felt so angry with her parents that sometimes she wanted to kill them, but she did not know why. She felt guilty, constantly, and told Piran she felt as if she carried within her "a perpetual sense of doom." Piran suspected Paula had also had these feelings as a child, but in an unconscious way, which made her feel as if she was always being punished for no good reason.

The parents often fought, and Paula's family life as a child was stormy and chaotic. There was much screaming and weeping and she told Piran that she felt her family was always "out of control." Her parents also ate too much, finding solace in food at all times of the day. Her father especially became grossly overweight. "In her mind," Piran says, "his obesity was connected with his difficulty in establishing relationships with people. She saw him as separated from other people by his layers of fat. She attributed to his fatness their own inability to be close." For Paula, food and eating and overweight all intermingled with a vague numbness, as if fat somehow could anesthetize the emotions. "They wanted her to eat *for them*," Piran says. "When she refused, it was not because she was not hungry, but because she wanted to defy them." The dinner table became an arena where her parents tried to control her.

There were noisy arguments as she resisted, not always knowing precisely what she was resisting, or why she felt compelled to defy them.

She actually showed more discernment and control with regard to her eating disorder than do most anorexics, and after several months of therapy with Piran she began to recognize her problem and to know what to do about it. Slowly, after nearly a year, Paula began to break the connection between fat and feelings.

One morning — Piran remembers it as the breakthrough day — Paula arrived for her appointment wearing a skirt. "She even wore makeup, which she had never done before. And she talked of job plans. She was also becoming a little more assertive. Before, she would never say anything she thought might hurt me. It was exciting the first time I heard her say, 'No!' and mean it." Soon after, Paula felt secure enough to put on a little weight, so that her breasts became fuller and her menses returned. "That day she arrived in a skirt, wearing makeup, that's when I knew we were getting somewhere. She's studying medicine now. She wants to become a doctor. She's dating again. And those little boots are gone."

Piran is a consultant to the National Ballet School in Toronto, where she conducts group sessions with the young dancers. Ballet demands a certain body shape that is pre-pubertal, which encourages eating and dietary practices Piran would classify as disorders. At the highest levels, ballet is extremely competitive — future primas may be selected for their body shape before they are even ten years old — and the womanly rounding of an aspiring ballerina's body as she enters her teens is something to be feared.

She finds the same problems with models and movie and television stars, all of whom strive for an unrealistic, unhealthy body shape. "You cannot have that recommended body shape without an eating disorder. There are standards of weight for different ages and heights, certain norms. The body tends to gravitate to a natural weight, just as it does to a natural height, and there is not much you can do about it, not when 99 per cent of all diets fail. When they do not fail, and a person is far below her normal weight, she gives up all other goals and maintaining the low weight becomes an obsession. And the brain keeps saying, 'Put the fat back on, put the fat back on.'"

Because thinness as fashion is an idea so widespread and entrenched, anorexia nervosa has become a two-edged sword affecting troubled women striving to be thin, and women striving to be thin who become troubled. There are the classic anorexics, women with deep-seated psychological problems who are pathologically obsessed with thinness, and the over-achievers who use anorexic tactics as a means to an end. In their pursuit of thinness, the dancers, and the models and movie and television stars, can slip over the edge and develop the same psychological problems as the classic anorexic.

Piran warns the young dancers at the National Ballet School of these dangers. She has also found a new practice which tends to encourage anorexia. Female bodybuilding attracts determined women who strive for a rippled, sinewy, pumped-up masculine body by hoisting weights for up to eight hours a day. The sport attracts classic anorexics, who find self-worth in exerting control over their body shapes, and the over-achievers, whose competitiveness pushes them on to be more rippled, more sinewy, more pumped-up than anyone else in the gym.

Elaborate studies done on starvation show people deprived of food tend to develop anorexia nervosa symptoms. In the early nineteen forties, a group of thirty-six male conscientious objectors were examined during the Second World War in what is now called "The Minnesota Studies." The men were put on a semi-starvation diet for six months in order to observe the psychobiological effects of starvation. The men soon became obsessed with food, and they began to display the peculiar anorexic features, such as mixing unusual food combinations, hoarding food, dawdling over their meals. Their concentration and sexual drive declined and they became increasingly inde-cisive, aloof, and depressed, all traits common to anorexics. After twelve weeks of rehabilitative "refeeding," the men returned to normal.

For women, Piran said, puberty is a crucial time, and not just for those who aspire to be dancers or models. "A lot of the eating disorders I see start at puberty, when the body changes, when girls normally put on fat and develop secondary sexual characteristics. Many of them have grown up isolated and have weak personalities. Puberty signals the start of adulthood and they can't assume the psychological role of being an adult woman. It's frightening. They can't deal with it. So, by starving themselves, they fight against puberty and the process of puberty reverses itself. The body fat drops below 7 per cent. Menstruation stops. By starving themselves they can avoid the issues of sexuality and all that it means —

socializing, growing, trusting. In a way, they're retarding themselves. If they start early enough they can stay looking like girls. It's like the child in *The Tin Drum*, the novel by Günter Grass about the boy who stops his own growth because he did not want to participate in adult life as he saw it. Actually, it's more likely to happen with girls than boys because male hormonal activity doesn't depend on body fat."

With boys, anorexic tendencies can be more easily camouflaged, showing up as anti-social behavior — delinquency, drug addiction. "When it's a good adaptation," Piran said, laughing, "it's computers." Not so with girls. "Girls usually are trained to handle problems within the home and they get more confused messages about their vocations, careers. You've got to look at people as you would an ecological system. The more ways a person has to cope, the better off they are, so that later, when they encounter problems, they can fall back on strengths and resources. It's an easier process for boys because they tend to have more options open to them. Boys usually are allowed to express their problems outside the family."

When Piran first met Ellen, she knew at once the young woman could break her heart. At that time three years ago, Ellen was twenty-four years old. She was pretty, with blonde hair, blue eyes, and the forlorn appeal of a waif. Piran thought she looked more like a twelve-year-old boy. Her hair was thin, brittle, falling out in patches. Her skin was so dry it looked cracked. She was five feet, four inches, but weighed about seventy pounds. She had not menstruated for nearly a decade. Her pulse was slow and her body temperature two degrees below normal, which made her hands feel cold to the touch. She had soft, downy hair on her cheeks, neck, forearms, and thighs — lanugo hair, the same fine, rudimentary fuzz found on a human fetus. She looked like a skeleton thinly covered in skin. The only parts of her that seemed alert, even vivid, were her eyes, which seemed oversized because the rest of her was so wasted.

Ellen was listening to the radio one day when she heard Paul Garfinkel being interviewed about anorexia nervosa. At the time, Garfinkel worked at the Clarke Institute of Psychiatry, where Piran also worked. Ellen could not believe that her entire life was being discussed on radio. Everything Garfinkel said seemed to be meant for her.

Ellen was the oldest child in an upper-middle-class family, with a younger brother and sister who had developed a close relationship, which Ellen felt excluded her. Her mother was a teacher, her father a sales agent. They were intellectual, but cold and aloof. Piran suspects that the parents, probably unwittingly, used Ellen to preserve the marriage, which was empty and rudderless. Even as a toddler, as soon as she learned to walk, Ellen tried to run away from home; the parents reacted by building a higher fence around the yard. Many times she was locked in her room, where her father played with her sexually. By the time she was seventeen, Ellen's favorite activity was to stand in the garden, often for most of the day. Other times she would walk, for hours, going nowhere. She never graduated from high school, though she had above-average intelligence. "She wasn't bright, but she was intelligent," Piran said. "Her thinking was concrete, not abstract. She really could only talk through her body. If she felt something, she had to show it physically. It would mean nothing to say that you cared for her. You had to *do* something."

For Ellen, anorexia became a full-time job, a career. She could talk forever about her thinness, her depressions, and a multitude of other symptoms that were as fascinating as they were repugnant, but she could not talk about herself. Whether it took the form of her standing alone in the garden or taking the long, aimless walks, the illness filled her days. Not eating became a challenge, weight loss became an achievement, and as she starved herself she felt she had some control of her life.

The day she heard Garfinkel being interviewed on the radio, she listened intently, and when the interview ended she immediately called and asked for help. Garfinkel referred her to Piran. Piran interpreted Ellen's call as "probably the healthiest thing she'd ever done." She met Ellen that week and, after one session, arranged for her to be hospitalized.

"She felt dead inside," Piran said. "She felt she had no life in her. She thought she didn't exist as a person. The therapy involved trying to show that you can talk to other parts of her beside her symptoms. It was difficult, because if you made the slightest mistake, if you did anything she could interpret as rejection, all the symptoms would come back. It might be something as innocent as my talking to another patient. She had this terrible *fragility*."

Piran tried repeatedly to place Ellen in another home, but her parents did not want to let her go. "She did all the housework. She cooked for them. Her parents couldn't let her go because they couldn't live together by themselves. She had become their servant, which often happens with anorexics. They are handy to have around." For a brief time, at a rehabilitation centre in Toronto, Ellen seemed to be making progress. She put on some weight, only a few pounds, but it strengthened her and she tried to see around the corners of her anorexia nervosa. She met a young man she liked and they went on dates, and, for a few months, Piran thought something remarkable might be happening.

Then, as abruptly as it had started, it ended. One day the young man suggested to Ellen that they not see so much of each other. He told her he wanted to keep seeing her, but they should date others, too. It was because of his parents, he told her. For Ellen, it was devastating, proof again that she could not trust anyone. She stopped eating entirely. "It was proof that she was not a person," said Piran, who arranged for Ellen to be readmitted to hospital. "She didn't want to see me any more either, because she could not trust me. Before she could trust someone, she had to idealize the person."

As Piran told Ellen's story, she broke off pieces of an empty Styrofoam cup she was twisting in her hands. She looked down and watched the pieces fall to the floor and her eyes filled with tears. "I really liked her. When she was seeing me, she probably developed the most intense relationship she ever had, but she had no good memories, no good feelings. Sometimes when I think about it, I think, how could anyone like that survive in this world? She was courageous. She tried very hard, *very* hard. She was just too weak."

Piran has not seen Ellen for nearly a year. She thought she might be back standing in her garden, or walking and walking.

Bruce
Enjoy the Time
You Have Left

BRUCE WANTED another game of cribbage.

Sitting on the edge of his bed in his room on the eleventh floor of the Norman Urquhart Wing, where thoracic patients either wait for the knife or recover from it, Bruce swung his attaché case to his lap, then snapped it open and removed several books. One was a book of plays, another a book on bridge, one of his passions. There was the novel *All the King's Men*, and a collection of writings by Henry David Thoreau. "I've always liked reading plays with lots of terse stage directions, or books with lots of dialogue. I've never much liked those long, rambling novels." Bruce picked up Thoreau and ran his thumb to the famous essay on Walden Pond. "For the first time in my life," he said, "I'm enjoying the descriptions."

He had been admitted to Toronto General the day before, May 7, for his second lung operation in five weeks, this time to remove a malignant cancer from his left lung. The first operation, on March 28, removed a cancer from his right lung. In January, he had been told there was no hope and he should prepare for death. He was not out of danger now, but his life had changed. He looked at things differently. He was less judgemental, more tolerant of people's weaknesses and peccadillos.

The second operation was scheduled for the next morning, but it hardly seemed to occupy his thoughts: "I can't believe you *skunked* me," he said. He shook his head in disbelief as he recalled the cribbage game the previous afternoon in the cafeteria on the ground floor of the Eaton Wing. Bruce is a competitive man. At marathon bridge sessions at his home in Oakville, sometimes he would get up to fetch a pickle or a piece of cheese, which involved walking around the table while everyone sorted their hands, then he would sit down and mutter, "A peek's as good as a trump." No one ever knew if he was joking.

"Let's play again," Bruce said, and we did, on his bed. He won.

The first signs of cancer had appeared the previous September, but Bruce had not recognized them as such. They appeared as pains in his ankles, knees, and wrists, pains that are often, but not always, related to an inchoate cancer. It is as if the body, having detected the onset of a sinister invasion, begins to panic. Bruce was in his mid-forties and he thought the signs might have meant the beginning of arthritis, or perhaps the ache of muscles and tendons rubbed raw from the tennis matches he played so vigorously at his club in Oakville. There was another sign, too, one that surprised Bruce, but only in retrospect, after the doctor had told him about it.

"Look at my fingers," he said, holding up his hands, the fingers spread apart at eye level, as if he were looking through a mask. "Do you notice anything?" The fingers looked normal, until Bruce said, "Now look at the tips of my fingers." The tips of his fingers were slightly swollen, knobby. Doctors refer to them as "clubbed" fingers. There is no adequate explanation for this symptom, but some oncologists believe a cancerous tumor produces a growth hormone, which may also explain the mysterious, arthritis-like swelling and pain in the ankles, knees, and wrists. The clubbing effect is peculiar to certain lung tumors, especially tumors that begin in the lungs, called primary lung tumors. Whatever the cause, Bruce seemed fascinated by it, as if he had stumbled upon a delightful piece of esoterica.

He had always been an intense man, brimming with ambition and ideas, though he was somewhat frail and accident-prone. Once he fell off the roof of his house and lost an eye. He loved politics and when he lived in western Canada he had worked as a strategist for various Progressive Conservative politicians, including E. Davie Fulton, a former cabinet minister. Most of his life he had worked as a management consultant, but in recent years he had teamed up with his wife, Rita, to sell real estate. They have two children, Tony, a bright young man who had finished private school and had gone off to university, and Lorrie, equally as bright and a gifted musician showing much promise with both piano and violin.

In January, Bruce went to his family doctor for a check-up. The pains in his ankles and knees that had appeared in September continued, but they were not in any way debilitating. His family doctor didn't suspect anything. Bruce felt fine. It was a routine annual check-up and everything appeared to be in order. Only at the end of the examination did the doctor suggest that he should have a chest X-ray, because he had not had one for several years, and because he was a smoker. He had started smoking when he was eighteen years old, living in Regina. He had frequently tried to quit, then would start again, and by his late teens he was smoking a package of cigarettes a day. After high school, he entered the Jesuit seminary in Guelph, Ontario, and he stopped smoking entirely. When he left the seminary, in his early twenties, he started smoking again. He had married Rita when he was twenty-five, and a year later he stopped smoking cigarettes and switched to a pipe. Years later, he switched to Colts, a thin cigarillo.

A week after his check-up, the doctor called Bruce to tell him to come and see him again. In his office, late that January, the doctor explained that the X-rays revealed a spot on his right lung. He told Bruce that he could not say for sure what it was, but that it had better be investigated further. He outlined the various tests that were required and suggested to Bruce that he go to Toronto General Hospital to see F. Griffith Pearson, the hospital's distinguished chief of surgery. "It was the first time I had heard Pearson's name mentioned," Bruce said. "He told me he'd be able to get me in to see Pearson and I remember being surprised that he could do it because Pearson's supposed to be one of the best lung fellows in the country."

But he did not go to Pearson, not immediately. He did not know what to do. He kept hearing about different doctors from relatives and friends and friends of friends and eventually he chose a thoracic surgeon in Hamilton, which was easier to get to from Oakville.

"He lined up more X-rays, and then there was more bad news. They found a spot on my other lung. I found out later that this was very disturbing because lung cancer does not spread from one lung to another lung, so the doctors were convinced the second cancer must have come from somewhere else — the stomach, the bowels, the liver. The tests were unbelievable! Barium X-rays. Enema-type X-rays. CT-scans.

Whole-body X-rays. Once they did a lung biopsy. They stuck a needle right into my lung to get a sample of the cancerous growth. It felt like a bee sting, although they had given me a local anesthetic. It was those enema-type tests, though, that were really uncomfortable. They'd fill me up with this fluid and tell me to hold it for twenty minutes while they took some pictures. They were convinced that the cancer had to come from somewhere else, that you couldn't get two cancers that started in each lung independently. And after all that, what did they find? They found *nothing.*"

After all the tests, Bruce found himself face to face with another doctor in Hamilton, this one a bright young surgeon who told him that he had cancers in both lungs, and that the situation was hopeless. "I remember his exact words," Bruce said. "He said, 'If you keep looking, you'll find a doctor who will operate, but the best advice I can give you is *don't do it.* What you have is inoperable. Enjoy what time you have left.'"

On his way home from Hamilton, Bruce wondered how he would tell his family. He liked the young doctor, though he felt he was overly clinical. Not cold, but "lacking warmth." Still, the doctor's words kept coming back to him — *enjoy what time you have left.* On an impulse, as he drove home down the main street of Oakville, he swung over to the curb in front of a music store and parked the car. He sat behind the wheel for a few minutes, then got out, walked into the store and bought a book of Scottish music. "I was really at the depths, but I decided I wanted to learn how to play the piano. I don't suppose this makes any sense. I have no ear for music at all. But I thought, if I haven't got much time I better learn how to play the piano."

The next day, Bruce went to see his family doctor and told him the news. There he found the warmth that he had missed the day before. When the doctor's secretary heard his news, she wept. The doctor told Bruce not to give up. He also told him he met once a month with a group of thoracic surgeons and he promised to mention Bruce's case at the next session.

While Bruce waited, he sat for hours at the keyboard of the baby grand in his living room, studying the basics of piano from an instruction book, trying to teach himself scales. His doctor did bring up his case at the monthly meeting of the thoracic surgeons, early in February, and after the meeting he told Bruce the consensus was that he should see Pearson

at Toronto General. He made the appointment and Bruce met
Pearson later that month.

F. Griffith Pearson is the most senior surgeon at the hospital,
a twenty-five-year veteran who has played an important role
in many of Toronto General's medical breakthroughs, including
the early experiments in hypothermia and in the development
of the pacemaker. He has taken part in most of the dramatic
lung and heart-lung transplant operations, including Tom
Hall's operation, when he worked throughout the night with
fellow surgeon Joel Cooper. Pearson, known to everyone as
"Griff," is the surgeon-in-chief, a man in his late fifties who
is personable, plain-spoken, and almost strikingly handsome.
When Bruce entered his office, off the main corridor of the
Bell Wing, which is reserved for chiefs of staff and senior
administrators, he was awestruck. "He was the perfect image
of what I thought a chief surgeon should be," he said. "If I
were a casting director I'd hire him immediately for the role
of chief surgeon."

One of the first questions Bruce asked was, "Can you operate
on me?"

Pearson, seated at his desk, wearing a white lab coat, looked
at him over the dark rims of his glasses and said, "Sure."

Pearson regularly performs six minor operations and four major
operations a week. His big operating day is Tuesday, when
he is busy in the operating room all day. He tries never to
schedule more than two major operations a day, but there are
times he can't avoid doing a third. "I wouldn't want to do
major cases on consecutive days. It takes a lot of concentration.
It wouldn't be good for the patients."

Pearson stretched his left leg out and rested it on a chair
as he talked. He had been walking with a decided limp for
more than a week, the result of an injury twenty years ago
to his kneecap, which he had re-injured ten years later. The
first accident had happened when he was tobogganing down
a hill with his children. He had stuck out his left foot to slow
the toboggan and caught his heel on a root under the snow,
wrenching the leg so badly that the kneecap was ripped from
its muscular attachments. He had also injured the ankle in
the same leg playing high-school hockey. His knee had been
repaired by Alan Gross, head of orthopedics at the hospital.

Having ready access to the best in the business is one of
the undefined perquisites of being a doctor at a major teaching
hospital. "Doctors are much better equipped to seek out the

best," Pearson said. "I would say it's impossible for patients always to be sure they are getting the best doctor. They might take the effort to get three opinions, but then find all three opinions are the same. There are a lot of surgeons who are very nice with patients and develop a substantial practice just because they have a nice manner, but they're not the top of their field. They might not even be good technical operators. The best available may be a real son of a bitch, but how's the patient to know this?"

As for the surgeon who advised Bruce not to bother looking for someone to operate on him, Pearson said it probably reflected inexperience. "It wasn't our opinion. And that's something else to bear in mind. Surgeons have different opinions." Bruce's situation was unusual, however, and a young surgeon might understandably be wary about recommending surgery. "We might see a case like Bruce's maybe four or five times a year," Pearson continued. "His wasn't the worst I've seen, but it was one of the bad ones. It wasn't a cancer that spread from the bowel or skin to the lung, one of the places where cancers that spread through the blood commonly land and grow. He had primary cancers in both his lungs, cancers that started independently of each other in each lung. Statistically it's not common at all, to have two primary cancers. In ten years, I've operated on about a thousand patients with cancer of the lung and maybe sixty or seventy were what we call 'second primaries.' With Bruce, it was a 'synchronous second primary,' which means that the cancers not only started independently of each other, in each of his lungs, but they appeared *at the same time*. It probably happens about fifteen times in fifteen hundred cases. Very unusual."

Pearson scheduled Bruce's operation for March 28, a Thursday, which meant Bruce was supposed to check in at the hospital Tuesday evening and be available all day Wednesday for a series of tests, get a good night's sleep, and be ready for the operation Thursday morning. Bruce got the date wrong and late Wednesday afternoon, when he was at his office, he got a call from the hospital telling him that the Admitting office was closing at six o'clock and he had better hurry if he wanted to be operated on the next day. He rushed home, packed a bag, and barely managed to get to the hospital in time. The panic of getting to the hospital helped to allay the usual fears of waiting for major surgery, but as a result of being a day late he also missed all the routine tests that had been scheduled. One of the important appointments Bruce missed was with the hospital physiotherapist, who was supposed to test his lung capacity and general fitness so as to provide a baseline for post-operative comparisons. After the operation, all they could do was guess, or ask Bruce what he used to be able to do. And the best Bruce could tell them was that he used to be able to play tennis and walk up and down a flight of stairs without puffing.

Pearson and Joel Cooper trekked into Bruce's room Wednesday evening and discussed the case with some medical students. Before Bruce went to sleep, a nurse came to shave his body for the operation. Early Thursday, another nurse nudged him awake and administered a sedative. No breakfast on the day of an operation. He remembers feeling relaxed as he was wheeled out of his room to the elevator, taken down to the operating-room floor, then wheeled along more corridors, lying on his back watching the lights in the ceilings pass by. In the operating room, the lighting was brighter, the temperature decidedly cooler.

Pearson expected that he would be able to remove both the cancers that morning, so he performed a midline incision in the chest, about fifteen inches long, the same incision used for heart bypass operations. After the cut, he sawed the breastbone in half and pried apart the ribs to expose both lungs.

Every surgeon has his own technique. Pearson prefers to push the ribs apart. Others, such as Cooper, probably because his hands are bigger, prefer to remove a rib to get inside. Sometimes when Pearson pushes a rib apart, it snaps, but the break is no cause for alarm. "It creates no more distress than the incision itself," Pearson said. "It heals as quickly as the incision and the patient usually never realizes one of the ribs snapped. It's especially common for the ribs of older patients to snap, especially women. Some older women can snap their ribs just by coughing."

When he was able to see inside, Pearson could confirm what the X-rays had indicated — both cancers were localized and operable. Both were irregularly rounded, about the size of ping-pong balls, which meant they had been there for several years. If Bruce had had his X-ray a year earlier, doubtless the cancer in the right lung would have been large enough to have been noticed. The cancer on the left lung, the second cancer, might have been missed by the X-rays because it was partially obscured by large blood vessels and the shadow of the heart. If the X-rays are taken in a slapdash manner, or if they are incompetently or sloppily interpreted, even cancers the size of ping-pong balls can be missed. The quality of the film is important, the angles are important — whether frontal or lateral. But ultimately, according to Pearson, "everything depends on how the radiologist interprets the X-ray. The lab technician who takes the X-rays doesn't interpret them. That's the radiologist's job, and he must be experienced. He's got to take an intense interest in what he is doing and report every detail."

As Pearson operates, he teaches. It is an instinctive thing to do at a teaching hospital. For nearly two hours, he maintained a running commentary, as he cut and cauterized: "The right lung has three lobes, the left two. . . . The left lung has an indentation, the cardiac depression, which makes room for the heart. . . . Each lung and each lobe has its separate blood supply and breathing tube. . . . The operation requires exposing these three components — arterial supply, venous supply, breathing tube — dividing them and closing the ends in a safe and appropriate way. . . . In an adult male, the right lung usually weighs about six hundred and twenty-five grams, the left five hundred and seventy grams. . . . Each lung contains three hundred million alveoli, tiny air sacs that give it a honeycomb appearance. . . . The respiratory surface of the lungs is between seventy and eighty square metres, about the size of a tennis court if laid flat. . . . The alveolus is the point at which the blood and inspired air are separated by a thin membrane that allows oxygen and nitrogen to diffuse into the blood and carbon dioxide and other gases to pass from the blood into the alveoli. . . . The wall is so thin you need an electron microscope to see it clearly. . . . Primary purpose of the lung is to bring air and blood into intimate contact so that oxygen can be added to the blood, and carbon dioxide can be removed. . . . This is achieved by two pumping systems, one moving a gas, the other a liquid. . . . Blood that's poor in oxygen but high in carbon dioxide is in contact with the air, which is high in oxygen and low in carbon dioxide, for less than a second. . . ."

Removing one of the lobes of a lung is called a "lobectomy." Removing an entire lung is called a "pneumonectomy." The lung itself is light and soft, spongy in texture, a mottled grey-pink in color. It can be handled almost roughly, and it is surprisingly large. Even a single lobe, when cut out and placed wriggling on a tray over the patient's legs, looks like a deflated football. "It's like a sponge with holes on the outside, covered by a thin skin," Pearson said. "You can depress it like a sponge, but air doesn't come out. It's not like a balloon. It's like a sponge, with very fine, myriad little spaces in it. . . ."

As Pearson worked, mostly standing at the head of the table, he would from time to time send samples of lung tissue to Pathology, where it was microscopically examined. Toronto General has an excellent, efficient pathology department, and the reports came back quickly, within five minutes. The pathologist, a woman, entered the operating room and stood stiffly just inside the door. She spoke as if reporting to a general on enemy troop movements: "Negative, doctor!" More bits of tissue were snipped from both lungs and sent off to Pathology. More negatives were reported, which was good news. It confirmed that the malignancy was confined to the tumor in the upper lobe of the right lung and the one in the lower lobe of the left lung.

It was crucial at this stage in the operation to examine both lungs. If only one of the cancers was confined and easily removable and the other had spread, it would be futile to proceed because the cancer that had spread would have to be treated differently — with radiation, chemotherapy, or a combination of both. If that was the case, Pearson would sew up the patient, and that would be the end of it. "Only if we think we can remove *both* tumors completely would we remove either one of them," Pearson explained. The right lung proved to be more complicated than he had expected, and the tumor would take longer to remove, so he decided to do the job in two stages. Bruce would need a second operation in about five weeks.

Time for a break. Pearson turned from the table, walked out of the operating room, pulled off his mask and gloves in the scrub room, and headed down a corridor to the Surgeons' Lounge. He wanted a coffee — and a smoke.

In the lounge, Al Shewchuk, the obstetrician who is the hospital's authority on in-vitro fertilization, walked over and offered Pearson his lighter. "Always a pleasure giving a lung surgeon a light," he said.

Surgeons tend to smoke more than physicians, an apparent paradox that became a lively topic for the morning break. Shewchuk, a cigarette smoker, suggested it is because surgeons basically are insecure. Pearson disagreed. More likely, he said, it is because surgeons tend to be striving, Type-A personalities. Pearson used to smoke cigarettes, but years ago, at Christmas, he announced to his children that he would quit. Actually, he made a bet with them. If he stopped for a year, they would have to pay him a dollar. If he could not stop, he would pay them a hundred dollars. He managed to stay off cigarettes for three days, then switched to a pipe. At the end of the year he won the bet.

Pearson knows the statistics on smoking and lung cancer. "We hardly ever see it in patients below the age of thirty," he said. "It starts showing up in the mid-forties and we really see a lot of it over age fifty. You can reduce your chances of getting it by quitting, but you never get to the same status as one who never smoked. The best a quitter can hope for — if he stops for ten years! — is to reach a point where he is only three times more likely to get lung cancer than one who had never smoked at all."

Doug Snell, an otolaryngologist, a specialist who treats ears and throats, listened to the discussion intently, then volunteered that he, too, used to smoke a pipe. "I stopped when I was forty-six years old, on the first day of June, 1972, at one o'clock in the afternoon. Thirteen years ago. I still miss it, every day."

"I wish you hadn't said that, Doug," Pearson interrupted, groaning softly.

It was Pearson's turn for a story and he told Snell and Shewchuk of the time he visited a lung patient he had operated on and found him smoking in his room — through a tube in his chest. "It was a rare instance, but I saw it. Now, *that* was an addiction."

"One thing I'll never give up is my Scotch at the end of the day," Shewchuk said. "Four ounces a day is good for you. You'll live longer than a teetotaller."

"You know," Pearson said, "it's harder for an alcoholic to stop smoking than to stop drinking."

Hearing this, Shewchuk challenged Pearson to another bet. "We'll set a date to quit smoking, let's say the end of June, on the honor system. First one to start buys the other a case of Royal Salute."

"Never heard of it."

"It's twenty-five-year-old Chivas Regal, seventy-five bucks a bottle."

"Holy Jesus, that's a thousand dollars a case!"

"End of June. We'll each stop for a year."

Pearson walked across the room and shook hands on it.

Pearson walked back to the operating room to finish up. When he was satisfied he had removed all of the tumors, the rest was a matter of putting everything back together and sewing up. A fairly routine matter, though the anesthetist warned, "Sometimes just when you think the worst is over a catastrophe happens." The blood pressure might suddenly drop to a perilous level, which requires fast action, a quick injection of a drug to constrict the blood vessels. "The worst thing I've seen at this point," the anesthetist said, "was a hole blown out of the bottom of a lung."

When Pearson removed the metal retractors that kept the chest cavity open during the operation, the ribs slowly moved back to their normal position. Pearson tied the breastbone in place with catgut, and after more cleaning, he injected painkiller around the lung so Bruce would not be too uncomfortable when he woke up. Then he began sewing up.

Pearson enjoys the operating room. "Most surgeons do," he said. "It's a break. It's peaceful. You're working at what you're trained to do." He recalled a recent operation that involved the removal of an esophagus, a long and delicate operation. He was assisted by a visiting American surgeon from Cape Cod, a man as experienced as himself, who had been doing surgery for twenty-five years. "Halfway through, suddenly he got very excited," Pearson said. "He was talking to a junior resident on the other side of the table and I heard him say, 'Can you imagine getting paid for doing this, doing what you love?' Most of us feel that way in the operating room. You can concentrate without being bothered by silly problems, though I don't think we'd want to stay up all night doing varicose veins."

Bruce stayed in hospital for twelve days and when it came time to leave, Pearson told him: "I want you to go home and get better fast because you're coming back in a month and we're going to do the other side." The month passed quickly, and early in May Pearson removed the other tumor, cutting away the lower lobe of the left lung. The second operation was easier than the first, though Bruce remembers one major difference. "One lung had to sustain me while they were working on the other, so they didn't want to put me very deeply to sleep," he said. "What they gave me really was like a local anesthetic, but they didn't want me to be conscious. They gave me some kind of spinal anesthetic, which I later heard was unusual and somewhat risky. The result was I woke up much faster and I was fully conscious in the recovery room. I wasn't foggy or punchy at all. I remember reading the newspaper and talking to the nurses in the recovery unit right after my operation. One of the nurses even gave me two real estate leads."

Pearson estimates the success rate for these lung operations at about 40 per cent, which means that 40 per cent of the patients have a life expectancy of five years. It also means that two-thirds of the patients are not cured. "One of the tumors could reappear, which means that when we operated they were too minuscule to be detected," he said. "They could appear anywhere, in the brain, in the liver, in the bones. We never cure anybody if we leave even one cell behind. Bruce will be on follow-up for the rest of his life. He'll come in every three months for the first year, then twice a year, and once a year after that. After five years, the patient comes in every two years. After ten years, some patients just forget to come back. Cancer of the lung usually declares itself as recurrent within two years. Bruce was lucky. The prognosis is much better if the cancer is primary, and hasn't spread. There are no guarantees, but if he goes two years without recurrence, the odds are much more in his favor."

As for Bruce's everyday prognosis, with a third of each lung removed, Pearson said, "He'll be able to do ordinary things without being aware of any embarrassment, but if he tries to run upstairs or play tennis he'll notice he's shortchanged in wind and endurance."

A year later, on a Monday afternoon in June, Bruce waited in the anteroom outside Pearson's office. He had had another chest examination two weeks ago and the radiologist said there was something on one of his lungs — a spot, a shadow — something that did not look encouraging. Bruce sat in a chair across from Pearson's secretary, waiting, drumming his fingers on a newspaper. His wife, Rita, was expected to arrive shortly with the new X-ray sheets from Toronto General's radiology department.

Pearson thought something might have gone wrong, but the spot or shadow Bruce's radiologist had worried about was merely what Pearson called "post-operative scar shadow." A false alarm.

After more than a year, Bruce has taught himself to play several pieces on the piano. One of them was "Lara's Theme," which he recorded on a cassette and gave to his daughter, Lorrie, at Christmas.

Two years after the operations, his check-ups had all been good. There were no signs of recurrence.

On a July morning, Bruce and Rita were in their backyard, relaxing by the pool. Rita stretched out on a chaise longue in a bikini and Bruce sat under the patio umbrella without a shirt, the scars of the two operations clearly visible. On the table was a tray of sandwiches, with a pitcher of lemonade and saucers of pickles, cucumbers, cheese, and celery.

Bruce talked about the nurses at Toronto General. "My local doctor had told me to expect a lot of efficiency there, but not a lot of warmth — *because it's TGH*. I guess that's the way it was, especially after they moved me from the step-down unit [where patients are sent immediately after an operation]. I really didn't care what they looked like or what their personalities were like. When you're that sick, all you want is competence. Sometimes they were distant, cool, but they were all highly trained and competent. When you cough, they come to help you cough. They'll smack you on the back to get the phlegm out. There was one Oriental nurse who was terrific. Once she came and stayed with me for a long time, until I finally got all the phlegm out. I can't tell you what a relief it was. Then I never saw her again. I heard that her mother died that day."

Bruce pulled out a letter he was going to send to a man who had shared his hospital room when he was in for his second operation. The man's name was Ben, and he also had an operation to remove a cancer on his lung. They had got to know each other well. Bruce leaned forward in his chair to read:

In Walden, Thoreau speaks of laying up treasures which moth and rust will corrupt and thieves break through and steal. It is a fool's life as they will find when they get to the end of it, if not before. Ben, I think that you and Marsha have been given an unusual opportunity to discover it now. With sharpened senses, you will see more stars, smell more flowers, hear more music, and feel more crackling snow under your skis than ever before.

You'll be given more time and, with God's blessing, the opportunity to spend it with your family and friends. There you will be reminded that people who listen receive greater respect than those who speak. Their talent is accepted, their values understood. They have no need to advertise. They have more friends. They are more pleasant to be with, and when they communicate everyone pays attention.

*I wish you well, Ben and Marsha. May the God of
Abraham, the God of Isaac and the God of Jacob be with
you always. May you see your children and your children's
children unto the third and fourth generation and may the
wind be always at your back and may He hold you in the
hollow of His hand.*

It was a hot summer afternoon but the backyard, shaded
as it was by the tall spruce trees, felt like a day at the cottage.
When Bruce finished reading, Rita smiled at him, then walked
to the edge of the pool and slid into the water. Bruce held
the letter to his knee and looked away from the light.

CHAPTER 17

Dear and Glorious Administrator

IT HAD BEEN one of those unpredictable, early October days, dark and windy, threatening rain. Now and then the clouds pushed apart and a cool autumn light broke through and splashed on the blue-and-white canvas tent in the hospital courtyard. The opening ceremony for Toronto General's new research building was scheduled for five o'clock and David Allen of Public Relations was taking no chances. Butane heaters blew hot air over the grass in the tent, making it feel like a dirigible about to ascend to the heavens.

For years research at the hospital had been hampered by lack of space. Research facilities were housed in various rooms scattered about the University of Toronto, some sixty-five thousand square feet in all, but only eight thousand square feet in the hospital itself. Surgeons had grown accustomed to leaving an operating room, bundling themselves into overcoats and galoshes, and heading across the street to another building to check the progress of some vital experimental work going on in a distant laboratory. In 1978, a report concluded that forty-five thousand to fifty thousand more square feet of research space would be required over the next decade. The hospital's board of trustees decided to redevelop the old College Wing, the original hospital building, to provide the space.

It soon became evident that this would not be good enough, not for W. Vickery Stoughton, the new president. He wanted nothing less than a world-class research facility, which he knew could never be achieved in a renovated patient wing. He listened intently to Charles Hollenberg, then chief of medicine, and Peter van Nostrand, head of the Research Development Committee, both of whom had been fighting for years for better research facilities. It did not take the new-breed, Harvard manager long in his turn to convince trustees that a new research facility should be built as quickly as possible, and on hospital property so as to provide convenient access for researchers. "It had been talked about for years," Allen said. "But it was only after Stoughton arrived that we got a hole in the ground."

On Wednesday, October 2, 1985, at five o'clock in the afternoon, the building that housed the Max Bell Research Centre and the Charlie Conacher Research Wing was officially opened, marred only by a gaggle of protesters outside hollering anti-abortion slogans at Premier David Peterson, one of the dignitaries on the dais inside the tent.

The new, seven-storey building would provide room for researchers to zero in on Toronto General's special areas of expertise: heart attacks and strokes, nutrition, single-lung and heart-lung transplants, human reproduction, molecular disease, joint and bone implants, spinal injuries resulting from injury and aging, and cancer detection and treatment. And diabetes, which had gained Toronto General and the University of Toronto a world reputation in the 1920s when Frederick Banting and Charles Best discovered insulin. The building cost $13.5 million, but it provided eighty hospital researchers with a hundred thousand square feet of space that they could get to without piling into their overcoats and galoshes.

Earlier in the day, in the Main Lecture Theatre in the hospital, Wilfred Bigelow hosted and narrated a show titled *Vignettes of Our Research Heritage*. Bigelow is among the hospital's most illustrious alumni, a doctor-researcher with a world reputation for his work in hypothermia — safely cooling the body to allow for open-heart surgery — and the development of the pacemaker, two projects pioneered at Toronto General. Before the show began, Bigelow looked out at those assembled in the theatre, which had just been handsomely refurbished, and sighed, "I love this old place." His job was to introduce some distinguished Toronto General alumni who had returned to the hospital for the opening ceremonies of the new research building. All of them had worked at the hospital between 1935 and 1965, a period Bigelow called Toronto General's "golden age of research."

It was a time when Edsel Ford of the Ford family in Detroit required surgery for a tumor in his stomach and scoured the world to find the best surgeon for the job. "He could have crooked his finger at any surgeon in the world," Bigelow said. "Instead, he invited Dr. Roscoe Tanner of Toronto General, who went to the Ford Hospital in Detroit and operated on Mr. Ford."

Bigelow also described the work of Duncan Graham and William Edward Gallie, who did their research at the hospital in the 1930s. It was Gallie who encouraged his surgeons to make use of animal research in the Banting Institute, where insulin was discovered in 1921. "In those days some still believed it was sacrilegious to consider the biochemistry and physiology of an animal as similar to man," Bigelow said.

The animal quarters were on the top floor of the Banting Institute, where the heating facilities were primitive and inadequate. Bigelow had worked there, under Gallie's supervision, using animals in experiments to reduce their oxygen requirements, an early form of hypothermia to allow open-heart surgery. One winter afternoon, he had noticed the animals were cooling much more slowly than they had previously, and he thought he had stumbled upon a medical breakthrough, possibly a discovery of global importance. He stopped the experiment in order to study why the one group of animals had somehow suddenly dropped their body temperatures so successfully. The study continued for months, until Bigelow reluctantly conceded that there was no breakthrough whatsoever, global or otherwise. The animals were merely adjusting to the subarctic environment of the top floor of the Banting Institute.

Next, Robert MacMillan, a cardiologist who helped to establish the world's first coronary care unit at Toronto General, followed Bigelow on the stage to tell how it had happened. MacMillan and Kenneth Brown, another cardiologist, had been working at the hospital on the use of anticoagulant drugs to treat patients with coronary artery disease in the 1950s. During one trial, MacMillan and Brown had been startled by the high mortality of patients admitted to hospital with heart attacks. They found that 40 per cent of the patients died and most deaths were unexpected, involving patients who appeared to be doing well until found dead by a nurse on morning rounds.

"The first thing for us to do was try to find why these patients died," MacMillan said. "This could only be done in an intensive care setting where nurses were in constant attendance, one to each patient, around the clock. Every heart beat had to be monitored and recorded for later analysis."

MacMillan and Brown found a vacant, four-bed room in the College Wing, next to a single room that could be used as a nursing station. There was no equipment on the market to monitor heart beats, so MacMillan and Brown approached John Scott, a Toronto General doctor who was an expert in elec-troencephalography, the study of electrical impulses in the brain. Scott provided them with an old, four-channel device that had been discarded because it could no longer adequately record brain waves. Scott modified the device to monitor heart beats, which are easier to record than brain waves. MacMillan and Brown soon turned the four-bed room into an intensive care unit for coronary patients, with equipment capable of tracing the heart beats of all four patients around the clock.

Because of budget restraints, however, the hospital could not also provide them with nurses, who were essential for the unit. Undeterred, Kenneth Brown approached one of his patients, a wealthy industrialist, and told him that he and MacMillan had everything going for the world's first coronary care unit except nurses.

"What's the problem?" the ailing industrialist asked.

"The hospital can't afford them," Brown said.

The industrialist asked for his chequebook, wrote out a cheque for $5,000, and handed it to Brown. "Now, go hire some nurses," he told him.

Brown showed the cheque to one of the hospital's senior administrators and asked if it was enough to hire nurses for the unit. The administrator, embarrassed that a patient had provided the money, said he would check the budget again. In a few days, he reported to Brown that he had managed to find just enough in the hospital budget to hire nurses for the unit, which duly opened in March 1962.

By the end of the year, MacMillan and Brown had determined the cause of most of the previously unexplained deaths. They collaborated on a medical journal report that said half the deaths were due to electrical abnormalities in the heart, which were treatable. Most of the other deaths were due to "pump failure," the result of heart muscle damage, which remains a coronary mystery. As a result of what they learned, however, over the next few years the mortality rate for coronary care patients in the hospital dropped from 40 per cent to 18 per cent.

MacMillan also mentioned William Boyd, a legendary figure at Toronto General who had studied psychiatry at medical school in his native Scotland, before becoming interested in pathology because no one else would do autopsies at the mental hospital where he worked. On his way to Canada on an ocean liner, Boyd assiduously prepared a hundred lectures on pathology, which he used for some time while teaching pathology in Winnipeg, where he was a huge success. He wrote textbooks on the subject, which were translated into several languages and earned him a world reputation. In 1937, Boyd moved to Toronto, where he became professor of pathology at the University of Toronto.

One of his minor obsessions was gardening. He especially enjoyed growing lilies, but because of wartime restrictions, imported lily bulbs were scarce and rationed one to a person. Boyd circumvented the pesty restrictions when he recruited everyone in his pathology department one cold March morning and had them trek *en masse* down to King Street, where they lined up for lily bulbs to bring back to the hospital. Boyd's garden bloomed in profusion that spring.

By the time Raymond Heimbecker took to the stage in the lecture theatre, the show had become something of a love-in. Heimbecker, who had been a senior member of Toronto General's cardiovascular staff until 1974, brought with him various props, including slides, old audio tapes, and the original artificial kidney, developed by another trail-blazing TGH scientist-surgeon, Gordon Murray. Although there has always been great competition for prestige and status — and often for funding — among scientific medicos, when they get together to party, there is also great affection, and respect. Gordon Murray's name brought the same audible sighs that the mention of Gordie Howe or Bobby Orr might bring at an old-timers' hockey reunion.

Heimbecker had worked with Murray as a junior intern in the late 1940s, the year after Murray had assembled the first artificial kidney ever used in North America. Heimbecker pointed to the kidney machine on a table beside the rostrum. It was about the size of a large waste-paper basket. Murray, an indefatigable researcher, had achieved medical fame a decade earlier when he developed heparin, the blood-thinner that became crucial to open-heart surgery. After treating more than four hundred patients at Toronto General with heparin, with spectacular results, Murray was invited to deliver the Hunterian Lecture before the Royal College of Surgeons in England in 1939. Soon after, he became engrossed in research that eventually resulted in the use of biological heart valves instead of metal or plastic heart valves, another world first for Toronto General.

Heimbecker reminisced about the good old days of the golden age of research at the hospital, when interns earned twenty-seven cents a day. He had brought his collection of slides, photographs of Toronto General in the 1930s, 1940s, and 1950s, and to break up the narrative he flashed old newspaper cartoons on the screen. He even played tapes he had made, using a homemade tape recorder, of an interns' party at the hospital in 1946. To the tune of "Waltzing Matilda," the interns sang in a scratchy chorus:

Resecting with Murray
Resecting with Murray
You'll come resecting with Murray and me . . .

During a break in the song, two intern-performers, barely audible on the old machine on a table on the stage, did a vaudevillian deadpan:

"Why is the elbow called the funny bone?"

"I don't know. Why is the elbow called the funny bone?"

"Because it borders on the humerus."

Bigelow is a warm and dignified man with almost matinee-idol good looks, even in his mid-seventies. He was born in Brandon, Manitoba, the son of a surgeon. He remembers his father as an outdoorsman, generous with his patients, and intensely curious. His early practice took him to small towns in Manitoba and even in the backwoods he struggled to bring to his patients the latest in medical knowledge and know-how. When he encountered a strange infection, he used a cotton swab to transfer the infected material to a test tube. Then, to keep the germ alive for investigation, he put the test tube in a special pocket he had sewn into his nightgown and slept with it in his armpit to maintain it at body temperature. The next morning, when the train left Brandon, the older Bigelow gave the tube to the conductor, who made sure it got to the bacteriology lab in Winnipeg.

In his book *Cold Hearts*, a funny and fascinating story of the development of hypothermia and the cardiac pacemaker, Bigelow mentions the expression his father often used in moments of exasperation: "To hell with it!" Bigelow's father told him that the exclamation, properly used, saves a lot of time and worry. In *Cold Hearts* he explains, "It is an acceptance of the fact that life is a gamble, and you can accept your losses as readily as your gains and not fret about it. . . . It is not possible to find a word in the English language to take the place of that phrase."

Bigelow's lifelong fascination with hypothermia, lowering the body temperature for therapeutic reasons, began in 1941. He was a resident at Toronto General, working under W. E. Gallie, the local legend who was then professor of surgery and surgeon-in-chief at the hospital. One day Bigelow had treated a young man from the north woods for frostbite — he had to amputate the man's gangrenous fingers — and later he approached Gallie and wondered aloud why in Canada, of all places, there was so little known about frostbite. "Why don't you make it your business to find out about it?" Gallie asked him. The question had inspired Bigelow to spend the next eighteen years researching hypothermia.

In 1946, he worked with Alfred Blalock, a pioneering heart surgeon at Johns Hopkins Hospital. Blalock became famous as the "Blue Baby Surgeon," having developed a technique that involved opening the chest, exposing the heart, and redirecting blood through the lungs to be oxygenated. It was still palliative surgery, providing relief without cure — the blue babies still had holes in their hearts — but it made life for them more comfortable. While watching Blalock at work, Bigelow says in *Cold Hearts*, "I became aware that surgeons . . . would never be able to correct or cure heart conditions unless they were able to stop the circulation of blood through the heart, open it, and operate in a bloodless field under direct vision."

Bigelow woke up one night with what he called "a simple and enchanting theory," a solution that did not require pumps or tubes. It was one of those eurekas that settle, full-blown, in one's head. It was, *cool the whole body, reduce the oxygen requirements, interrupt the circulation, and open the heart.* "The thinking may not sound particularly courageous today," he explains in *Cold Hearts*. "However, one must realize that in those days a fall in body temperature was considered dangerous — something to be carefully avoided in surgery and in the treatment of injury."

The first time he used the technique was on a dog in his lab in Toronto, which was really only a storage room in the basement of the Banting Institute. "It was strange to see the heart beating so slowly and deliberately and to feel cool tissues and cool blood. . . . What a thrill to look inside a beating heart!"

In 1950, when he was ready to start work on humans, Bigelow presented a paper on the technique to the American Surgical

Association in Colorado Springs. It was the first time in medical history that someone had suggested a surgical technique involving total body cooling. "It was a blasphemy," he says in *Cold Hearts*. As it turned out, Bigelow's paper started a wave of hypothermia research around the world.

The pacemaker, a device that electronically stimulates the heart, was an offshoot of Bigelow's hypothermia research. Again, the beginnings were simple, the result of a researcher's childlike curiosity. One morning in 1949, Bigelow was in his laboratory performing open-heart surgery on a dog that had been cooled in refrigeration blankets and ice bags. Toward the end of the surgery, just as he was about to start certain tests, the dog's heart stopped beating, and would not respond to cardiac massage.

Bigelow describes the scene in *Cold Hearts*:

I looked at the heart. It was quiet, cool, pink, and the muscle was firm. It was of normal appearance in all respects. What was wrong with the little rascal? Out of interest and in desperation, I gave the left ventricle a good poke with a probe I was holding. There was an immediate and sudden strong contraction that involved all chambers — then it returned to a standstill. I did it again, with the same result. What an unexpected observation!

I poked it regularly every second. Lo and behold, it resembled a normal beating heart. Were these phony beats or real contractions expelling blood into the circulation? A technician acting as anesthetist said, "Hey, I'm getting a blood pressure here."

Perhaps Bigelow's strangest and most obsessive research project was his quest to unlock the secret of hibernation. If there was a magic elixir that allowed certain animals to sleep away entire winters, tolerating extremely low temperatures, it might be used with great success on surgical patients to achieve a deeper and safer hypothermia than anyone imagined. Bigelow had a hunch that groundhogs had the answer.

There are two types of animals, warm-blooded and cold-blooded, or what are scientifically known as *homeotherms* and *poikilotherms*. Humans and other warm-blooded animals are homeotherms, which means we have a heat-regulating system that maintains a constant body temperature. Poikilotherms do not, and their body temperatures adjust to whatever temperatures they are exposed to, which can be as low as a few degrees above freezing. A true hibernating animal, such as the groundhog, is a homeotherm in summer and a poikilotherm in winter. The groundhog has a built-in wake-up thermostat that rouses it when the temperature falls to near zero, to save him from freezing. (Bigelow maintains that bears are not true hibernating animals because they retain a temperature-control system in winter, though in *Cold Hearts* he said "no research worker had ever come forward and taken the rectal temperature of a sleeping bear in his den.")

Bigelow recruited helpers to round up groundhogs wherever they could find them. He established a groundhog farm at Collingwood, Ontario, and at one time he had four hundred groundhogs in his collection. Gradually, Bigelow became "overwhelmingly impressed" with a mysterious "brown fat" in the groundhog's hibernating gland. "The unusual tolerance to low body temperature that these animals demonstrated was clearly related to this gland," he said. "It reaches its maximum size just before the onset of hibernation, and it rapidly diminishes in size after hibernation." For ten years he worked to identify and isolate a chemical hormone from the blood of the groundhog's hibernating gland, hoping to find a "hibernating hormone" that could be injected into human patients.

He thought he had it once. The team had come up with an extract from the brown fat and blood of a hibernating groundhog that it identified as "1-butyl, 2-butoxy-carbonyl-methyl-phthalate." They had it examined by scientists at the National Research Council in Ottawa, who declared it was indeed "a pure substance." Applications were made at once to patent the extract, which the team named "hibernin." Just before the discovery was to be announced to the world, a letter arrived from Washington, D.C., that said 1-butyl, 2-butoxy-carbonyl-methyl-phthalate had already been patented, twenty years earlier — as a plasticizer.

Eh?

It turned out that the extracting process that brought forth hibernin used a small, one-inch section of plastic tubing, the formula for which was, yes — 1-butyl, 2-butoxy-carbonyl-methyl-phthalate. As Bigelow ruefully explains in the book, "You could buy our precious hormone . . . by the barrel."

Another grand instance of, "To hell with it!"

It was a good day for W. Vickery Stoughton. Any new chief executive officer who can throw up a $13.5-million research building with a minimum of fuss and delay and without much financial strain on the institution earns a gold star on his personal CEO's report card. And he was still a young man, only thirty-nine years old.

Stoughton had not made any wrong moves in his first five years at Toronto General, nothing to embarrass himself, nothing that would be a blemish on his record when he moved on. And those close to him had no doubt that some day he would be moving on. When he had first appeared before the hospital's board of trustees as a candidate for the job of president, Stoughton told the august members that every organization benefits from a change in leadership every ten years. "It's just something I happen to believe in," he said. "It's not something I learned in an MBA program."

Running a thousand-bed hospital is never a cinch, either, whether you try to play it safe or risky. Even the quiet times are like the quiet times rounding Cape Horn. After five years at Toronto General, Stoughton had won over the doctors, the nurses, and the other administrators and managers. He had done it mainly by playing tough and fair, staying outside and above the frays, never appearing to take sides, but always manoeuvring and manipulating and being what he likes to call "pro-active." It means taking the initiative, and it means finding how things can be done, not why things can't be done.

He began by delegating authority, decentralizing power, and improving communications. The best example is nursing, which in every hospital is regarded as dripping with potential as a huge power base, loaded with possibilities as a force for hospital reform, brimming with new ideas for patient-care improvement, but somehow always kept in check — fragmented, impotent. Soon after Stoughton arrived, the head nurses became "nursing managers," which was far from being a sop or merely a cosmetic change. It gave nurses control of money, a say in the running of the hospital, and effective countervailing leverage against the well-entrenched power of the doctors. It helped even things up in the hospital. Not everyone was happy with the move, but no one complained too loudly, or dared to suggest openly that Stoughton was wrong. So well did he work behind the scenes that most people at the hospital did not even notice his fingerprints.

Stoughton also encouraged group practices among doctors within the hospital, another move that streamlined the organization and improved communication. A few specialties had formed group practices before Stoughton arrived, but most doctors operated as individuals, as private entrepreneurs, a clumsy and outdated system that has been described as "an army of pushcart vendors in an age of supermarkets." In a group practice, doctors' incomes are pooled and a minimum is agreed upon, perhaps $90,000 or $100,000 a year. Anything left over usually goes to research or an academic enrichment fund. When a patient is referred to, say, Orthopedics, he usually is referred to a specific doctor, but in Orthopedics there are specialties within the specialty, so the group will redirect him to the most qualified person — an orthopedist who does hip replacements, or one that treats sports injuries. Because it is a group practice, with all income pooled, there is no economic incentive to individual doctors to get as many patients as they can. The system has obvious benefits to patients — they get to the proper doctors — and it makes things easier for the president, because it is administratively more efficient.

"If you've got six hundred doctors in the hospital practising as individuals, you've got no organizational structure whatsoever," Stoughton said. "Every time you want to make a decision, make a change, you've got to convince every doctor who's impacted by it. Group practices create all sorts of good things — sharing research, sharing patient referrals, building management structures within the groups."

The move to group practices erodes doctors' independence, but it is a trend in hospitals and it will continue. The mystique of medicine is shifting slowly away from individual doctors, the dear and glorious physicians, to the hospital itself. Not that long ago, in a life-threatening crisis, the plea was, "Send for the doctor!" Now it is, "Take him to the hospital!" And the age of the doctor as the only uniquely learned person in the community is a distant, rustic memory. More and more big, modern hospitals are being run by non-medical administrators, specially trained management artists who know more about balance sheets than about operating-room procedures (but more about operating-room procedures than most doctors know about balance sheets). The best of them, like Stoughton, have studied and apprenticed in hospital management, a new profession as demanding and esoteric as the most abstruse medical specialty.

It was about time.

In Canada, Heward Grafftey trenchantly described the imbecilities and horrors of the old and (one hopes) fading hospital system in a book he wrote in 1972 titled *The Senseless Sacrifice: A Black Paper on Medicine*. "Doctors rarely have to account to anybody except other doctors," he said. "Boards of Governors take them at their word and together with the administrator, rubber-stamp decisions they would never even entertain in their own world of business."

He recalled a large hospital in Montreal that was engaged in an expansion program and the board of governors was trying to decide how many elevators were needed in the new building. The architects recommended a certain number of elevators, but a doctor representing the medical staff on the board vetoed the recommendation, arguing that the money could be better spent on modern lab equipment. "A year after the expansion was completed," Grafftey said, waits for elevators were so long that hospital efficiency was seriously impaired as exasperated crowds of staff, visitors, and even patients backed up down the halls. Soon the order went out for more elevators. The spectacle of demolition workers tearing down the centre of a modern hospital with all its high cost in-put was enough to give any cost engineer a lifetime of sleepless nights." The fiasco wasted more than $2 million.

It reminded Grafftey of his first year as a member of Parliament, when he sat on the Estimates Committee of the House of Commons, which examines government expenditures department by department. One day a naval officer appeared to testify on the cost of a submarine chase-type destroyer, which originally had been estimated to cost $4 million but which ended up costing $18 million. "The admiral dutifully explained to us that technological advances during construction necessitated many design changes and thus the necessity for soaring costs," Grafftey wrote. "Under questioning by the committee, the admiral, rather than resorting to clear language and clear answers, somehow or other conveyed the impression he wasn't very impressed with the patriotism of members of parliament who seemed overly concerned with dollars and cents when the defence of freedom was involved. Hospital administrators, trustees and governors are, likewise, made to feel at a disadvantage with medical staff when matters of life and death are being discussed. There seems to be an impression in the medical establishment that any great emphasis on organization, control, efficiency and costs infringes on the quality of health and medical care, that somehow or other efficiency and high standards of care are incompatible."

Grafftey concluded: "By insisting on dominating hospitals' front offices, too many doctors are forgetting how to practise medicine. Their administrative bumbling has resulted in such inefficiencies and chaotic control at the hospital level that if continued they will sadly and cruelly nullify many of the benefits modern medical advances and discoveries should have long since conferred on all the peoples of North America."

Stoughton is not under the thumb of the doctors. Early in 1985, when he foresaw a $2-million deficit looming at the hospital, he acted quickly to avert it. He got rid of sixty people, some by attrition, some by layoffs. He imposed a tough, across-the-board 2 per cent reduction of expenses in all departments in the hospital. By midsummer the crisis had been averted.

In Ontario early in 1986, when doctors and the provincial government were on a collision course over the opting-out issue — the government had announced it would bring in legislation to prevent doctors from billing patients more than the public health insurance plan specified — Stoughton steered a neutral course.

The debate inflamed the old passions that had greeted the introduction of medicare to Canada twenty-five years earlier in Saskatchewan. The doctors took out full-page newspaper advertisements to push their case against the government, which they accused of "humiliating" the profession and stripping it of its independence. They warned that banning "extra-billing" would demoralize doctors and cripple health care. They threatened slowdowns, walkouts, and civil disobedience.

At one session in a government committee room, spokesmen for the doctors harangued the politicians for nearly three hours. The official submission of the Ontario Medical Association asked, "What kind of doctors will be produced during the first century of enslavement following centuries of freedom and independence?" They accused the government of being "intransigent," of using its power "to bring an honorable profession to its knees." They categorized themselves as "shackled," "resentful," "humiliated," and "disgruntled."

It was as if the doctors were caught in a time warp.

"These are the actions of responsible men and women driven to desperation by the prospect of losing their civil rights, professional freedom, and human dignity," the doctors argued. "We who have inherited the stewardship of a centuries-old noble profession feel a solemn obligation to honor our commitment by preserving the integrity of our profession for future generations. It is our duty to ourselves, to medical students now in training and to those yet unborn who will carry on our profession in the twenty-first century to resist, in any and every possible way, this mortal attack on our professional freedom."

At the end of the session, Murray Elston, the Minister of Health, displayed a remarkable calm. He said, "We have not heard anything new today."

Stoughton stayed out of the rumble. When the Ontario Medical Association hired a film crew to prepare promotional material for the doctors' cause, Stoughton allowed the cameras in the hospital, but warned the doctors that they were to be identified only as University of Toronto doctors, not Toronto General Hospital doctors. "I don't know if they'll do it," he admitted privately, "but I have to at least put the message across." Once, when someone mentioned in conversation in his office that doctors contribute generously out of their own pockets to hospital research and academic enrichment funds, Stoughton suggested that their motives were not entirely altruistic.

"If you're a surgeon out practising in the community, your overhead's going to be about 45 per cent," he said. "If you come into the hospital, the overhead will be less than 20 per cent. And you're going to have a lot of patients referred to TGH because there are good physicians here. So if doctors in one of the group practices give $100,000 to an academic enrichment fund, that's about 20 per cent of their total income, roughly what they're saving on overhead. And they get a 50 per cent tax deduction for doing it, so I don't feel sorry for them at all."

Stoughton continued to push forward improvements, including a new system of distributing drugs and medication within the hospital, and a new computer system that eventually will have bedside computer screens in every patient room, allowing doctors and nurses to call up in an instant any information they need on a patient's medical history, diagnosis, and treatment. The computer system will take about eighteen months to install, at a cost of nearly $10 million, but Stoughton promised that within five years it would pay for itself by normal attrition of unnecessary staff. Besides saving money, he said, the bedside computers would allow nurses to spend more time with patients and less with hospital forms and charts.

Stoughton's boldest move came in February 1986, at a regular meeting of the board of trustees. Extra chairs were hauled in to accommodate an overflow crowd, all because of one item on the agenda — item 3d. It dealt with a merger of Toronto

General Hospital and Toronto Western Hospital, the ninety-year-old, 600-bed institution several blocks to the west.

Talks on the merger had gone on for months. Indeed, soon after his installation as president Stoughton had begun to explore mergers with several Toronto hospitals, believing that hospital consolidations would provide better patient care and save enormous amounts of money by avoiding competition and duplication. He would have loved a merger between Toronto General and the Hospital for Sick Children across the street, but that was not to be. By November 1985, rumors of a merger were flying at both hospitals, which prompted Stoughton to write a public memo to all hospital staff in Toronto General's inter-office newsletter *Generally Speaking*. "Merger discussions tend to create the opportunity for many rumors," he said. "The process also brings out concerns on the part of individuals concerning opportunity for input. Medical Departmental Chairmen, Division Heads and Vice-Presidents have been aware of the discussions and each has been asked to consider whether a consolidation might make it easier to improve and maintain current patient care, teaching and research programs. Some of them have indicated that such a decision would create new and appropriate opportunities; others have stated that they see no immediate benefit." He stressed that any merger "would not result in bed reductions, hence job security should not be a concern."

On the afternoon of February 11, 1986, at five o'clock, the trustees assembled in the boardroom at Toronto General. A similar meeting had also begun in the boardroom at Toronto Western Hospital. This was to be the debate, then the vote, though David Allen of Public Relations had already had printed a news release that began: "The Toronto General Hospital and the Toronto Western Hospital have voted in favor of merging the two institutions. . . ."

Stoughton took his seat at the middle of the long table, next to Alf Powis, the chairman. One of the first questions was how much money a merger would save. Stoughton answered that, using conservative estimates, cost-savings and cost-avoidance would amount to about $3.5 million. "We intend to stay lean and mean," he said.

There was some concern that the merger was being rushed, that it was a *fait accompli*, but Stoughton and Powis assured everyone that the decision was in the hands of the trustees. Around the table, one by one, various spokesmen reported on the moods of their departments. The two biggest departments,

Medicine and Surgery, were overwhelmingly opposed to the merger, though most of the smaller departments favored it. In an earlier show of hands, only twenty-five of a hundred and eighty doctors had favored the merger. It was the same at Toronto Western, where sixty doctors had opposed the merger and only twenty-three had favored it.

Stoughton worked his considerable charm on the meeting, listening, answering questions, careful not to intrude too heavily, playing out the line. The mood swung from mildly skeptical to querulous to suspicious. Stoughton listened, replying only when asked, usually prefacing his remarks by saying, "Isn't it right, Jim, that . . ." As it grew dark outside and the streetlights came on, little agreements erupted, then pockets of consensus.

Someone asked, "Will the marriage be consummated by the vote today?"

"It will still require legislative approval," Powis replied, "but if we pass this motion, we are committing ourselves to the merger. It would mean that tomorrow Vic will be acting CEO of Toronto Western."

"Why now?" another member wanted to know.

"Why not?" Powis replied.

When the vote finally was taken, only two board members opposed the merger.

It had been such a dazzling performance by Stoughton that, as the meeting ended, one of the members moved that the board formally express its thanks to the president for his patience. After the meeting, Powis and Stoughton shook hands with the trustees, said goodbye, then walked down the corridor, past the portraits of their predecessors, for a celebratory drink in the president's office. The two men could find no ice cubes and no mix in the office cabinet, but they found some glasses, wiped them clean with a paper towel, then poured themselves a couple of fingers of warm Scotch and clinked their glasses in a toast.

"We downed 'em neat," Powis said.

Three weeks later, on Saturday, March 1, David Allen logged more overtime. He was in the hospital kitchen, making arrangements with Nutrition to bake a birthday cake. He wanted to make absolutely sure the order was not messed up. The cake was for W. Vickery Stoughton, who had just turned forty.